How to Teach English to a Spanish Speaker Level 1
Second Edition

Dr. Ephrain Tristan Ortiz

Copyright © 2019 Dr. Ephrain Tristan Ortiz

All rights reserved.

ISBN: 9781798961186

DEDICATION

To everyone using my How to English to a Spanish Speaker books out of a compassionate desire to help others live a more enriching life and find more doors of opportunity. I wish you success, fulfillment and lots of fun! Thank you and God bless you and guide you!

Christian missionary Toni (third from the left) teaches English with my books in Tecate, Mexico. Here she is pictured with some of her students.

The Church Behind Bars ministry in Florida, USA uses this book to teach English as a Second Language to prison inmates, who greatly enjoy the learning method in "How to Teach English to a Spanish Speaker." Their first graduating class is scheduled to complete Level 1 in December, 2023. Level 2 is next!

CONTENTS

	INTRODUCTION - HOW THIS LANGUAGE LEARNING METHOD WORKS	1
	CRASH COURSE IN SPANISH READING	10
LEVEL 1:	LESSON 1	13
LEVEL 1:	LESSON 2	20
LEVEL 1:	LESSON 3	26
LEVEL 1:	LESSON 4	33
LEVEL 1:	LESSON 5 (LESSONS 1 – 4 REVIEW)	40
LEVEL 1:	LESSON 6	49
LEVEL 1:	LESSON 7	54
LEVEL 1:	LESSON 8	61
LEVEL 1:	LESSON 9	68
LEVEL 1:	LESSON 10 (LESSONS 6 – 9 REVIEW)	75
LEVEL 1:	LESSON 11	84
LEVEL 1:	LESSON 12	90
LEVEL 1:	LESSON 13	96
LEVEL 1:	LESSON 14	103
LEVEL 1:	LESSON 15 (LESSONS 11 – 14 REVIEW)	109
LEVEL 1:	LESSON 16	116
LEVEL 1:	LESSON 17	124
LEVEL 1:	LESSON 18	132
LEVEL 1:	LESSON 19	139
LEVEL 1:	LESSON 20 (LESSONS 16 – 19 REVIEW)	145
LEVEL 1:	LESSON 21	153
LEVEL 1:	LESSON 22	169
LEVEL 1:	LESSON 23	176
LEVEL 1:	LESSON 24	184

LEVEL 1:	LESSON 25 (LESSONS 21 – 24 REVIEW)	191
LEVEL 1:	LESSON 26 (REVIEW CONTINUATION)	198
LEVEL 1:	LESSON 27	216
LEVEL 1:	LESSON 28	223
LEVEL 1:	LESSON 29	232
LEVEL 1:	LESSON 30 (LESSONS 26 – 29 REVIEW)	239
LEVEL 1:	LESSON 31	245
LEVEL 1:	LESSON 32	251
LEVEL 1:	LESSON 33	276
LEVEL 1:	LESSON 34	283
LEVEL 1:	LESSON 35 (LESSONS 31 – 34 REVIEW)	290
LEVEL 1:	LESSON 36	298
LEVEL 1:	LESSON 37	306
LEVEL 1:	LESSON 38	325
	ABOUT THE AUTHOR	334

INTRODUCTION – HOW THIS LANGUAGE LEARNING METHOD WORKS

Welcome to Level 1 of my Teach English to a Spanish Speaker series! You can easily use this book to expertly teach English to friends, family, business associates, employees, etc. in an enjoyable way that gets fast and effective results. Each student begins to participate in English conversation in the first line of the first lesson and will continue to do so throughout the course of this book!

Each student will immediately begin using the most common grammatical words used in conversation and master these through practical and fun conversations and dialogues. New information will spiral and cling to previously learned information providing an automatic review of earlier lessons while learning new material. The student will be trained to actually think in English instead of translating. Classrooms just aren't meant for learning to speak a second language.

I remember once when I taught karate years ago, one of my teen students was attending a fancy private high school where he was studying Spanish. He was scoring straight A's in this class and was well into his third year of classroom Spanish at this $35,000 a year school. (This was back in 1995. I cringe thinking how much their tuition is now!). His mom would often boast to me, "My son is getting really good at Spanish; he is reading, writing and speaking it. He could teach you a few things."

Being a strong silent Clint Eastwood type back then I didn't stoop to argue. Well one day I brought this sharp but classroom-trained young man a page of Spanish math homework I was using to teach a bilingual first grade classroom in San Jose, CA. I found that he couldn't understand what it said! He began saying, "Well this must be some sort of command verb and this must be a plural noun, but I don't know what this word is and, eh, well uh. . . ."

He finally gave up and his 12 year old brother who had been watching all this said, "Ha ha ha. You can't even read a first grade Spanish page. Ha ha."

You learned your native language by being immersed in an environment where you could learn the meaning of everything through context. Think about it; when you were a toddler did your mom ever tell you, "Today we are going to study imperative verbs"? or "Let's learn definite and indefinite articles today"? If you had gotten that kind of language instruction as a toddler, you would have worn out the knees of your pants from crawling away from such mental torture.

You can teach a Spanish speaker to speak English effectively through this instructional series. I developed the concepts, strategies and teaching techniques in this manual from 20 years teaching English to Spanish speaking students of all ages in a variety of learning environments.

This manual contains specific prompts and commands for the instructor and all the correct answers the student should give. Many tips are at the beginning of lessons as well as reading lessons that reinforce the speaking lessons. I also include reading practice in "high frequency" English words which are found the most in English literature and conversation.

Your student will get a strong sense of accomplishment upon the completion of this book. This book will get him/her to an advanced beginner level, which will allow the student to speak better than a university second language student in the middle of his second year. He/she will confidently be able to communicate in the community in daily tasks, errands, and basic social conversation.

Additional English words and phrases that the student learns through daily living will attach themselves effectively to the grammatical foundations he has developed in this book. Another benefit of this course is that it trains the student to become a more effective English learner!

The book's instructional method is a user friendly, layman's method of teaching the English language to a Spanish speaker. It makes use of the following instructional strategies so your student learns quickly and effectively, while having a fun learning experience. Here are the strategies I'll be employing in this program so as to give you great results:

Deliberate Spiraling Recall- According to research on foreign language learning, the student forgets new information (such as a new word or grammatical rule) within five to seven minutes. It is important then, that the new information is reviewed and used again before this time period.

The time period then lengthens to twice that time and the information is covered again until the student remembers it permanently. While this new information is being mastered, previous information (previously learned words, grammatical rules, etc.) are beginning reviewed as well. New and semi new information is constantly being reviewed in a "spiraling" manner until the student becomes fluent in the use of all the information and can retain it permanently.

***Appropriate Pace Design*-** Students of the Teach English to a Spanish Speaker method participate in challenging sessions that will last only 35 – 40 minutes at a time. Students enter the lesson "fresh" and complete the lesson "fresh". In this way, they do not need to worry about forgetting new information due to mental exhaustion or boredom. "Fried brains" are not found in this method! (Not even lightly boiled ones. ☺)

In fact, students often feel mentally invigorated by the sessions, which causes them to get used to English speaking as being a positive, refreshing experience.

Such students are more apt to enjoy practicing their English in the community as opposed to those poor university or adult school students who suffer through awful two and a half hour "marathon" classes a couple of days a week. Is it any wonder many of them see second language learning as mentally torturing and discouraging? The Teach English to a Spanish Speaker method recommends offering sessions that are expertly timed to give your student the most effective language instruction that will mentally stimulate and energize him or her. Try this method and see!

***Colloquial Synergistic Enhancement*-** Whoa, that's one fancy term! Sorry about that. But it does sound good, doesn't it? This just means that this program will use many colloquial words and expressions, all of which are time-tested as providing the Spanish speaker with a greater understanding of the culture, thought and emotions behind the American English language. This greatly enhances learning, as well as increases the level of interest and enjoyment in the student's lessons.

To "synergize" means "to enhance the effectiveness of an active agent". The colloquial words and expressions enhance the effectiveness of the Teach English to a Spanish Speaker program, which for us is the "active agent".

***Adaptive Anticipatory Retrieval*-** This aspect of our teaching method often excites students and brings a kind of novelty to their language sessions. Anticipatory retrieval is when a student is given a prompt which they are to respond to in English. The possible answer is not one they have actually been taught, but they can "adapt" the English they know to respond correctly. For instance:

Instructor (In English): Are you going to see your father today?

Student: (Answers in English) No. I'm going tomorrow.

Instructor: (In English) And your sister? Is she going tomorrow?

Student: (In English) No. She is going today.

In the above scenario, the student hadn't been taught to respond to the prompt, "And your sister? Is she going tomorrow?" But the student knew how to answer because previously learned English (various forms of "to go") allowed him to "anticipate" what the answer could be. With adaptive anticipatory recall, the student is taught to actually think in the second language, rather than mentally translate during conversation!

HOW TO USE THIS BOOK

You can teach a parent, aunt/uncle, cousin, friend or any other Spanish speaking person how to speak and understand English better than a year of adult school could teach them simply by using this book regularly with them, 35 – 40 minutes a day (this includes both conversation practice & reading practice), for a couple of months.

The lessons are easy to follow but there are some important things you should know before you begin. Each lesson may be done in person or even over the telephone or computer, if the reception is good. It is recommended for you to have the student practice speaking and reading in each session.

Daily practice is recommended but if that isn't possible, then 3 days a week can work as long as the student is given a copy of the lesson sheets so he can practice on the days when you don't have sessions with him.

How long will it take for my student to make progress?

It takes between 2 – 4 months for beginning students to master the level one instruction from this book, depending on how often the sessions are each week. They will have the proficiency of an advanced beginner and will be well able to communicate for most needs that may arise in their community. Their conversational proficiency will be equal to or higher than someone in adult school for one and a half years.

In order for your student to progress that quickly, 3 or more weekly practice sessions are strongly recommended. It is a commitment from you and the student; yes. But you will help someone live a life with much more opportunity and enjoyment, and you will have the satisfaction of teaching someone the English language better than someone with a bunch of certificates teaching a roomful of tired working students a couple of nights a week for two hours + a night with a boring, useless state program. I've been there, I've done that.

If you are doing lessons by phone, it would be good for your student to have a copy of this book or at least of the lesson so he may do the reading portion of this book with you.

What if my student has taken English classes before?

Start with lesson one, even if your student has had English classes before. Learning the basics that the Teach English to a Spanish Speaker program teaches will help the student master more advanced material later. If it seems too easy for your student at the time, let them know that lessons will get more challenging within 1 ½ to 2 weeks.

If you wish, you can do two lessons a day with an experienced student for lessons 1 through 6. Doubling up on lessons past this point is not recommended.

How do I know when my student is ready to move on to the next lesson?

Stay on a lesson until your student responds correctly at least 85% of the time. Once this happens, you may move on to the next lesson the following day. For example, let's say you are teaching your uncle José Lesson 22 and he gets half of the answers correct. The following day you have him do Lesson 22 with you again. And if on the second day he doesn't reach 80% do it the following day and as many days as he needs until he does, so he can pass to the next lesson.

Among my personal students, the longest I've ever seen anyone take in passing a lesson from English Level 1 has been four tries. Let the student know that taking extra days on a lesson is normal and completely okay. You can mix in small pieces of review with repeat lessons so the student doesn't get bored. Remember, teaching should be at the student's pace, not the instructor's.

IMPORTANT: Every 5 or 6 lessons, you'll find a review lesson (which are longer than the rest). I recommend that you take a couple of days on each review lesson. Since this is material they've already passed on, you don't have to follow the 85% rule on these review lessons. But that's your call.

How do I use this book with my student?

In each lesson you will see sentences and phrases in bold print and regular print. You are to read the bold print lesson prompt to your student. The lesson prompts you'll be given are in basic Spanish and at higher levels, will use more and more English.

"Wait a minute," you may be asking. "I don't know how to read Spanish."

Don't worry; Spanish is a very phonetic language which is easy to read. I'll show you soon. The student can even help you.

If however, you insist you won't be able to read the Spanish prompts, then have the student read them! Simply cover up the answer (which is on the right side in normal print) with a page. After the student reads the prompt, wait to see if he gives the right answer. If he does, then uncover the answer which you covered. If it's right, go on the next line. If it isn't, then correct the student.

But let's get back to learning how the lesson prompts work.

For example here you are telling the student to say "Hello. How are you today?":

YOU SAY THIS:	THEY SHOULD SAY THIS:
Diga en inglés, "Hola. ¿Cómo está hoy?"	Hello. How are you today?

After reading the prompt (in bold print) on the left side, check the answer on the right side (in regular print) with what the student said. If the student answered correctly, continue to the next prompt. If the student made a mistake, correct them and have them do it again. That's it. Continue until you finish the lesson. When the speaking lesson is over, do the reading page which follows and you and your student are well on your way!

Again, if you don't think you'll be able to reach the Spanish prompt **Diga en inglés, "Hola. ¿Cómo está hoy?"** then put the page in front of your student (while you have the "Hello. How are you today?" covered). See if he gets the right answer and says, "Hello. How are you today?"

Now of course when you teach someone something new for the first time you'll have to give some command words which your student won't repeat. For example:

YOU SAY THIS:	THEY SHOULD SAY THIS:
En inglés, "Buenas tardes" se dice "Good afternoon". Repita: "good afternoon".	Good afternoon.

When you have command words mixed in with what your student is supposed to say, your student should only say what is in quotation marks. In this example above you are saying, **In English, "Buenas tardes" is said "Good afternoon". Repeat, "Good afternoon."** The student would then simply say, "Good afternoon." Here is another example.

YOU SAY THIS:	THEY SHOULD SAY THIS:
Diga otra vez "Te veré más tarde".	See you later.

This command means **Tell me again, "See you later"**. IMPORTANT! – Pause for a moment before prompts in quotation marks. This will better help your student know what to say. Example:

YOU SAY THIS:	THEY SHOULD SAY THIS:

| Diga (pause) "Buenos días". | Good morning. |

"(Pause)" will not be in your commands because of the space they would take to type in the commands. Just remember to pause for a moment before anything in quotation marks so your student can understand the prompt better.

Sometimes you may be given only command words to say to your student. Here´s an example of this.

YOU SAY THIS:	THEY SHOULD SAY THIS:
Pregúnteme si me gustaría ir con ustedes.	Would you like to come with us?

The command "Pregúnteme si me gustaría ir con usedes" means "Ask me if I´d like to come with you". The answer to this command would then be to say, "Would you like to come with us?"

There will be times in the program when the conversation starts moving at a fast pace and using command words like "diga" (say) or "cómo se dice" (how does one say) would slow down the fluency of the speaking so I'll use a "no command" prompt. It will look like this:

YOU SAY THIS:	THEY SHOULD SAY THIS:
Pregúnteme si me gustaría ir con ustedes.	Would you like to come with us?
Sí.	Yes.
¿A qué hora?	At what time?

You'll notice above that there was one command (pregúnteme si me gustaría ir con ustedes). Afterwards when you said "Sí" the student automatically said "yes". And when you asked "¿A qué hora?" the student automatically asked "At what time?" This is when the program gets real fun, when you get a bunch of prompts which aren't commands; you'll fire away something in Spanish and the student instinctively fires them back at you in English!

What additional teaching tips can you offer?

If your student makes a mistake, patiently correct him and allow him to say the sentence or word again correctly. Help the student with correct pronunciation of words too. Watch out for the following:

The short i as in "bit". Many Spanish speakers will say "beet". Help them relax their jaw so it is pronounced as in "bit".

Words that start with s, as "Spanish". Many Spanish speakers will say "Espanish". Help them take out the "E" sound by stressing the "S" strongly, as if they were hissing like a snake. Eg. – "Ssspanish." Over the next couple of months they can gradually reduce this stress as they eliminate adding the "e" before the s.

The short a as in "bat". Spanish speakers often say "bot". Have the student tighten the lower part of their mouth as he says the "a" sound.

The short y as in "yet". Your student may pronounce it almost like a "j", saying "jet". Help them tighten the lower part of their mouth out so the "y" sound comes out crisp and clear.

Words that have the "th" as in "thanks" are often said "tanks" by Spanish speakers. Help your student pinch his tongue between his teeth so as to pronounce this consonant blend softly. "Th" not "T".

Words with the "s" sound at the end often have this sound dropped. Many Spanish speakers will say "It cost more here" instead of "It costs more here".

I'll remind you of all these throughout the lessons, as well as share other teaching tips.

Watch for these things and don't be lazy about having the student pronounce the word over again.

Try to stick to the lesson. Even though you may want to speak socially with your student if they are a relative, amigo or compadre, wait till the lesson is over. ¿Entiende?

What else should I know?

You should read through each speaking/listening lesson before beginning it with your student. In this way your instruction can flow easier and you will be better prepared to help your student by understanding the lesson beforehand. Watch for the prompts that don't have commands. They are fun to do, especially if you know they are coming.

Each speaking/listening lesson is followed by a one page reading lesson. Read the instructions on what to do for each one since they vary slightly. If you are working with your student by phone, he or she will need a copy of this book too, so he or she can read out loud to you.

The lessons are written out as if they were for one student or a small group of students. If you and your student or students are consistent in studying every week, you will see excellent results. And you will change lives for the better!

Perhaps you don´t know how to read Spanish but still want to read the instructional prompts. Let me give you a crash course in Spanish reading so you are able to read the instructional prompts. If you can read Spanish you can skip the crash course and go right to lesson one. Otherwise continue to the crash course in Spanish reading.

CRASH COURSE IN SPANISH READING

Spanish is very easy to learn to read. If you want to read the basic Spanish commands for the Spanish speaker to respond in English this will help you. After a few lessons, you´ll be reading Spanish effortlessly. It is a phonetic language. Words are pronounced the way they are written.. Over the course of the entire Teach English to a Spanish Speaker program, the Spanish commands will gradually reduce and be replaced by English commands. Let's begin.

Spanish is a phonetic language. Words are pronounced the way they are spelled. Let's start with the vowels.

The "a" sound in Spanish is always pronounced like the "a" in the word "father".

The "e" sound in Spanish is always pronounced like the "e" in the word "egg".

The "i" sound in Spanish is always pronounced like the sound made by "ee" as in "bee".

The "o" sound in Spanish is always pronounced like the long "o" sound in words like "coat" and "boat" but it is cut off before you hear a slight "w" sound. When you say words like "coat" slowly, you'll notice a slight "w" at the end. The Spanish "o" stops before you can hear that. A simple way to learn this if you are confused is to simply ask a Spanish speaker to say the word "Alfonso". Listen to how he pronounces the "o" in this name. That's how you'll pronounce all the "o"s.

The "u" sound in Spanish is always pronounced like the "oo" in "broom".

Almost all the consonants in Spanish are pronounced as they are in English.

The "h" in Spanish is always silent.

The "j" makes a strong, nasal "h" sound as in "Bach" or "achtung".

The "ll" in Spanish makes the "y" sound.

Now with what you know, read these sentences:

Esta es mi amiga Julia Hernandez. Ella es muy hermosa. Ella es la hermana de Hilda.

(This is my friend Julia Hernandez. She is very lovely. She is Hilda´s sister.)

That wasn't too bad! The "h" in "Hernandez", "hermosa", "hermana" and "Hilda" were all silent. The "J" in "Julia" made the "ch" sound like in "Bach" or "Achtung!" The "ll" in "Ella" was pronounced as a "y". Good job!

Now we have a few more things we need to know. The "c" makes the "k" sound unless it is before an "I" or an "e". Then it becomes a soft c, which makes an "s" sound.

The "z" in Spanish also makes the "s" sound.

Say these words:

        cinco   centavo   cerveza

In the same way, a "g" will become soft when it is next to an "I" or an "e". It will sound like the "h" in English.

Say these words:

        gelatina   gente   Gerardo

Now there are times when a hard "g" sound is needed before an "I" or an "e". In order for the "g" to remain a hard "g", it needs a "u" between it and the "I" or "e".

Say these words (the "g" stays hard and the "u" is silent):

        guisar   Aguilar   merengue

In a similar way, sometimes a hard "c' sound is needed before an "I" or an "e". This is made with a "qu" before the "I" or "e".

Say these words:

        aquí   queso   que

The "ñ" makes as "ny" sound.

Say these words:

        año   niña   piña

The "x" is somewhat rare in Spanish so let me prepare you for that. The "x" in most cases will be like the "j", which means is has a sound like the "ch" in Bach or achtung.

Say these words:

                        Mexico   mexicana   Xavier

Well that's it in a taco shell. I've taught you what you need, grasshopper. We're not going to spend more time on this, seeing as this is NOT a Spanish instruction book. We are learning to teach someone to speak English quickly. Feel free to review these Crash Course Spanish reading pages as you wish but I'm going to have you jump in and teach the lessons now.

Just jump right in and read the Spanish instructor prompts in bold print in the lessons. You will improve quickly and your student can help you. Listen to see if they answer you in English correctly. That's what counts. Remember what they should say is in regular print to the right of the bold print command.

When you complete the book, you will be reading Spanish like a pro and your student will be speaking English like a semi pro!

LEVEL 1: LESSON 1

Teaching Tip: Many Spanish speakers pronounce words having a short "a" sound as if they had an "ah" or "aw" sound. They pronounce words like "Spanish" and "basket" as if they were "Spawnish" and "bawsket"(as in "awful"). To correct this, you can have the student occasionally place his fingers on both sides of the jaw line, on the sides of the chin when the short "a" sound in a word is pronounced.

If the short "a" is pronounced correctly, the facial muscles should push the fingers to the side. If the student pronounces the "a" sound like an "aw" sound (as in the word "paw") then the facial muscles will push the fingers downward. Placing the fingers on both sides of the jaw line can help remind the student to pronounce the short "a" correctly.

Read through the lesson first. Then begin the lesson with your student. You read the bold print (or point to it) and the student is expected to respond with what you see in the normal print to the right.

Feel free to do this lesson or any other one as many times as needed for the student to feel comfortable moving on to the next one. Scoring 85% correct answers means the student is ready to move onto the next lesson. Are you ready? Begin!

Discúlpeme se dice "Excuse me". Repita "Excuse me". Excuse me.
Repita "me". Me.
Ahora repita "Ex". Ex.
Excuse. Excuse.
Excuse me. Excuse me.
¿Cómo se dice "discúlpeme" en inglés? Excuse me.
"español" se dice "Spanish". Repita "Spanish". Spanish.
Diga "Discúlpeme"en inglés. Excuse me.
¿Cómo se dice "español"? Spanish.
La palabra "entiende" es "understand"en inglés. Repita "understand". Understand
Ahora repita "stand". Stand.

Under. Under.
Understand. Understand.
Un. Un.
Under. Under.
Understand. Understand.
¿Cómo se dice "entiende"? Understand.
En inglés, "usted" se dice "you." Repita "you". You.
Ahora diga "Usted entiende". You understand.
¿Cómo se dice "español" en inglés? Spanish.
Usted entiende. You understand.
Usted entiende español. You understand Spanish.
Repita "do". Do.
¿Cómo se dice "Usted entiende"? You understand.
La palabra "do" va en frente para preguntar si alguien entiende. Se dice "Do you understand?" Repita "Do you understand"? Do you understand?
¿Cómo se dice, "¿Entiende usted?"en inglés? Do you understand?
¿Cómo se dice "con permiso" o "discúlpeme"? Excuse me.
Ahora pregunte "¿Entiende usted?" Do you understand?
¿Cómo se dice "español" en inglés? Spanish.
Pregúnteme si yo entiendo. Do you understand?
Pregúnteme si yo entiendo español. Do you understand Spanish?
La palabra "No" se dice "no" en inglés. Diga "no". No.
"Señor" se dice "Sir". Repita "sir". Sir.
¿Cómo se dice "no, señor"? No, sir.
Diga "Señor" en inglés. Sir.
Ahora diga "no". No.
No, señor. No, sir.
¿Cómo se dice "Con permiso, señor"? Excuse me, sir.
¿Entiende usted? Do you understand?
¿Entiende usted español? Do you understand Spanish?
"Yo" es "I" en inglés. Repita "I". I.
¿Cómo se dice "yo" en inglés? I.
La palabra "Entiendo" también se dice "understand". Repita "understand". Understand.
Ahora diga, "Yo entiendo". I understand.
Yo entiendo español. I understand Spanish.
Otra vez diga "Yo entiendo". I understand.

Usted entiende. You understand.
Yo entiendo. I understand.
Con permiso. Excuse me.
¿Entiende usted? Do you understand?
¿Entiende usted español? Do you understand Spanish?
No, señor. No, sir.
¿Cómo se dice "Yo entiendo"? I understand.
"Yo no entiendo" se dice "I don't understand". Repita "I don't understand". I don't understand.
Repita "I don't." I don't.
Ahora diga que usted no entiende. I don't understand.
Otra vez "Yo no entiendo." I don't understand.
Repita "don't". Don't.
Repita "Don't understand". Don't understand.
Repita "Do". Do.
Ahora diga "Don't". Don't
¿Cómo se dice "Yo no entiendo"? I don't understand.
español. Spanish.
No, señor. No, sir.
Yo no entiendo español. I don't understand Spanish.
Ahora pregunte "¿Entiende usted?" Do you understand?
¿Entiende usted español? Do you understand Spanish?
No. Yo no entiendo. No. I don't understand.
Yo no entiendo español. I don't understand Spanish.
"inglés" se dice "English". Repita, "English". English
Repita "lish". lish
Diga "Eng". Eng
English. English.
Yo entiendo. I understand.
Yo entiendo inglés. I understand English.
Yo no entiendo inglés. I don't understand English.
Repita "understand English". Understand English.
Ahora repita, "I don't understand English." I don't understand English.
Usted entiende inglés. You understand English.
¿Cómo se dice "Con permiso" en inglés? Excuse me.
¿Usted entiende inglés? Do you understand English?
"Un poco" se dice "a little". ¿Cómo se dice "un poco"? A little.

Otra vez. "Un poco." A little.
Diga en inglés, "Yo entiendo un poco". I understand a little.
Yo entiendo inglés. I understand English.
Un poco. A little.
Un poco (de) inglés se dice "a little English". Repita "a little English". A little English.
Yo entiendo un poco de inglés. I understand a little English.
mexicano o mexicana se dice "Mexican". Diga "Mexican". Mexican.
Repita "can". Can.
Ican. Ican.
Mexican. Mexican.
"Usted es" se dice "You are". ¿Cómo se dice en inglés, "usted es"? You are.
Repita conmigo "are". Are
Say "you are". You are.
Say "Usted es mexicano". You are Mexican.
Diga "usted es". You are.
¿Cómo se dice en inglés las palabras "es usted"? Are you.
Pregunte en inglés, "¿Es usted mexicano?" Are you Mexican?
¿Entiende usted inglés? Do you understand English?
¿Entiende usted español? Do you understand Spanish?
¿Es usted mexicano? Are you Mexican?
"Sí" se dice "yes" en inglés. ¿Cómo se dice "sí" en inglés? Yes.
Diga "sí" en inglés. Yes.
La palabra "señorita" se dice "Miss" en inglés. Diga "Señorita" en inglés. Miss.
Ahora diga "Sí, señorita." Yes, miss.
Pregunte en inglés, "¿Es usted mexicano? Are you Mexican?
Conteste en inglés, "Sí señorita." Yes, miss.
¿Entiende usted español? Do you understand Spanish?
No. Yo no entiendo. No. I don't understand.
Yo no entiendo español. I don't understand Spanish.
Yo entiendo un poco de inglés. I understand a little English.
Yo entiendo un poco de español. I understand a little Spanish.
Perdón. Excuse me.
Perdón, señorita. Excuse me, miss.
¿Entiende usted? Do you understand?
¿Entiende usted inglés? Do you understand English?
¿Entiende usted español? Do you understand Spanish?

No entiendo español. I don't understand Spanish.
¿Entiende usted inglés? Do you understand English?
Yo entiendo un poco. I understand a little.
¿Es usted mexicano? Are you Mexican?
Sí señorita. Yes, miss.
¿Entiende español, señor? Do you understand Spanish, sir?
¿Entiende inglés, señor? Do you understand English, sir?

End of the speaking/listening lesson. Continue with the reading for Lesson 1.

Reading for Lesson 1

You can copy this page or have the student read off your book or computer screen. Read each word first. Have the student read these short sentences after you.

Reading Practice
Excuse me.

Yes?

Do you understand Spanish?

No, I don´t understand Spanish. Are you Mexican?

Yes. I understand a little English.

Now the student will read some words with short vowel sounds. These are only an exercise to help with pronunciation. The student does not need to know the meanings of these words yet. Make sure the vowel "a" is read as in "bat" (not "bot") and the vowel "I" is read as in "bit" (not "beet").

Short Vowel Sounds

Aa

bat	cat	fat
hat	mat	lag
pat	rat	sat
vat	pal	rag

Ee

bet	debt	get
jet	met	let
net	pet	set
vet	wet	tell

Ii

bit	fit	hit
kit	lit	grit
mitt	knit	pit
quit	sit	grill

Oo

bought	caught	dot
fought	got	rot
hot	jot	lot
not	pot	sought

Uu

but	cut	gut
hut	jut	shut
mutt	nut	putt
rut	butt	funny

LEVEL 1: LESSON 2

Teaching tip: Watch for the student omitting the "m" sound in "I'm". If he starts doing this, stop him immediately and have him pronounce the word again after you. Say "I'm" with the "m" sound twice as long as you would normally say it so the student can do the same. Are you ready? Begin!

¿Cómo se dice "español" en inglés? Spanish.
Ahora diga "inglés". English.
Yo entiendo. I understand.
Yo entiendo inglés. I understand English.
Un poco. A little.
Un poco de inglés. A little English.
Entiendo un poco de inglés. I understand a little English.
¿Entiende usted? Do you understand?
Pregúnteme si yo entiendo inglés. Do you understand English?
Pregúnteme si yo entiendo español. Do you understand Spanish?
Conteste "No entiendo". I don't understand.
No entiendo español. I don't understand Spanish.
No entiendo inglés. I don't understand English.
Entiendo un poco. I understand a little.
No entiendo inglés. I don't understand English.
Entiendo español. I understand Spanish.
Entiendo un poco de español. I understand a little Spanish.
Usted es. You are.
Usted es mexicano. You are Mexican.
¿Es usted mexicano? Are you Mexican?
Conteste, "Sí, señorita". Yes, miss.
Diga "Señor" en inglés. Sir.
No, señor. No sir.

Señorita. Miss.
Con permiso, señorita. Excuse me, miss.
Entiendo inglés. I understand English.
Un poco. A little.
Entiendo un poco de inglés. I understand a little English.
¿Es usted mexicano? Are you Mexican?
Sí, usted es mexicano. Yes, you are Mexican.
"You are" se dice también "you're" cuando se utiliza contracción.
Diga "You are". You are.
Ahora diga "you're". You're.
Es como decir "del" en vez de "de el". Repita "you're". You're.
Ahora diga "Usted es mexicano" utilizando la contracción. You're Mexican.
Otra vez "You're Mexican". You're Mexican.
"Yo soy colombiano" se dice "I'm Colombian". Repita "I'm Colombian. I'm Colombian.
"Yo soy" se dice "I am". Diga "I am". I am.
Diga "I am Colombian". I am Colombian.
Para utilizar la contracción se dice "I'm Colombian". Diga "I'm Colombian". I'm Colombian.
La "m" se tiene que escuchar en la palabra "I'm". Diga "I'm." I'm.
Otra vez diga "I'm". I'm.
Diga "I'm Colombian". I'm Colombian.
Otra vez diga en inglés "Yo soy colombiano". I'm Colombian.
Usted entiende español. You understand Spanish.
¿Entiende usted? Do you understand?
¿Entiende usted español? Do you understand Spanish?
No, señor. No, sir.
No entiendo. I don't understand.
Hola se dice "hello" en inglés. Diga "hola". Hello.
Lo. Lo.
Hel. Hel.
Hello. Hello.
Hola, señorita. Hello, miss.
Señora se dice "ma'am" cuando no le está llamando con su apellido. Diga "ma'am". Ma'am.
Hola, señora. Hello, ma'am.
"¿Cómo está?" se dice "How are you?". Repita, "How are you?" How are you?

Pregúnteme en inglés como estoy. How are you?
Diga en inglés, "cómo". How.
¿Cómo está? How are you?
Sin usar la contracción, diga en inglés, "Usted es". You are.
Ahora pregunte en inglés, "¿Es usted? Are you?
¿Cómo se dice en inglés la palabra "Cómo"? How.
¿Cómo está usted? How are you?
Hola, señora. Hello, ma'am.
Hola, señorita. Hello, miss.
¿Cómo está usted? How are you?
"Gracias" se dice "thanks" en inglés. Diga gracias. Thanks.
Diga "Th" suavemente. Th.
Otra vez "th". Th.
Thanks. Thanks.
"Bien" se dice "fine" en inglés. Diga "fine". Fine.
¿Cómo cree que se dice en inglés, "Bien, gracias"? Fine, thanks.
Hola, señor. Hello, sir.
¿Cómo está? How are you?
Bien, gracias. Fine, thanks.
"Estoy bien" se dice "I'm fine". Diga "I'm fine". I'm fine.
¿Cómo está usted? How are you?
Estoy bien, gracias. I'm fine, thanks.
En inglés "Adiós" se dice "Goodbye". Diga adiós en inglés. Goodbye.
Repita "bye". Bye.
Otra vez diga "bye". Bye.
Ahora diga "Good". Good.
Otra vez diga "Good". Good.
Goodbye. Goodbye.
Diga "adiós" en inglés. Goodbye.
Hola. Hello.
Hola, señor. Hello, sir.
Pregunte en inglés, "¿Cómo está? How are you?
Conteste en inglés, "Bien, señorita." Fine, miss.
Gracias. Thanks.
Estoy bien. I'm fine.
Adiós, señora. Goodbye, ma'am.
No entiendo. I don't understand.

¿Es usted mexicano? Are you Mexican?
Sí, señora. Yes, ma'am.
Adiós, señora. Goodbye, ma'am.
Con permiso, señora. Excuse me, ma'am.
¿Entiende? Do you understand?
Oh, usted entiende inglés. Oh, you understand English.
Sí. Entiendo inglés. Yes, I understand English.
Cuando estamos hablando de una acción, "bien" se dice "well". Repita "well". Well.
En inglés, "Muy" se dice "very". Repita, "very". Very.
Diga "muy bien" en inglés. Very well.
Otra vez repita "very well". Very well.
Ahora diga "Entiendo muy bien" en inglés. I understand very well.
¿Cómo está, señora? How are you, ma'am?
Bien gracias. Fine thanks.
Estoy bien. I'm fine.
Muy bien, gracias. Very well, thanks.
Entiendo muy bien. I understand very well.
No entiendo. I don't understand.
¿Entiende usted español? Do you understand Spanish?
Sí. Entiendo español. Yes. I understand Spanish.
Entiendo inglés. I understand English.
Un poco. A little.
Yo soy colombiano. I'm Colombian.
Entiendo un poco de inglés. I understand a little English.
Entiendo un poco. I understand a little.
Para decir "No muy bien" en inglés, se dice "Not very well". Repita, "Not very well". Not very well.
Repita "not". Not.
Not very. Not very.
Not very well. Not very well.
¿Cómo se dice "no muy bien" en inglés? Not very well.
Entiendo un poco de inglés. I understand a little English.
Entiendo un poco. I understand a little.
No muy bien. Not very well.
Diga "Hola" en inglés. Hello.
Adiós. Goodbye.
Hola, señorita. Hello, miss.

¿Cómo está? How are you?
Estoy bien, gracias. I'm fine, thanks.
¿Es usted colombiano? Are you Colombian?
Sí. Soy colombiano. Yes, I'm Colombian.
¿Entiende inglés? Do you understand English?
Entiendo un poco de inglés. I understand a little English.
Usted entiende inglés muy bien. You understand English very well.
Gracias, señorita. Thanks, miss.
Adiós. Goodbye.

End of the speaking/listening lesson. Continue with the reading for Lesson 2.

Reading for Lesson 2

Have your student reread Reading for Lesson 1, but this time by himself. Correct any mistakes and have the student reread wherever necessary. After you are done, read each word/phrase/sentence below first and have the student read after you.

Reading Practice
Excuse me.
Spanish.
I understand.
I understand Spanish.
Excuse me, sir. Do you understand Spanish?
Yes, I understand.
I understand a little. Not very well.
How are you?
I'm fine, thanks. And you?
I am well too, thanks.
That is good.
Are you Mexican?
Yes, I am.
Do you understand English?
Yes. I understand English very well.
You understand English very well.
Thanks. I understand a little Spanish. Not very well.
You're Mexican.
Yes, I'm Mexican.
Hello.
Well, goodbye.

High Frequency English Words

Have the student read these after you. These will be regularly seen in the program. The student does not need to be given the meanings of these yet.

the	of	and
to	a	to
that	is	was
he	for	it
with	as	his

LEVEL 1: LESSON 3

Teaching tip: Many Spanish speakers will pronounce the English short "i" sound as an "ee" sound. So they will pronounce the word "bit" as "beet". What can help is showing them to put the backs of their fingers under their chin and pronounce the "i" sound. The muscles under the chin should push downwards against the fingers. Don't let the student say "Tanks" or "Tank you" instead of "Thanks" or "Thank you"!

Diga la palabra "inglés" en inglés. English.
Ahora diga "Yo entiendo inglés". I understand English.
Entiendo un poco. I understand a little.
Entiendo un poco de inglés. I understand a little English.
Say "no muy bien" in English. Not very well.
No entiendo. I don't understand.
No muy bien. Not very well.
Con permiso. Excuse me.
¿Cómo está? How are you?
¿Cómo está, señor? How are you, sir?
"Estoy bien, gracias" se dice "I'm fine, thanks". Repita "I'm fine, thanks". I'm fine, thanks.
Estoy bien, gracias. I'm fine, thanks.
Si quiere ser más cortés se dice "thank you" en vez de "thanks". Es como decir "Se lo agradezco." Diga "Se lo agradezco" en inglés. Thank you.
Otra vez diga "Thank you". Thank you.
Thank. Thank.
Repita "Thank you". Thank you.
Diga otra vez en inglés, "Se lo agradezco". Thank you.
Se lo agradezco, señora. Thank you, ma'am.
Say "Hola" in English. Hello.
Hola, señora. Hello, ma'am.

Adiós. Goodbye.
Adiós, señora. Goodbye, ma'am.
Otra manera de despedirse es decir "See you later". Es muy informal, y es como decir "Te veré más tarde". Repita "See you later". See you later.
¿Cómo está? How are you?
Bien, gracias. Fine, thanks.
Te veré más tarde. See you later.
No entiendo inglés. I don't understand English.
¿Entiende inglés? Do you understand English?
Entiendo un poco de inglés. I understand a little English.
¿Es usted colombiano? Are you Colombian?
¿Es usted colombiano, señor? Are you Colombian, sir?
Pregúntele a una señorita lo mismo. Are you Colombian, miss?
Sí, soy colombiana. Yes, I'm Colombian.
Recuerde que "soy" se dice "I'm" cuando utiliza la contracción. Diga "soy" en inglés. I'm.
Soy mexicana. I'm Mexican.
Ahora diga "Usted es" utilizando la contracción. You're.
Say "mexicano" in English. Mexican.
Usted es mexicano. You are Mexican.
Soy colombiano. I'm Colombian.
¿Es usted mexicana, señora? Are you Mexican, ma'am?
"No. Yo soy norteamericana" en inglés se dice, "No. I'm American". Repita, "No. I'm American". No, I'm American.
Diga "can". Can.
Erican. Erican.
American. American.
Soy norteamericana. I'm American.
¿Entiende español? Do you understand Spanish?
Un poco. A little.
No muy bien. Not very well.
"No soy norteamericano" se dice "I'm not American". Repita, "I'm not American". I'm not American.
Not American. Not American.
I'm not American. I'm not American.
"¿Y usted?" se dice "and you?" Diga "And you?" And you?
And. And.

And you? And you?
¿Cómo se dice "Y" en inglés? And.
¿Y usted? And you?
¿Y usted, señor? And you, sir?
Y. And
¿Y usted? And you?
Soy mexicano. ¿Y usted? I'm Mexican. And you?
Usted es mexicano. You're Mexican.
Yo no soy mexicano. I'm not Mexican.
Usted no es mexicana. You're not Mexican.
No soy norteamericano. I'm not American.
¿Y usted? And you?
No soy norteamericano. I'm not American.
"Pero" se dice "but" en inglés. ¿Cómo se dice "pero" en inglés? But.
Pero yo entiendo. But I understand.
Diga la palabra "Y". And.
Pero yo entiendo. But I understand.
Pero yo entiendo inglés. But I understand English.
Repita "but". But.
Ahora diga "don't". Don't.
Not. Not.
Pero entiendo inglés. But I understand English.
Entiendo un poco de inglés. I understand a little English.
No entiendo. I don't understand.
No entiendo muy bien. I don't understand very well.
No muy bien. Not very well.
¿Y usted? And you?
Pregunte en inglés, "¿Es usted norteamericana, señora?" Are you American, ma'am?
¿Es usted mexicana? Are you Mexican?
¿Entiende español? Do you understand Spanish?
Te veré más tarde. See you later.
Para decir "no" cortésmente se dice "I'm sorry" que también quiere decir "Lo siento". Repita, "I'm sorry". I'm sorry.
Diga, "Lo siento" en inglés. I'm sorry.
Repita, "Ry". Ry.
Sor. Sor.
Sorry. Sorry

I'm sorry. I'm sorry.
Diga en inglés, "No. Lo siento." No. I'm sorry.
No entiendo español. I don't understand Spanish.
No. Lo siento. No entiendo español. No. I'm sorry. I don't understand Spanish.
Diga en inglés, "Te veré más tarde". See you later.
"Por favor" se dice "please" en inglés. Diga "please". Please.
Repita "Ease". Ease.
Please. Please.
Ahora diga, "Con permiso" en inglés. Excuse me.
Utilizando la contracción, diga "Usted es". You're.
Ahora haga lo mismo con "Yo soy". I'm.
¿Cómo se dice "No entiendo" en inglés? I don't understand.
No, señorita. No miss.
No entiendo inglés. I don't understand English.
Lo siento. I'm sorry.
Lo siento. No entiendo inglés. I'm sorry. I don't understand English.
No soy mexicana. I'm not Mexican.
Usted no entiende español. You don't understand Spanish.
Usted no es mexicana, señorita. You're not Mexican, miss.
Usted no es norteamericano, señor. You're not American, sir.
Soy mexicano. ¿Y usted? I'm Mexican. And you?
¿Es usted norteamericana? Are you American?
Lo siento. No entiendo. I'm sorry. I don't understand.
¿Cómo está? How are you?
Estoy bien, gracias. I'm fine, thanks.
Adiós. Goodbye.
Te veré más tarde. See you later.
¿Cómo está? How are you?
Estoy bien, gracias. I'm fine, thanks.
Con permiso. Excuse me.
Gracias. Thanks.
Con permiso, señor. Excuse me, sir.
Por favor, señor. Please, sir.
¿Es usted mexicano? Are you Mexican?
Conteste "Sí, señorita" en inglés. Yes, miss.
¿Cómo se dice "No entiendo español" en inglés? I don't understand Spanish.
No entiendo muy bien. I don't understand very well.

Entiendo un poco. I understand a little.
No muy bien. Not very well.
Diga "Not". Not.
Repita, "Not very well". Not very well.
Entiendo un poco de inglés. I understand a little English.
Señorita. Miss.
Hola, señorita. Hello, miss.
¿Cómo está? How are you?
Estoy bien, gracias. ¿Y usted, señor? I'm fine, thanks. And you, sir?
¿Entiende español? Do you understand Spanish?
No entiendo español. I don't understand Spanish.
¿Es usted mexicano? Are you Mexican?
Sí. Yes.
Pero entiendo inglés. But I understand English.
Diga "Un poco" en inglés. A little.
Ahora diga "No muy bien" en inglés. Not very well.
Pero usted entiende inglés muy bien. But you understand English very well.
Gracias, señorita. Thanks, miss.
"You speak" quiere decir "Usted habla" en inglés. Repita "You speak". You speak.
Usted habla. You speak.
¿Cómo se dice, "Usted habla muy bien" en inglés? You speak very well.
Por favor, señorita. Please, miss.
Adiós, señor. Goodbye, sir.
Adiós, señorita. Goodbye, miss.
Te veré más tarde. See you later.
¿Es usted mexicana? Are you Mexican?
Sí, soy mexicana pero entiendo inglés. Yes I'm Mexican but I understand English.
No muy bien. Not very well.
Usted habla muy bien inglés. You speak English very well.
Gracias. Thanks.

End of the speaking/listening lesson. Continue with the reading for Lesson 3.

HOW TO TEACH ENGLISH TO A SPANISH SPEAKER LEVEL 1

Reading for Lesson 3

Read each word first. Have the student read each one after you. Do the same for the Reading Practice phrases and the High Frequency English Words.

More Short Vowel Reading Practice

Aa

ban	can	Dan
fan	Jan	man
pan	ran	tan
van	land	drag

Ee

den	hen	Jen
Ken	men	pen
wren	ten	when
well	went	bent

Ii

bin	fin	kin
pin	sin	tin
win	grip	slip
chin	grin	hip

Oo

con	fawn	Don
gone	John	lawn
pawn	Ron	won
knot	rod	solid

Uu

bun	done	fun
gun	none	pun
run	sun	ton
nun	bump	lump

Reading Practice

Hello, how are you?

Very well, thanks. And you?

Fine, thanks.

You speak English very well.

Thank you. I speak a little. And you? Do you understand Spanish?

Not very well.

High Frequency English Words

on	be	at
by	I	this
had	not	are
but	from	or
have	an	they

LEVEL 1: LESSON 4

Teacher note: Review the teaching tips covered so far and be sure to continue applying them in this lesson, and the ones that follow. You'll also notice that we are using some commands in English. Over time these will increase so as to immerse the student in more English during the lessons. Be careful not to let the student say "turd" instead of "third" in this lesson!

Diga "hola" en inglés. Hello.

Say "adiós" in English. Goodbye.

Now say "Te veré más tarde" in English. See you later.

Diga "Hola" en inglés otra vez. Hello.

¿Cómo está? How are you?

Bien, gracias. Fine, thanks.

Estoy bien, gracias. I'm fine, thanks.

¿Y usted? And you?

Muy bien. Very well.

Yo soy mexicano. I'm Mexican.

Soy mexicano, señorita. I'm Mexican, miss.

Pero entiendo un poco de inglés. But I understand a little English.

¿Es usted norteamericana, señora? Are you American, ma'am?

Usted no es mexicana. You're not Mexican.

¿Entiende español, señorita? Do you understand Spanish, miss?

Sí, pero no muy bien. Yes, but not very well.

No entiendo español. I don't understand Spanish.

Lo siento. No entiendo español. I'm sorry. I don't understand Spanish.

Lo siento. I'm sorry.

En inglés "¿Cómo te va?" se dice "How's it going?". Repita "How's it going?" How's it going?

Pregúnteme cómo me va. How's it going?

Repita otra vez "How's it going?" How's it going?
"Todo bien" se dice "It's going well". Diga "It's going well" It's going well.
¿Cómo se dice que "Todo bien" en inglés? It's going well.
Pregúnteme otra vez cómo me va. How's it going?
Otra vez diga "¿Cómo te va?" How's it going?
Todo bien. It's going well.
Todo bien, gracias. It's going well, thanks.
Para decir "Usted habla" en inglés, se dice "You speak". Repita "You speak". You speak.
Diga esta combinación de sonidos "Sp". Sp.
Ahora diga "speak". Speak.
Usted habla. You speak.
Usted entiende. You understand.
Usted habla. You speak.
Usted habla muy bien. You speak very well.
Hola, ¿cómo te va? Hello, how's it going?
Say "Muy bien, gracias" in English. Very well, thanks.
Now say, "Todo bien, gracias" in English. It's going well, thanks.
Ahora diga en inglés, "Usted habla muy bien". You speak very well.
Otra vez en inglés, "Usted habla muy bien inglés". You speak English very well.
"Yo hablo" se dice "I speak" en inglés. ¿Cómo se dice "yo hablo"? I speak.
Yo hablo un poco. I speak a little.
Yo hablo un poco de inglés. I speak a little English.
Hablo un poco. I speak a little.
Pero. But.
No entiendo. I don't understand.
Entiendo un poco. I understand a little.
Pero no hablo. But I don't speak.
No hablo muy bien. I don't speak very well.
No entiendo. I don't understand.
Entiendo un poco pero no hablo muy bien. I understand a little but I don't speak very well.
No soy norteamericano. I'm not American.
No soy mexicana. I'm not Mexican.
Lo siento. No entiendo. I'm sorry. I don't understand.
Diga lo siguiente con entonación de pregunta: "¿Usted no entiende español?" You don't understand Spanish?

¿Perdón? Excuse me?
¿Usted no entiende español? You don't understand Spanish?
Sí. Entiendo un poco. Yes. I understand a little.
Y hablo un poco. And I speak a little.
Pero no muy bien. But not very well.
Entiendo un poco de español. I understand a little Spanish.
Pero no hablo muy bien. But I don't speak very well.
Entiendo inglés. I understand English.
No soy norteamericano. I'm not American.
¿Y usted? And you?
Sí. Soy norteamericana. Yes. I'm American.
Y hablo inglés. And I speak English.
Pero no hablo español. But I don't speak Spanish.
Lo siento. No hablo español. I'm sorry. I don't speak Spanish.
Por favor. Please.
"Tercer" se dice "Third" en inglés. Repita "Third". Third.
Tercer. Third. Sin embargo al usarlo en numeraciones que no tengan que ver con días, se dice **"tres"**
"Cincuenta" se dice "fifty" en inglés. Repita "fifty". Fifty
Diga esta combinación de sonidos, "fif". Fif.
Ty. Ty.
Fifty. Fifty.
"Cincuenta y tres" se dice "Fifty third". Diga "Fifty third". Fifty third.
"Street" quiere decir "calle" en inglés. Repita "street". Street.
Repita, "Fifty Third Street". Fifty Third Street
Calle Cincuenta y tres. Fifty Third Street
Otra vez diga "Fifty Third Street". Fifty Third Street.
La dirección "Norte" se dice "North" en inglés. Diga "North". North.
"La Calle cincuenta y tres Norte" se dice "North Fifty Third Street". Repita "North Fifty Third Street". North Fifty Third Street.
La Calle Cincuenta y tres Norte. North Fifty Third Street
Say in English, "North Fifty Third Street". North Fifty Third Street.
"Park" quiere decir "parque". ¿Cómo se dice "parque" en inglés? Park.
"Park Street" quiere decir "La Calle Parque" en inglés. Repita, "Park Street". Park Street.
¿Cómo se dice "La Calle Parque Norte" en inglés? North Park Street.
"Where" quiere decir "donde". Diga "where". Where.

Say "donde" in English. Where.

"Where is?" quiere decir "¿dónde está?" en inglés. Repita "Where is?" Where is?

Repita, "Where is North Fifty Third Street?" Where is North Fifty Third Street?

Pregúnteme en inglés, "¿Dónde está la Calle Cincuenta y tres Norte? Where is North Fifty Third Street?

¿Dónde está la Calle Cincuenta y tres Norte? Where is North Fifty Third Street?

Por favor. Please.

¿Dónde está la Calle Parque? Where is Park Street?

Por favor. Please.

"Avenida" se dice "avenue" en inglés. Repita "avenue". Avenue

Nue. Nue.

Av. Av.

Ave. Ave.

Avenue. Avenue

Avenida Parque. Park Avenue.

¿Dónde está la Avenida Parque? Where is Park Avenue?

¿Dónde está la Avenida Parque, por favor? Where is Park Avenue please?

"Here" quiere decir "aquí" Diga "here". Here.

"Está" se dice "It is". Repita "It is". It is.

Está. It is.

Aquí. Here.

Está aquí. It is here.

Repita lo mismo pero con la contracción. Se dice "It's here". It's here.

Está aquí. It's here.

¿Dónde está la Calle Cincuenta y tres Norte? Where is North Fifty Third Street?

Por favor. Please.

¿Dónde está la Calle Cincuenta y tres Norte? Where is North Fifty Third Street?

Está aquí. It's here.

Está aquí, señor. It's here, sir.

Para preguntar "¿está aquí?" se dice "Is it here?" Pregunte si está aquí. Is it here?

Sí. Está aquí. Yes. It's here.

¿Está aquí? Is it here?

Para decir "No, no está aquí" se dice, "No, it's not here." Repita, "No, it's not here". No, it's not here.

En inglés, se dice "no" solo una vez. Luego "not". Repita otra vez, "No, it's not here." No, it's not here.

No, no está aquí. No, It's not here.

Ahora diga simplemente, "No está aquí" en inglés. It's not here.
No está aquí. It's not here.
No, no está aquí. No, it's not here.
"Over there" quiere decir "por allá" en inglés. Repita "over there". Over there.
¿Cómo se dice "por allá" en inglés? Over there.
"It´s over there" quiere decir "Está por allá". ¿Cómo se dice "Está por allá" en inglés? It's over there.
¿La Calle Parque? Está por allá. Park Street? It's over there.
¿La Calle Cincuenta y tres Norte? Está por allá. North Fifty Third Street? It´s over there.
No está por allá. It's not over there.
Está aquí, señor. It's here, sir.
No está por allá. It's not over there.
La Avenida Parque está aquí. Park Avenue is here.
¿Dónde está la Calle Cincuenta y tres Norte? Where is North Fifty Third Street?
Por favor. Please.
No está aquí, señor. It's not here, sir.
Está por allá. It's over there.
Y la Avenida Parque está aquí. And Park Avenue is here.
Hola, señor. Hello, sir.
¿Cómo está? How are you?
Bien, gracias. ¿Y usted? Fine, thanks. And you?
Estoy bien. ¿Es usted mexicano? I'm fine. Are you Mexican?
Sí, soy mexicano. Yes, I'm Mexican.
Soy norteamericana. ¿Usted entiende inglés? I'm American. Do you understand English?
Yo entiendo un poco. I understand a little.
Pero usted habla muy bien inglés. But you speak English very well.
Gracias. Thanks.
Discúlpeme. Excuse me.
¿Dónde está la Calle Cincuenta y tres Norte, por favor? Where is North Fifty Third Street, please?
La Calle Cincuenta y tres Norte no está por allá. North Fifty Third Street is not over there.
Está aquí. It's here.
¿Y la Calle Parque? And Park Street?
Está por allá. It's over there.

Lo siento. No entiendo. I'm sorry. I don't understand.
Adiós. Goodbye.
Te veré más tarde. See you later.

End of the speaking/listening lesson. Continue with the reading for Lesson 4.

Reading for Lesson 4

Read each phrase or sentence and have the student read each one after you. Do the same for the High Frequency English Words.

Reading Practice
How are you, sir?
I'm fine, thank you. And you?
Fine, thanks. Do you speak English?
Yes. I speak English very well.
Are you from the United States?
Yes, I am. And you? Where are you from?
I am from Mexico. I speak Spanish. Do you speak Spanish too?
I speak a little. Only a little. I don't speak Spanish very well.
Are you Mexican?
Yes, but I speak English.
You speak English and Spanish.
You're American.
Yes, I am.
I'm American but I speak a little Spanish.
Excuse me. Where is North Fifty Third Street?
It's over there. It's not here.
And Park Avenue? Where is it?
It's here. It's not over there.
I'm sorry. I don't understand you.
You don't understand English?
I don't understand English very well.
Never mind. Goodbye.
Okay. See you later.

High Frequency English Words

which	one	you
were	her	all
she	there	would
their	we	him
been	has	when

LEVEL 1: LESSON 5 (LESSONS 1 – 4 REVIEW)

Teaching tip: This lesson is a little longer. You can spend 1 – 2 days or more on this review, depending on how well the student has mastered the material. Reviewing the reading lessons that went with lessons 1 – 4 can be of help also. Remember, a student should not move ahead until he or she responds correctly at least 85% of the time.

Hola Richard. ¿Cómo está? Hello Richard. How are you?
Muy bien, gracias. ¿Y usted, Martha? Very well, thanks. And you, Martha?
Muy bien. Very well.
Say in English "Perdón. ¿Habla español?" Excuse me. Do you speak Spanish?
Now answer "Sí, pero no muy bien." Yes, but not very well.
Yo hablo español muy bien. I speak Spanish very well.
Pregúnteme en inglés "¿Es usted mexicano?" Are you Mexican?
No, soy norteamericano. No, I'm American.
Pero entiendo un poco de español. But I understand a little Spanish.
Yo hablo y entiendo inglés bien. I speak and understand English well.
Adiós. Goodbye.
¿Cómo se dice "Te veré más tarde"? See you later.
Usted habla inglés muy bien, señorita. You speak English very well, miss.
Se lo agradezco. Thank you.
De nada. You're welcome.
Usted no es mexicano. You're not Mexican.
Pero habla español muy bien. But you speak Spanish very well.
Yo hablo inglés y español. I speak English and Spanish.
Lo siento. No hablo español. I'm sorry. I don't speak Spanish.
Usted no habla español. You don't speak Spanish.
Repita lo mismo pero con entonación de pregunta: "¿Usted no habla español?" You don't speak Spanish?
Diga la palabra "inglés" en inglés. English.

Ahora diga "Yo entiendo inglés". I understand English.
Entiendo un poco. I understand a little.
Entiendo un poco de inglés. I understand a little English.
Say "no muy bien" in English. Not very well.
No entiendo. I don't understand.
No muy bien. Not very well.
Con permiso. Excuse me.
¿Cómo está? How are you?
¿Cómo está, señor? How are you, sir?
"Estoy bien, gracias" se dice "I'm fine, thanks". Repita "I'm fine, thanks". I'm fine, thanks.
Estoy bien, gracias. I'm fine, thanks.
Si quiere ser más cortés se dice "thank you" en vez de "thanks". Es como decir "Se lo agradezco". Diga "Se lo agradezco" en inglés. Thank you.
Otra vez diga "Thank you". Thank you.
Repita, "Thank". Thank .
Ahora repita, "Thank you". Thank you.
Diga otra vez en inglés, "Se lo agradezco". Thank you.
Se lo agradezco, señora. Thank you, ma'am.
Say "Hola" in English. Hello.
Hola, señora. Hello, ma'am.
Adiós. Goodbye.
Adiós, señora. Goodbye, ma'am.
Otra manera de despedirse es decir "See you later". Es muy informal, y es como decir "Te veré más tarde". Repita "See you later". See you later.
¿Cómo está? How are you?
Bien, gracias. Fine, thanks.
Te veré después. See you later.
No entiendo inglés. I don't understand English.
¿Entiende inglés? Do you understand English?
Entiendo un poco de inglés. I understand a little English.
¿Es usted mexicano? Are you Mexican?
¿Es usted mexicano, señor? Are you Mexican, sir?
Pregúntele a una señorita lo mismo. Are you Mexican, miss?
Sí, soy mexicana. Yes, I'm Mexican.
Recuerde que "soy" se dice "I'm" cuando utiliza la contracción. Diga "soy" en inglés. I'm.

Soy mexicana. I'm Mexican.
Ahora diga "Usted es" utilizando la contracción. You're.
Say "mexicano" in English. Mexican.
Usted es mexicano. You are Mexican.
Soy mexicano. I'm Mexican.
¿Es usted mexicana, señora? Are you Mexican, ma'am?
"No. Yo soy norteamericana" se dice, "No. I'm American".
Soy norteamericana. I'm American.
¿Entiende español? Do you understand Spanish?
Un poco. A little.
No muy bien. Not very well.
Diga, "No soy norteamericano". I'm not American.
"¿Y usted?" se dice "And you?" Diga "And you?" And you?
And. And.
And you? And you?
¿Cómo se dice "Y" en inglés? And.
¿Y usted? And you?
¿Y usted, señor? And you, sir?
Y. And
¿Y usted? And you?
Soy colombiano. ¿Y usted? I'm Colombian. And you?
Usted es mexicano. You're Mexican.
Yo no soy mexicano. I'm not Mexican.
Usted no es colombiana. You're not Colombian.
No soy norteamericano. I'm not American.
¿Y usted? And you?
No soy norteamericano. I'm not American.
Pero yo entiendo. But I understand.
Pero entiendo inglés. But I understand English.
Entiendo un poco de inglés. I understand a little English.
No entiendo. I don't understand.
No entiendo muy bien. I don't understand very well.
No muy bien. Not very well.
¿Y usted? And you?
¿Es usted norteamericana, señora? Are you American, ma'am?
¿Es usted mexicana? Are you Mexican?
¿Entiende español? Do you understand Spanish?

Para decir "no" cortésmente se dice "I'm sorry". Esto también quiere decir "Lo siento". Repita, "I'm sorry". I'm sorry.
Lo siento. I'm sorry.
No. Lo siento. No. I'm sorry.
No entiendo español. I don't understand Spanish.
No. Lo siento. No entiendo español. No. I'm sorry. I don't understand Spanish.
Diga en inglés, "Te veré más tarde". See you later.
Diga "Por favor" en inglés. Please.
Ahora diga, "Con permiso" en inglés. Excuse me.
Utilizando la contracción, diga en inglés, "Usted es". You're.
Ahora haga lo mismo con "Yo soy". I'm.
No entiendo. I don't understand.
No, señorita. No, miss.
No entiendo inglés. I don't understand English.
Lo siento. I'm sorry.
Lo siento. No entiendo inglés. I'm sorry. I don't understand English.
No soy mexicana. I'm not Mexican.
Usted no entiende español. You don't understand Spanish.
Usted no es mexicana, señorita. You're not Mexican, miss.
Usted no es norteamericano, señor. You're not American, sir.
Soy colombiana. ¿Y usted? I'm Colombian. And you?
¿Es usted norteamericana? Are you American?
Lo siento. No entiendo. I'm sorry. I don't understand.
¿Cómo está? How are you?
Estoy bien. Gracias. I'm fine. Thanks.
Adiós. Goodbye.
Te veré más tarde. See you later.
Con permiso. Excuse me.
Gracias. Thanks.
Con permiso, señor. Excuse me, sir.
Por favor, señor. Please, sir.
¿Es usted mexicano? Are you Mexican?
Sí, señorita. Yes, miss.
No entiendo español. I don't understand Spanish.
No entiendo muy bien. I don't understand very well.
Entiendo un poco. I understand a little.
No muy bien. Not very well.

Entiendo un poco de inglés. I understand a little English.
Hola, señorita. Hello, miss.
¿Cómo está? How are you?
Estoy bien, gracias. ¿Y usted, señor? I'm fine, thanks. And you, sir?
¿Entiende español? Do you understand Spanish?
No entiendo español. I don't understand Spanish.
¿Es usted mexicano? Are you Mexican?
Sí. Yes.
Pero entiendo inglés. But I understand English.
Diga "Un poco" en inglés. A little.
Ahora diga "No muy bien". Not very well.
Pero usted entiende muy bien inglés. But you understand English very well.
Gracias, señorita. Thanks, miss.
¿Cómo se dice "Usted habla" en inglés? You speak.
Usted habla muy bien. You speak very well.
Por favor, señorita. Please, miss.
Adiós, señor. Goodbye, sir.
Adiós, señorita. Goodbye, miss.
Te veré más tarde. See you later.
¿Es usted mexicana? Are you Mexican?
Sí, soy mexicana pero entiendo inglés. Yes I'm Mexican but I understand English.
No muy bien. Not very well.
Usted habla muy bien inglés. You speak English very well.
Gracias. Thanks.
Diga "hola". Hello
Say "adiós" in English. Goodbye
Now say "te veré más tarde". See you later.
¿Cómo está? How are you?
Bien, gracias. Fine, thanks.
Estoy bien, gracias. I'm fine, thanks.
¿Y usted? And you?
Muy bien. Very well.
Yo soy colombiano. I'm Colombian.
Soy colombiano, señorita. I'm Colombian, miss.
Pero entiendo un poco de inglés. But I understand a little English.
¿Es usted norteamericana, señora? Are you American, ma'am?
Usted no es mexicana. You're not Mexican.

¿Entiende español, señorita? Do you understand Spanish, miss?
Sí, pero no muy bien. Yes, but not very well.
No entiendo español. I don't understand Spanish.
Lo siento. No entiendo español. I'm sorry. I don't understand Spanish.
Pregúnteme cómo me va. How's it going?
¿Cómo se dice que "Todo bien"? It's going well.
Pregúnteme otra vez cómo me va. How's it going?
Todo bien, gracias. It's going well, thanks.
Usted habla. You speak.
Usted entiende. You understand.
Usted habla muy bien. You speak very well.
Hola, ¿como te va? Hello, how's it going?
Say "Muy bien, gracias" in English. Very well, thanks.
Todo bien, gracias. It's going well, thanks.
Usted habla inglés muy bien. You speak English very well.
Yo hablo un poco. I speak a little.
Yo hablo un poco de inglés. I speak a little English.
Hablo un poco. I speak a little.
Pero. But.
No entiendo. I don't understand.
Entiendo un poco. I understand a little.
Pero no hablo. But I don't speak.
No hablo muy bien. I don't speak very well.
No entiendo. I don't understand.
Entiendo un poco pero no hablo muy bien. I understand a little but I don't speak very well.
No soy norteamericano. I'm not American.
No soy mexicana. I'm not Mexican.
Lo siento. No entiendo. I'm sorry. I don't understand.
Diga lo siguiente con entonación de pregunta: "¿Usted no entiende español?" You don't understand Spanish?
¿Perdón? Excuse me?
Sí. Entiendo un poco. Yes. I understand a little.
Y hablo un poco. And I speak a little.
Pero no muy bien. But not very well.
Entiendo un poco de español. I understand a little Spanish.
Pero no hablo muy bien. But I don't speak very well.

Entiendo inglés. I understand English.
No soy norteamericano. I'm not American.
¿Y usted? And you?
Sí. Soy norteamericana. Yes. I'm American.
Y hablo inglés. And I speak English.
Pero no hablo español. But I don't speak Spanish.
Lo siento. No hablo español. I'm sorry. I don't speak Spanish.
Por favor. Please.
Calle Cincuenta y tres. Fifty Third Street
Otra vez diga "Fifty Third Street". Fifty Third Street.
La Calle Cincuenta y tres Norte. North Fifty Third Street
La Calle Parque. Park Street.
La Calle Parque Norte. North Park Street
Say "dónde" in English. Where.
¿Dónde está la Calle Cincuenta y tres Norte? Where is North Fifty Third Street?
Por favor. Please.
¿Dónde está la Calle Parque? Where is Park Street?
Avenida Parque. Park Avenue.
¿Dónde está la Avenida Parque? Where is Park Avenue?
¿Dónde está la Avenida Parque, por favor? Where is Park Avenue please?
Está aquí. It is here.
Repita lo mismo pero con la contracción. Se dice "It's here". It's here.
Está aquí. It's here.
Say "Por favor" in English. Please.
¿Dónde está la Calle Cincuenta y tres Norte? Where is North Fifty Third Street?
Está aquí, señor. It's here, sir.
Pregunte si está aquí. Is it here?
Sí. Está aquí. Yes. It's here.
Otra vez pregunte, "¿Esta aquí?" Is it here?
Conteste, "No, no está aquí". No, it's not here.
Ahora diga simplemente, "No está aquí." It's not here.
¿Cómo se dice "por allá" en inglés? Over there.
¿Cómo se dice "Está por allá"? It's over there.
¿La Calle Parque? Está por allá. Park Street? It's over there.
¿La Calle Cincuenta y tres Norte? Está por allá. North Fifty Third Street? It's over there.
No está por allá. It's not over there.

Está aquí, señor. It's here, sir.
La Avenida Parque está aquí. Park Avenue is here.
¿Dónde está la Calle Cincuenta y tres Norte? Where is North Fifty Third Street?
No está aquí, señor. It's not here, sir.
Está por allá. It's over there.
Y la Avenida Parque está aquí. And Park Avenue is here.
Hola, Señor. Hello, sir.
¿Cómo está? How are you?
Bien, gracias. ¿Y usted? Fine, thanks. And you?
Estoy bien. ¿Es usted colombiano? I'm fine. Are you Colombian?
Sí, soy colombiano. Yes, I'm Colombian.
Soy norteamericana. ¿Entiende inglés? I'm American. Do you understand English?
Yo entiendo un poco. I understand a little.
Pero habla inglés muy bien. But you speak English very well.
Gracias. Thanks.
Discúlpeme. Excuse me.
¿Dónde está la Calle Cincuenta y tres Norte, por favor? Where is North Fifty Third Street, please?
La Calle Cincuenta y tres Norte no está por allá. North Fifty Third Street is not over there.
Está aquí. It's here.
¿Y la Calle Parque? And Park Street?
Está por allá. It's over there.
Lo siento. No entiendo. I'm sorry. I don't understand.
Adiós. Goodbye.
Te veré más tarde. See you later.

End of the speaking/listening lesson. Continue with the reading for Lesson 5.

Reading for Lesson 5

Have the student read the following phrases and sentences out loud. See if he can do this without help. Then have him try to reread all the high frequency English words for the previous four chapters out loud by himself. Correct him as needed.

<u>Reading Practice</u>
Hello, ma'am.
Hello. How are you?
I'm fine, thanks. And you?
I'm fine *too (también)*.
Excuse me, where is Park Street?
It's here, ma'am.
Where is North Fifty Third Street?
It's there.
I'm sorry, sir. I don't understand.
You don't understand English?
I understand a little bit.
Do you understand Spanish?
Yes.

High Frequency English Words

the	of	and	to	a
in	that	is	was	he
for	it	with	as	his
on	be	at	by	I
this	had	not	are	but
from	or	have	an	they
which	one	you	were	her
all	she	there	would	their
we	him	been	has	when

LEVEL 1: LESSON 6

Teaching tip: Your student will run into a lot of words that will have the "th" sound in this lesson, and the few lessons that follow. It will be common for him to pronounce this sound as a hard "t". Have him slow down the pronunciation, pausing the syllables. For example, when saying "Something to eat", have him say "Some.....thhhing to eat." And don't let the student get away with saying "You welcome" instead of "You're welcome"!

En inglés, "You're welcome" quiere decir "De nada". Repita, "You're welcome." You're welcome.
¿Cómo se dice "De nada" en inglés? You're welcome.
Say again, "You're welcome". You're welcome.
Say "Hola" in English. Hello.
Now ask this in English, "¿Entiende usted español?" Do you understand Spanish?
Answer in English, "Entiendo un poco". I understand a little.
Y hablo un poco. And I speak a little.
No muy bien. Not very well.
¿Y usted? And you?
¿Entiende inglés? Do you understand English?
Lo siento. No entiendo. I'm sorry. I don't understand.
No soy norteamericano. I'm not American.
Y no entiendo. And I don't understand.
No soy norteamericano y no entiendo. I'm not American and I don't understand.
Say "Lo siento" in English. I'm sorry.
Now say in English, "Pero usted habla muy bien". But you speak very well.
How do you say "Se lo agradezco" in English? Thank you.
De nada. You're welcome.
¿Cómo está? How are you?
Estoy bien, gracias. ¿Y usted? I'm fine, thanks. And you?
¿Cómo le va? How's it going?

Todo bien, gracias. It's going well, thanks.
Vamos a usar "tres" en vez de "tercio". Diga en inglés "Calle Cincuenta y tres Norte". North Fifty Third Street.
Repita, "North". North.
Fifty Third Street. Fifty Third Street.
Una vez más, diga, "Calle Cincuenta y tres Norte" en inglés. North Fifty Third Street.
Now say"Avenida Parque" in English. Park Avenue.
Pregunte en inglés,"¿Dónde está la Avenida Parque?" Where is Park Avenue?
Now say "Por favor" in English. Please.
Pregunte en inglés, "¿Dónde está la Calle Cincuenta y tres Norte?" Where is North Fifty Third Street?
Conteste en inglés, "Está aquí." It's here.
La Calle Cincuenta y tres Norte está aquí. North Fifty Third Street is here.
Ask in English, "¿Queda aquí?" Is it here?
Answer in English, "No. Está por allá." No. It's over there.
No está por allá. It's not over there.
Y no está aquí. And it's not here.
La Calle Cincuenta y tres Norte no está aquí. North Fifty Third Street is not here.
Pero la Avenida Parque está aquí. But Park Avenue is here.
Se lo agradezco, señorita. Thank you, miss.
De nada. You're welcome.
Ask in English, "¿Dónde está la Calle Cincuenta y tres Norte por favor? Where is North Fifty Third Street, please?
"Yo no sé" se dice "I don't know". Repita "I don't know". I don't know.
Repita, "Know". Know.
Repeat, "Don't know". Don't know.
Now repeat, "I don't know." I don't know.
¿Cómo se dice "Yo no sé" en inglés? I don't know.
Ahora diga "Yo sé". I know.
Pregúnteme dónde está la Calle Parque. Where is Park Street?
Say "Yo no sé" in English. I don't know.
Oh, yo sé. Oh, I know.
Say in English, "Está por allá." It's over there.
Gracias. Thanks.
De nada. You're welcome.
Yo sé. I know.
Para decir "Usted sabe" se dice "You know". Repita "You know". You know.

Ahora pregunte, "¿Entiende usted?" Do you understand?

¿Cómo cree que se dice "¿Sabe usted?" en inglés? Do you know?

Otra vez repita "Do you know?" Do you know?

No, no sé. No, I don't know.

No está por allá. It's not over there.

Gracias. Thanks.

De nada. You're welcome.

Las palabras "Yo quiero" se dicen "I want" en inglés. Repita, "I want". I want.

¿Cómo se dice "Yo quiero" en inglés? I want.

Ahora diga "Usted quiere" en inglés. You want.

Say "Yo quiero" in English. I want.

Yo sé. I know.

Yo no sé. I don't know.

Yo no quiero. I don't want.

Usted quiere. You want.

¿Quiere usted? Do you want?

Las palabras "Le gustaría" se dice "You would like" en inglés. Repita "You would like". You would like.

Diga, "You". You.

Repeat, "You would". You would.

You would like. You would like.

Diga otra vez en inglés, "Le gustaría". You would like.

La palabra "comer" se dice "to eat" en inglés. Repita "to eat". To eat

Otra vez diga "to eat". To eat.

¿Cómo se dice "Comer" en inglés? To eat.

Le gustaría comer. You would like to eat.

Para decir la palabra "algo" se dice "something". Repita, "something." Something

Diga "thing". Thing

Diga "some". Some

Ahora diga "something". Something.

Repita lo siguiente, "Something to eat". Something to eat.

Para decir "Le gustaría comer algo", se dice "You would like something to eat."

Esto no es pregunta. Repita "You would like something to eat." You would like something to eat.

Otra vez diga, "You would like something to eat." You would like something to eat.

¿Cómo se dice "Le gustaría comer algo" en inglés? You would like something to eat.

Repita "You would like something to eat." You would like something to eat.

Ahora diga "Something to eat".   Something to eat.
Repita "Would like". Would like.
Ahora diga "you would like".   You would like.
Repita "You would like something to eat." You would like something to eat.
Para preguntarle a alguien "¿Cómo le va?" se dice "How's it going?" Repita, "How's it going?" How's it going?
Say again, "How's it going?" How's it going?
¿Cómo se dice en inglés, "Hola, ¿cómo le va?"? Hello, how's it going?"
Again say, "Hello, how's it going?" Hello, how's it going?
Hola, ¿cómo le va? Hi, how's it going?
"Todo bien" quiere decir, "It's going well". Repita, "It's going well." It's going well.
Pregunte en inglés, "¿Cómo le va? How's it going?
Diga en inglés que todo le va bien. It's going well.
Todo bien, gracias. ¿Y usted? It's going well, thanks. And you?
¿Cómo está? How are you?
La palabra "too" quiere decir "también". Repita "Too". Too.
Diga, "también" en inglés. Too.
¿Qué dices cuando alguien te dice "Gracias"? You're welcome.
"cubano" se dice "Cuban". Repita, "Cuban". Cuban.
Diga "Yo soy cubano" en inglés. I'm Cuban.
Ahora diga "Yo soy cubano también". I'm Cuban too.
¿Usted también? You too?
Sí. Yes.
Ahora diga la palabra "calle" en inglés. Street.
La palabra "esa" se dice "that". Repita, "that". That.
Say "Esa calle" in English. That street.
Now say, "¿Dónde está esa calle?" Where is that street?
Say "Calle Cincuenta y tres Norte". North Fifty Third Street
Repita "Fifty Third". Fifty Third.
Now repeat "North Fifty Third Street". North Fifty Third Street.

End of the speaking/listening lesson. Continue with the reading for Lesson 6

Reading for Lesson 6

Read the following numbers and say the letters of the alphabet with the student. After this, have the student read the sentences, phrases and English High Frequency Words at the bottom.

The Alphabet

Aa	Bb	Cc	Dd	Ee	Ff	Gg
Hh	Ii	Jj	Kk	Ll	Mm	Nn
Oo	Pp	Qq	Rr	Ss	Tt	Uu
Vv	Ww	Xx	Yy	Zz		

Reading Practice

Excuse me, do you know where North Fifty Third Street is?

I'm sorry. I don't know.

Do you speak English?

I understand a little and I speak a little, but not very well.

I understand English very well. I speak English very well too.

Where is North Fifty Third Street?

I know. It's over there. It's not here.

Okay. Thank you.

You're welcome.

Goodbye.

See you later.

High Frequency English Words

who	will	more
no	if	out
so	said	what
up	its	about
into	than	them

LEVEL 1: LESSON 7

Teaching tip: This lesson has a lot of practice in pronouncing what every Spanish speaker needs: practice in the "th" sound. Have your student take all these "th" words slowly so the sound does not come out like a hard "t".

Ask in English, "¿Dónde está la Calle Cincuenta y tres Norte? ¿Dónde está esa calle?" Where is North Fifty Third Street? Where is that street?
Again, ask, "¿Dónde está la Calle Cincuenta y tres Norte? ¿Dónde está esa calle?" Where is North Fifty Third Street? Where is that street?
Por favor. Please.
Conteste en inglés, "Está por allá". It's over there.
¿Y la Avenida Parque? And Park Avenue?
¿Queda aquí? Is it here?
Diga en inglés, "Está por allá también." It's over there too.
¿Queda aquí? Is it here?
Answer in Engish, "No, no está aquí". No, it's not here.
Se lo agradezco, señor. Thank you, sir.
¿Cómo se dice "De nada" en inglés? You're welcome.
¿Habla español? Do you speak Spanish?
Usted habla. You speak.
Usted habla muy bien. You speak very well.
Usted habla muy bien también. You speak very well too.
Yo entiendo un poco. I understand a little.
Y hablo un poco. And I speak a little.
Usted quiere. You want.
Le gustaría. You would like.
Algo. Something.
Para preguntarme si quiero comer algo, se dice, "Do you want something to eat?"
Repita, "Do you want something to eat?" Do you want something to eat?

Pregúnteme si yo quiero comer algo. Do you want something to eat?
Again ask in English, "¿Quiere comer algo?" Do you want something to eat?
Ahora pregunte en inglés, "¿Le gustaría comer algo?" Would you like something to eat?
Sí. Me gustaría comer algo. Yes. I would like something to eat.
La contracción de "I would" es "I'd". Diga "I'd". I'd.
Se necesita escuchar la "d". Repita, "I'd." I'd.
Ahora usando esta contracción, diga, "Me gustaría." I'd like.
Repita en inglés, "I'd like". I'd like.
¿Cómo se dice "Me gustaría comer algo" en inglés? I'd like something to eat.
Ahora diga otra vez en inglés, "Sí. Me gustaría comer algo." Yes. I'd like something to eat.
¿Cómo se dice "I'd" sin la contracción? I would.
Repita "I would". I would.
Ahora diga "I'd". I'd.
La palabra, "beber" se dice "to drink" en inglés. Repita, "to drink". To drink.
¿Qué quiere decir "to drink" en inglés? Beber.
¿Cómo se dice "Beber" en inglés? To drink.
¿Le gustaría beber algo? Would you like something to drink?
Sí. Me gustaría beber algo. Yes. I'd like something to drink.
Ask in English, "¿Quiere beber algo?" Do you want something to drink?
No gracias. No thanks.
¿Le gustaría comer algo? Would you like something to eat?
Sí. Me gustaría. Yes. I would.
Ask in English, "¿Le gustaría comer algo?" Would you like something to eat?
Repeat this word, "something". Something.
Now ask, "Would you like something to eat?" Would you like something to eat?
Sí. Me gustaría. Yes. I would.
No, se lo agradezco. Pero me gustaría beber algo. No, thank you. But I'd like something to drink.
Lo siento. No entiendo. I'm sorry. I don't understand.
¿Dónde está la Avenida Norte? Where is North Avenue?
¿Dónde está la Avenida Norte, por favor? Where is North Avenue, please?
¿Sabe usted? Do you know?
Lo siento. No sé. I'm sorry. I don't know.
No está aquí. It's not here.
Y no está por allá. And it's not over there.

Ask in English, "¿Le gustaría comer algo?" Would you like something to eat?
Answer in English, "Sí, me gustaría." Yes. I would.
Sí. Me gustaría comer algo. Yes. I'd like something to eat.
¿Dónde le gustaría comer? Where would you like to eat?
Repita en inglés, "Where would you". Where would you.
Ahora repita, "Like to eat". Like to eat.
¿Dónde le gustaría comer? Where would you like to eat?
Restaurante se dice "Restaurant". Restaurant.
Diga "Res". Res
Ahora "Resta" Resta
Repita "Restaurant". Restaurant
"Un restaurante" se dice "A restaurant". Repita "A restaurant". A restaurant
¿Cómo se dice "un"? A
La palabra "en" se dice "at". Repita "at". At
"En un" se dice "At a". Diga "At a". At a.
Ahora diga "En un restaurante". At a restaurant.
En un restaurante, por favor. At a restaurant, please.
¿Dónde le gustaría comer? Where would you like to eat?
¿En un restaurante? At a restaurant?
Sí. En un restaurante. Yes, at a restaurant.
A mí me gustaría comer también. I'd like to eat too.
Say "También" in English. Too.
Now say again, "A mí me gustaría comer también." I'd like to eat too.
La pregunta "¿Cuándo?" se dice "When?" Repita "When?" When?
¿Cómo se dice "¿Cuándo?" en inglés? When?
No sé. I don't know.
A mí también me gustaría comer. I'd like to eat too.
La palabra "Ahora" se dice "Now". Repita "Now". Now.
Say "Ahora" in English. Now.
¿Dónde le gustaría comer? Where would you like to eat?
¿Cuándo? When?
¿Cuándo le gustaría comer? When would you like to eat?
Ahora. Now.
A mí también me gustaría comer. I'd like to eat too.
¿Cuándo le gustaría comer? When would you like to eat?
Para contestar "Ahora no" diga "Not now". Not now.
Otra vez diga "Not now". Now now.

Say this in English: "Ahora no." Not now.
En inglés "Más tarde" se dice "Later". Diga "Later". Later.
Repita "er" sin pronunciar la "e". "R". R.
Ahora diga "late". Late.
Diga "later". Later.
Más tarde. Later.
Pregunte en inglés, "¿Le gustaría beber algo? Would you like something to drink?
Conteste en inglés, "Sí. Me gustaría." Yes. I would.
¿Cuándo? When?
No sé. I don't know.
No sé. Más tarde. I don't know. Later.
No gracias. Pero me gustaría comer algo. No thanks. But I'd like something to eat.
Me gustaría comer algo. I'd like something to eat.
¿Dónde le gustaría comer? Where would you like to eat?
¿Dónde? Where?
En un restaurante. At a restaurant.
Pero más tarde. But later.
¿Cuándo le gustaría beber algo? When would you like something to drink?
Pregunte "¿Cuándo?" en inglés. When?
Conteste en inglés, "Ahora no". Not now.
Más tarde. Later.
¿Dónde? Where?
¿Cuándo? When?
¿Cuándo le gustaría comer? When would you like to eat?
Ahora no. Not now.
Ahora no, señorita. Not now, miss.
Más tarde. Later.
Más tarde, por favor. Later, please.
¿Dónde? Where?
¿Dónde le gustaría comer? Where would you like to eat?
En un restaurante. At a restaurant.
En inglés "De acuerdo" se dice "Okay". Repita "Okay". Okay.
¿Cómo se dice "De acuerdo"? Okay.
Ahora diga "De acuerdo. En un restaurante." Okay. At a restaurant.
No, no en un restaurante. No, not at a restaurant.
Para responder con las palabras "No quiero" se dice "I don't want to". Repita "I don't want to". I don't want to.

Esto quiere decir que "No quiero hacerlo". Diga otra vez "I don't want to." I don't want to.

Ahora repita en partes. Primero con "I don't". I don't.

Diga "I don't want to". I don't want to.

En inglés cuando se dice "I want to", quiere decir "Quiero hacerlo." Diga " I want to". I want to.

¿Cómo se dice en inglés, "No quiero hacerlo"? I don't want to.

Say "Me gustaría beber algo" in English. I'd like something to drink.

De acuerdo. Okay.

A mí también me gustaría beber algo. I'd like something to drink too.

¿Cuándo le gustaría beber algo? When would you like something to drink?

Más tarde. Later.

No. Ahora. No. Now.

¿Ahora? De acuerdo. Now? Okay.

¿Le gustaría beber algo en un restaurante? Would you like something to drink at a restaurant?

Conteste en inglés, "Sí. Me gustaría." Yes. I would.

De acuerdo. Okay.

Pero a mí también me gustaría comer algo. But I'd like something to eat too.

Sí señorita. Pero más tarde. Yes, miss. But later.

Se lo agradezco, señor. Thank you, sir.

De nada. You're welcome.

End of the speaking/listening lesson. Continue with the reading for Lesson 7.

Reading for Lesson 7

Let the student know what each Long vowel sounds like before reading. As in other lessons, the student is to read the word after you.

Long A, Long I, and Long O:
_ a _ e, _ i _ e and _ o _ e

Long A: _ a _ e

skate	late	mate
fate	rate	hate
Kate	date	gate
Nate	wade	crate

Long O: _ o _ e

dole	hole	mole
pole	role	stole
sole	Nicole	note
wrote	vote	tote

Long I: _ I _ e

white	file	five
strive	mile	Nile
pile	bite	tile
vile	while	kite

Long E: ee

bee	beet	fee
feet	meet	greet
see	sheet	tee
wee	flee	glee

Long U:

cube	cubic	fume
perfume	mule	Yule
molecule	huge	music
musician	Jupiter	Jewish

Reading Practice

Would you like to drink something at a restaurant?
Yes, *but (pero)* I'd like to eat something too.
Okay.
And you?
No thanks. I don't want to.
Would you like to have something to eat at a restaurant?
Yes, I would. But not now. Later.
Later? Okay, but when?
I don't know. Maybe *at six o'clock (a las seis)*.
Six o'clock?
Yes, six o'clock.

LEVEL 1: LESSON 8

Teaching tip: Don't let your student get away with saying "More later" for "Más tarde"! Let him know that the "er" in "later" means "más" already. When he says "More later" it's as if he's saying "Más más tarde" in Spanish!

Say in English, "Me gustaría comer". I'd like to eat.
Now ask "¿Dónde le gustaría comer?" Where would you like to eat?
Answer "En un restaurante." At a restaurant.
Ahora diga, "A mí también me gustaría comer". I'd like to eat too.
¿Cuándo? When?
¿Cuándo le gustaría comer? When would you like to eat?
Ahora. Now.
A mí me gustaría comer ahora. I'd like to eat now.
¿A usted le gustaría comer algo también? Would you like something to eat too?
Sí. Me gustaría. Yes. I would.
No, se lo agradezco. No, thank you.
Pero me gustaría beber algo. But I'd like something to drink.
A mí me gustaría beber algo también. I'd like something to drink too.
¿Cuándo? When?
Conteste "Más tarde". Later.
Quiero comer más tarde. I want to eat later.
¿Dónde le gustaría comer? Where would you like to eat?
¿Por allá? Over there?
No. Por allá no. No. Not over there.
Aquí. Here.
Ahora no. Not now.
Aquí no. Not here.
¿Dónde? Where?
En un restaurante, por favor. At a restaurant, please.

De acuerdo. Okay.
Gracias. Thanks.
De nada. You're welcome.
A mí me gustaría comer aquí. I would like to eat here.
Pero yo no quiero. But I don't want to.
¿Dónde le gustaría comer? Where would you like to eat?
"En el hotel" se dice "at the hotel". Repita "at the hotel". At the hotel.
The. The
Repeat, "The hotel". The hotel.
Now repeat, "At the hotel". At the hotel.
The hotel. The hotel.
Me gustaría comer en el hotel. I would like to eat at the hotel.
En un restaurante. At a restaurant.
En un hotel. At a hotel.
En el hotel. At the hotel.
Lo siento. No quiero. I'm sorry. I don't want to.
Pregunte en inglés, "¿Cuándo le gustaría comer?" When would you like to eat?
¿Dónde le gustaría comer? Where would you like to eat?
¿Qué le gustaría comer? What would you like to eat?
Pregúnteme qué me gustaría comer. What would you like to eat?
No sé. I don't know.
¿Dónde le gustaría comer? Where would you like to eat?
¿En un restaurante? At a restaurant?
¿En el hotel? At the hotel?
De acuerdo. Se lo agradezco, señor. Okay. Thank you, sir.
Me gustaría beber algo. I'd like something to drink.
¿Qué le gustaría beber? What would you like to drink?
"Té helado" se dice "iced tea" en inglés. Repita, "iced tea". Iced tea.
La "d" suena como una "t". Repita, "Iced". Iced.
Iced tea. Iced tea.
"Algo" quiere decir "some". ¿Cómo se dice "algo"? Some.
Ahora para decir "algo de té helado" se dice "some iced tea. Repita, "some iced tea". Some iced tea.
Té helado. Iced tea.
Algo de té helado. Some iced tea.
Ahora repita, "I'd like some iced tea." I'd like some iced tea.
"Vino" es "wine" en inglés. ¿Cómo se dice "vino" en inglés? Wine.

Algo de té helado. Some iced tea.

Algo de vino. Some wine.

Me gustaría algo de vino. I'd like some wine.

En un restaurante. At a restaurant.

¿Qué le gustaría beber? What would you like to drink?

¿Le gustaría algo de vino? Would you like some wine?

Sí, me gustaría. Yes, I would.

Sí. Me gustaría algo de vino. Yes. I'd like some wine.

Me gustaría algo de té helado. I'd like some iced tea.

"Some beer" quiere decir "algo de cerveza". Repita "some beer". Some beer.

¿Cómo se dice "cerveza" en inglés? Beer.

Algo de cerveza. Some beer.

Algo de vino. Some wine.

Algo de té helado. Some iced tea.

Me gustaría algo de cerveza. I'd like some beer.

Pero me gustaría algo de vino. But I would like some wine.

¿Y usted? And you?

Quiero algo de té helado, por favor. I want some iced tea, please.

¿Dónde? ¿En el hotel? Where? At the hotel?

En el hotel no. Not at the hotel.

En un restaurante, por favor. At a restaurant, please.

Pero más tarde. But later.

Ahora no. Not now.

De acuerdo. Okay.

Me gustaría comer algo. I'd like something to eat.

A mí también me gustaría comer algo. I'd like something to eat too.

Me gustaría beber algo. I'd like something to drink.

¿Le gustaría beber algo? Would you like something to drink?

No. Se lo agradezco. No thank you.

Ahora no. Más tarde. Not now. Later.

Pero me gustaría comer algo. But I would like something to eat.

¿Le gustaría comer ahora? Would you like to eat now?

Sí. Me gustaría. Yes, I would.

¿Dónde le gustaría comer? Where would you like to eat?

En un restaurante, por favor. At a restaurant, please.

De acuerdo. ¿Cuándo? Okay. When?

Ahora, por favor. Now, please.

En el Restaurante Avenida Parque. At the Park Avenue Restaurant.
El Restaurante Avenida Parque. The Park Avenue Restaurant.
En el restaurante. At the restaurant.
En el Restaurante Avenida Parque. At the Park Avenue Restaurant.
¿Dónde está el Restaurante Avenida Parque? Where is the Park Avenue Restaurant?
Está por allá. It's over there.
En la Avenida Parque. On Park Avenue.
Diga otra vez "En la Avenida Parque". On Park Avenue.
¿Qué le gustaría comer? What would you like to eat?
Yo no sé. I don't know.
De acuerdo. ¿Qué le gustaría beber? Okay. What would you like to drink?
No sé. ¿Y usted? I don't know. And you?
¿A usted le gustaría algo de vino? Would you like some wine?
¿Algo de cerveza? Some beer?
No. Se lo agradezco. Ahora no. No, thank you. Not now.
¿Le gustaría comer algo? Would you like something to eat?
No gracias. No thanks.
Diga, "Usted no quiere comer." You don't want to eat.
Ahora con entonación de pregunta, "¿Usted no quiere comer?" You don't want to eat?
Ahora no, gracias. Not now, thanks.
Me gustaría algo de vino. I'd like some wine.
Pero más tarde. But later.
En el hotel. At the hotel.
En el hotel en la Avenida Parque. At the hotel on Park Avenue.
Pero me gustaría beber algo ahora. But I'd like something to drink now.
Me gustaría beber algo ahora. I'd like something to drink now.
De acuerdo. Okay.
¿Qué le gustaría comer? What would you like to eat?
Yo no sé. I don't know.
De acuerdo. ¿Qué le gustaría beber? Okay. What would you like to drink?
Algo de vino. ¿ Y usted? Some wine. And you?
Yo quiero algo de té helado. I want some iced tea.
Y usted, ¿Roberto? ¿Qué le gustaría beber? And you, Roberto? What would you like to drink?
Yo no sé. ¿Y usted? I don't know. And you?
¿Le gustaría algo de vino? Would you like some wine?

¿Algo de cerveza? Some beer?
No gracias. No thanks.

End of the speaking/listening lesson. Continue with the reading for Lesson 8.

Reading for Lesson 8

Have your student read after you in the Reading Practice and High Frequency English Words below. Then have your student read the entire page by herself. Make corrections as needed.

Reading Practice

Hi, how are you? I'm fine, thanks. And you?
Very well.
Do you understand Spanish, miss?
Yes, but not very well. I'm not Mexican. I'm American.
Do you understand English, sir? I understand a little.
Would you like to have something to eat?
Yes, I would. Thanks.
Where would you like to eat? At the hotel?
No, not at the hotel. At the restaurant, please.
You speak Spanish very well.
Thank you.
You're welcome.
Excuse me. Where is the Columbus Hotel? Is it here?
No, it's not here. It's over there.
Ah, yes. Thank you. Good bye.
See you later.
Where is George?
I don't know.
Do you know?
Yes, I do. He's over there.
I see him now *(Lo veo ahora)*. Thanks.
Would you like to have something to drink?
Yes.
Some beer? Some wine?
Okay. Some wine, please.
I'd like some wine, please.
Where would you like to eat?
I'd like to eat at the restaurant.
Okay.
I'd like to eat too.
When? When would you like to eat?
Later.
Well, I would like to eat now.
Not now. Later.

High Frequency English Words

can	only	other
new	some	could
time	these	two
may	then	do
first	any	my

LEVEL 1: LESSON 9

It's common for Spanish speakers to pronounce the word "lunch" with a Spanish "o" sound. You can do a vocal exercise to help correct this. Have the student place his hand about an inch and a half below his chin with the palm down. Have him make the "u" sound as in "jump" and relax his jaw so it touches his hand. He can do this several times and also when he gets to the word "lunch". Note: In the following lessons the student will be practicing using "at a" and "at an", which is why we'll be using "at a Chinese restaurant" and "at an Italian restaurant". Everything has a reason here!

"En un restaurante chino" se dice "at a Chinese restaurant" en inglés. Repita, "at a Chinese restaurant". At a Chinese restaurant.

Repita, "At a". At a.

At a Chinese. At a Chinese.

At a Chinese restaurant. At a Chinese Restaurant.

¿Cómo se dice, "En un restaurante chino" en inglés? At a Chinese restaurant.

"Almorzar" se dice "to have lunch". Diga, "to have lunch". To have lunch.

Say again, "To have lunch". To have lunch.

Acuérdese que "I'd like" quiere decir "Me gustaría". Repita, "I'd like". I'd like.

Say in English, "I'd like to have lunch". I'd like to have lunch.

Say "Me gustaría almorzar" in English. I'd like to have lunch.

Ask in English, "¿Dónde? Where?

Answer in English, "En un restaurante chino". At a Chinese restaurant.

Say, "Almorzar" in English. To have lunch.

Now say, "Almorzar en un restaurante chino" in English. To have lunch at a Chinese restaurant.

Diga en inglés, "Me gustaría almorzar en un restaurante chino." I would like to have lunch at a Chinese restaurant.

En un restaurante chino. At a Chinese restaurant.

"Dos cervezas" se dice "two beers" en inglés. Repita, "two beers". Two beers

Say in English, "I would like two beers please." I would like two beers please.
Now say, "I would like to have lunch". I would like to have lunch.
¿Cómo se dice "almorzar" en inglés? To have lunch.
Diga en inglés, "Me gustaría almorzar". I'd like to have lunch.
Say in English, "Me gustaría almorzar en un restaurante chino". I'd like to have lunch at a Chinese restaurant.
Now say, "Me gustaría comer algo". I'd like something to eat.
Ask in English, "¿Le gustaría comer ahora?" Would you like to eat now?
Answer in English, "Sí. Me gustaría almorzar". Yes, I'd like to have lunch.
Say, "Me gustaría almorzar ahora". I'd like to have lunch now.
Ask, "¿Dónde le gustaría almorzar?" Where would you like to have lunch?
¿En un restaurante? At a restaurant?
No, en el hotel. No, at the hotel.
En el hotel en la Calle Norte. At the hotel on North Street.
A mí me gustaría almorzar también. I'd like to have lunch too.
Pero más tarde. But later.
Me gustaría comer algo. I'd like something to eat.
En el hotel en la Calle Norte. At the hotel on North Street.
Me gustaría almorzar. I'd like to have lunch.
¿Le gustaría beber algo ahora? Would you like something to drink now?
Sí. Me gustaría. Yes. I would.
Dos cervezas, por favor. Two beers, please.
¿Qué le gustaría beber? What would you like to drink?
¿Le gustaría beber algo? Would you like something to drink?
"Claro" se dice "sure" en inglés. ¿Cómo se dice "claro" en inglés? Sure.
¿Qué le gustaría beber? What would you like to drink?
¿Cuándo le gustaría beber algo? When would you like something to drink?
¿Le gustaría beber algo? Would you like something to drink?
Claro. Sure.
¿Le gustaría algo de cerveza? Would you like some beer?
Claro. Sure.
Dos cervezas, por favor. Two beers, please.
¿Cómo se dice "dos" en inglés? Two.
Say "Dos cervezas" in English. Two beers.
Dos cervezas, por favor. Two beers, please.
How does one say "También" in English? Too.
¿Cómo se dice cuando es más que una cerveza? Beers.

¿How does one say "Cerveza" in English? Beer.
Now say "Cervezas" in English. Beers.
Dos cervezas, por favor. Two beers, please.
Dos cervezas, por favor, señorita. Two beers, please, miss.
La palabra "O" se dice "or" en inglés. Repita, "or". Or
¿Cómo se dice la palabra "o" en inglés? Or.
Pregunte esto en inglés, "¿Le gustaría algo de cerveza? Would you like some beer?
Claro. Sure.
¿O algo de vino? Or some wine?
Me gustaría algo de vino. I'd like some wine.
¿Y usted? And you?
Me gustaría algo de té helado. I'd like some iced tea.
Diga, "Yo quiero" en inglés. I want.
No quiero. I don't want.
Quiero comer en un restaurante chino. I want to eat at a Chinese restaurant.
Me gustaría. I'd like.
"At an Italian restaurant" quiere decir "en un restaurante italiano". Diga, "at an Italian restaurant". At an Italian restaurant.
Repita, "At an". At an.
At an Italian. At an Italian.
At an Italian restaurant. At an Italian restaurant.
¿Cómo se dice "¿En un restaurante italiano?" en inglés? At an Italian Restaurant?
Ahora diga, "Me gustaría almorzar en un restaurante italiano". I'd like to have lunch at an Italian restaurant.
¿Dónde? Where?
En un restaurante italiano. At an Italian restaurant.
En un restaurante chino. At a Chinese restaurant.
No en un restaurante chino. Not at a Chinese restaurant.
En un restaurante italiano, por favor. At an Italian restaurant, please.
De acuerdo. Okay.
¿Cómo se dice, "Me gustaría algo de vino" en inglés? I'd like some wine.
¿A usted le gustaría algo de vino? Would you like some wine?
No. Se lo agradezco. No, thank you.
Me gustaría algo de cerveza. I'd like some beer.
Dos cervezas, por favor. Two beers, please.
Dos cervezas, por favor, señorita. Two beers, please miss.
¿Vino o cerveza? Wine or beer?

No sé. I don't know.
Me gustaría algo de té helado. I'd like some iced tea.
Lo siento. No entiendo. I'm sorry. I don't understand.
Me gustaría algo de té helado. I'd like some iced tea.
¿Qué le gustaría comer? What would you like to eat?
¿Qué quiere comer usted? What do you want to eat?
"Hacer" se dice "to do" en inglés. Por favor diga, "to do". To do.
¿Cómo se dice "hacer" en inglés? To do.
Pregunte, "¿Qué quiere hacer usted?" What do you want to do?
Diga "Hacer" en inglés. To do.
¿Qué quiere hacer usted?" What do you want to do?
Me gustaría almorzar. I'd like to have lunch.
¿Qué le gustaría hacer? What would you like to do?
Me gustaría beber algo. I'd like to have something to drink.
¿Cuándo? When?
¿Dónde? Where?
En el hotel. At the hotel.
El hotel. The hotel.
En el hotel. At the hotel.
How does one say "No en el hotel" in English? Not at the hotel.
En un restaurante. At a restaurant
En un restaurante chino. At a Chinese restaurant.
En un restaurante italiano. At an Italian restaurant.
En el restaurante. At the restaurant.
¿Dónde? Where?
En el restaurante. At the restaurant.
¿Qué le gustaría hacer? What would you like to do?
¿Le gustaría almorzar? Would you like to have lunch?
¿Qué quiere hacer? What do you want to do?
"To buy" quiere decir "comprar" en inglés. Repita, "to buy". To buy.
¿Cómo se dice "comprar" en inglés? To buy.
"Comprar algo" se dice "to buy something". Repita, "to buy something". To buy something.
Say in English, "Me gustaría comprar algo." I'd like to buy something.
¿Cómo se dice "Comprar" en inglés? To buy.
Say in English, "Comprar algo". To buy something.
Me gustaría comprar algo. I'd like to buy something.

Comprar. To buy.

Hacer. To do.

Hacer algo. To do something.

Comprar algo. To buy something.

Ask in English, "¿Qué quiere hacer?" What do you want to do?

Quiero comprar algo aquí. I want to buy something here.

Say in English, "Hola, ¿cómo está?" Hi, how are you?

Bien, gracias. ¿Y usted? ¿Cómo le va? Fine, thanks. And you? How's it going?

Todo bien, gracias. It's going well, thanks.

¿Cómo le va? How's it going?

Muy bien, gracias. Very well, thanks.

End of the speaking/listening lesson. Continue with the reading for Lesson 9.

Reading for Lesson 9

Have your student read the following sentences out loud to you. If he makes a mistake, help him correct it before reading any further. The text in parenthesis is only for the reader to understand some new vocabulary. They are to read only the English out loud.

Reading Practice
Hi, how's it going?
Fine, thank you. And you?
I'm doing well, thanks. Say hello to my friend Mark.
Hello Mark.
Hi. Do you speak Spanish?
Yes, but only a little.
You speak Spanish very well.
Thanks. And you speak English well too.
You speak and understand Spanish very well. I only speak and understand a little.
Where are you from?
I'm from Mexico City (Soy de la Ciudad de México).
Do you speak English?
Yes, I speak English very well.
Excuse me. Do you know where North Fifty Third Street is?
I'm sorry. I'm not from here. I don't know where it is. *Maybe (Tal vez)* it's there.
Okay. Thank you.
Do you know where Park Avenue is?
Yes. It's here.
Excuse me, where is North Fifty Third Street?
I don't know. I'm sorry.
That's okay.
I'll see you later *then (entonces).*
Okay, sure.
Do you understand Spanish?
Yes, but not very well.
I understand English very well.
What would you like to do?
I'd like to eat.
Where would you like to eat?
At a restaurant.
I'd like to eat too.
Where? Where would you like to eat?
I'd like to eat at a Chinese restaurant.
That's fine with me (Está bien conmigo).

I'd like to eat now. Would you like to have something to eat too?
Yes. I would.

LEVEL 1: LESSON 10 (LESSONS 6 – 9 REVIEW)

Teaching tip: You can spend 1 – 3 days or more on this review, depending on how well the student has mastered the material. Reviewing the reading lessons that went with lessons 6 – 9 can be of help also. Remember, a student should not move ahead until he or she responds correctly at least 85% of the time.

Say "Hola" in English. Hello.
Ask in English, "¿Entiende usted español?" Do you understand Spanish?
Answer in English, "Entiendo un poco". I understand a little.
Y hablo un poco. And I speak a little.
No muy bien. Not very well.
Repeat, "You speak very well". You speak very well.
Se lo agradezco. Thank you.
De nada. You're welcome.
¿Y usted? And you?
¿Entiende inglés? Do you understand English?
Lo siento. No entiendo. I'm sorry. I don't understand.
No soy norteamericano. I'm not American.
Y no entiendo. And I don't understand.
No soy norteamericano y no entiendo. I'm not American and I don't understand.
Pero usted habla muy bien. But you speak very well.
Se lo agradezco. Thank you.
De nada. You're welcome.
¿Cómo está? How are you?
Estoy bien, gracias. ¿Y usted? I'm fine, thanks. And you?
Ask in English, "¿Dónde está la Avenida Parque?" Where is Park Avenue?
Now answer in English, "Está aquí." It's here.
¿Y la Calle Cincuenta y tres Norte? And North Fifty Third Street?
La Calle Cincuenta y tres Norte está aquí. North Fifty Third Street is here.

¿Queda aquí? Is it here?
No. Está por allá. No. It's over there.
No está por allá. It's not over there.
Y no está aquí. And it's not here.
Pero la Avenida Parque está aquí. But Park Avenue is here.
Pregúnteme en inglés dónde está la Calle Parque. Where is Park Street?
¿Queda aquí? Is it here?
Conteste "Yo no sé". I don't know.
Ahora conteste, "Oh, yo sé". Oh, I know.
Está por allá. It's over there.
Ahora pregunte, "¿Entiende usted?" Do you understand?
¿Cómo se dice "¿Sabe usted?" Do you know?
No, no sé. No, I don't know.
No está por allá. It's not over there.
Yo quiero. I want.
Yo sé. I know.
Yo no sé. I don't know.
Usted quiere. You want.
¿Quiere usted? Do you want?
¿Dónde está la Calle Cincuenta y tres Norte? Where is North Fifty Third Street?
¿Dónde está esa calle? Where is that street?
¿Esta calle? This street?
No, esa calle. No, that street.
Está por allá. It's over there.
¿Y la Avenida Parque? And Park Avenue?
¿Quéda aquí? Is it here?
Diga en inglés, "Está por allá también." It's over there too.
Ask in English, "¿Quéda aquí?" Is it here?
Answer in English, "No, no está aquí". No, it's not here.
Usted habla inglés muy bien. You speak English very well.
Gracias. Usted habla muy bien también. Thanks. You speak very well too.
Yo entiendo un poco. I understand a little.
Y hablo un poco de inglés. And I speak a little English.
¿Le gustaría comer algo? Would you like something to eat?
Sí. Me gustaría. Yes. I would.
No, se lo agradezco. Pero me gustaría beber algo. No, thank you. But I'd like to have something to drink.

Ask in English, "¿Dónde está la Avenida Norte?" Where is North Avenue?
Answer in English, "Lo siento. No sé". I'm sorry. I don't know.
No está aquí. It's not here.
Y no está por allá. And it's not over there.
¿Dónde le gustaría comer? Where would you like to eat?
¿En un restaurante? At a restaurant?
Sí. En un restaurante. Yes, at a restaurant.
How does one say in English, "A mí también me gustaría comer". I'd like to eat too.
¿Cuándo le gustaría comer? When would you like to eat?
Ahora. Now.
¿Cuándo? When?
Ahora no. Not now.
Más tarde. Later.
Ahora no, señorita. Not now, miss.
Más tarde, por favor. Later, please.
¿Dónde? Where?
¿Dónde le gustaría comer? Where would you like to eat?
En un restaurante. At a restaurant.
No, no en un restaurante. No, not at a restaurant.
Diga "I don't want to". I don't want to.
Me gustaría beber algo. I'd like something to drink.
De acuerdo. Okay.
A mí también me gustaría beber algo. I'd like something to drink too.
Pero más tarde. But later.
No. No.
Ahora. Now.
¿Ahora? De acuerdo. Now? Okay.
Repeat in English, "¿Would you like to have something to drink at a restaurant?" Would you like to have something to drink at a restaurant?
Conteste en inglés, "Sí. Me gustaría." Yes. I would.
Pero a mí me gustaría comer algo también. But I'd like to have something to eat too.
A mí me gustaría comer ahora también. I'd like to eat now too.
Say in English, "Quiero comer más tarde". I want to eat later.
¿Dónde le gustaría comer? Where would you like to eat?
Aquí no. Not here.
¿Dónde? Where?
¿Allá? Over there?

No. Allá no. No. Not over there.
En un restaurante, por favor. At a restaurant, please.
A mí me gustaría comer aquí. I would like to eat here.
Pero yo no quiero. But I don't want to.
Me gustaría comer en el hotel. I would like to eat at the hotel.
Me gustaría beber algo en el hotel. I'd like to have something to drink at the hotel.
¿Qué le gustaría beber? What would you like to drink?
Ahora repita, "I'd like some iced tea". I'd like some iced tea.
Me gustaría algo de vino. I'd like some wine.
¿Y usted? ¿Qué le gustaría beber? And you? What would you like to drink?
¿Le gustaría algo de vino? Would you like some wine?
Sí, me gustaría. Yes, I would.
Me gustaría algo de cerveza. I'd like some beer.
Quiero algo de té helado, por favor. I want some iced tea, please.
¿Dónde? ¿En el hotel? Where? At the hotel?
En el hotel no. Not at the hotel.
En un restaurante, por favor. At a restaurant, please.
¿Qué le gustaría comer? What would you like to eat?
No sé. ¿Y usted? I don't know. And you?
¿A usted le gustaría algo de vino? Would you like some wine?
No, se lo agradezco. Ahora no. No, thank you. Not now.
¿Usted no quiere comer? You don't want to eat?
Ahora no, gracias. Not now, thanks.
Me gustaría algo de vino. I'd like some wine.
Pero más tarde. But later.
En el hotel. At the hotel.
En el hotel en la Avenida Parque. At the hotel on Park Avenue.
De acuerdo. ¿Qué le gustaría beber? Okay. What would you like to drink?
Yo quiero algo de té helado. I want some iced tea.
¿Y usted, Roberto? ¿Qué le gustaría beber? And you, Roberto? What would you like to drink?
Yo no sé. ¿Y usted? I don't know. And you?
Me gustaría almorzar en un restaurante chino. I would like to have lunch at a Chinese restaurant.
Me gustaría comer algo. I'd like something to eat.
¿Le gustaría comer ahora? Would you like to eat now?
Sí, me gustaría almorzar. Yes, I'd like to have lunch.

Me gustaría almorzar ahora. I'd like to have lunch now.

¿Dónde le gustaría almorzar? Where would you like to have lunch?

¿En un restaurante? At a restaurant?

No, en el hotel. No, at the hotel.

En el hotel en la Calle Norte. At the hotel on North Street.

A mí también me gustaría almorzar. I'd like to have lunch too.

Pero más tarde. But later.

Me gustaría comer algo. I'd like something to eat.

¿Cómo se dice "claro" en inglés? Sure.

Say in English, "Dos cervezas, por favor, señorita". Two beers, please, miss.

Now say in English, "Me gustaría algo de té helado". I'd like some iced tea.

How does one say in English, "Quiero comer en un restaurante chino"? I want to eat at a Chinese restaurant.

Say in English, "Me gustaría almorzar en un restaurante italiano". I'd like to have lunch at an Italian restaurant.

Lo siento. No entiendo. I'm sorry. I don't understand.

Ask in English, "¿Qué le gustaría comer?" What would you like to eat?

Now ask in English, "¿Qué quiere comer usted?" What do you want to eat?

How does one ask in English, "¿Qué quiere hacer usted?" What do you want to do?

¿Qué le gustaría hacer? What would you like to do?

Me gustaría beber algo en el restaurante. I'd like to have something to drink at the restaurant.

¿Cuándo? When?

¿Dónde? Where?

En el hotel. At the hotel.

No en el hotel. Not at the hotel.

En un restaurante. At a restaurant.

En el restaurante. At the restaurant.

Me gustaría comprar algo. I'd like to buy something.

¿Cómo se dice "Hacer algo"? To do something.

Pregunte, "¿Qué quiere hacer?" What do you want to do?

Me gustaría comprar dos cervezas. I'd like to buy two beers.

Para preguntar "¿Con quién?" se dice, "With whom?" Repita, "With whom?" With whom?

¿Entiende inglés? Do you understand English?

Me gustaría comer algo. I'd like to eat something.

¿Con quién? With whom?

¿Dónde está la Avenida Parque? Where is Park Avenue?
¿Sabe usted dónde está la Avenida Parque? Do you know where Park Avenue is?
¿Sabe usted dónde está la Calle Cincuenta y tres Norte? Do you know where North Fifty Third Street is?
¿Dónde está esa calle? Where is that street?
¿Dónde está el Restaurante Avenida Parque? Where is the Park Avenue Restaurant?
Me gustaría almorzar ahora. I'd like to have lunch now.
¿Con quién? With whom?
¿Le gustaría almorzar también? Would you like to have lunch too?
De acuerdo. Se lo agradezco. Okay. Thank you.
De nada. You're welcome.
¿Qué le gustaría hacer? What would you like to do?
Me gustaría comprar algo. I'd like to buy something.
¿Cuándo? When?
¿Qué le gustaría comprar? What would you like to buy?
¿Con quién? With whom?
"Conmigo" se dice, "With me". Repita, "With me". With me.
¿Con quién? With whom?
¿Conmigo? With me?
Me gustaría comprar algo de vino. I'd like to buy some wine.
O algo de cerveza. Or some beer.
Quiero comprar dos cervezas. I want to buy two beers.
Diga en inglés, "Me gustaría beber algo." I'd like to have something to drink.
Ahora diga en inglés, "Me gustaría beber algo con usted." I'd like to have something to drink with you.
Pero aquí no. But not here.
Y no por allá. En el hotel. And not over there. At the hotel.
No, no en el hotel. No, not at the hotel.
No sé. Me gustaría comer en un restaurante. I don't know. But I'd like to eat at a restaurant.
De acuerdo. En un restaurante. Okay. At a restaurant.
¿Dónde está el Hotel Parque? Where is the Park Hotel?
¿Sabe usted dónde está el hotel? Do you know where the hotel is?
Está por allá. En la Avenida Parque. It's over there. On Park Avenue.

End of the speaking/listening lesson. Continue with the reading for Lesson 10.

Reading for Lesson 10

Have the student reread all the high frequency English words (75) covered so far. Correct him/her if there are any mistakes. Here they are for easy reference:

the	of	and	to	a
in	that	is	was	he
for	it	with	as	his
on	be	at	by	I
this	had	not	are	but
from	or	have	an	they
which	one	you	were	her
all	she	there	would	their
we	him	been	has	when
who	will	more	no	if
out	so	said	what	up
its	about	into	than	them
can	only	other	new	some
could	time	these	two	may
then	do	first	any	my

Now have the student read the section below.

Who or Whom?

I would like to have lunch at a Chinese restaurant.
With whom?
With him (Con él). I would like to have lunch with him.

I would like to eat at an Italian restaurant.
With whom?
With her (Con ella). I would like to have lunch with her.

I want to eat now.
With whom?
With her. I want to eat with her.

I want to drink something now.
With whom?
With him. I want to drink something with him.

Who is he? He is Roberto.
Who is she? She is Monica.

Who is there? Roberto is there.
Who is Cuban? Mario is Cuban.

If you can replace the word with "he'" or "'she," **use who.** (Si puedes replazar la palabra con "he" o "she", usa "who".)

If you can replace it with "him" or "her," **use whom**. (Si puedes replazar la palabra con "him" o "her", usa "whom".)

LEVEL 1: LESSON 11

Teaching tip: Make sure to stop completely (at the period) after the word "no" in sentences like, "No. At eight o'clock. It may be good to even stop for a couple of seconds so the student will not think you are saying a poor grammar phrase like "No at eight o'clock." So make sure to stop at the period for extra time in sentences like "No. At eight o'clock."

Para decir "Mucho más tarde" se dice "Much later". Diga, "Much later". Much later.
Me gustaría hacer algo. I'd like to do something.
¿Cuándo? When?
Más tarde. Mucho más tarde. Later. Much later.
¿Cómo se dice "mucho más tarde" en inglés? Much later.
Pregunte en inglés, "¿De acuerdo?" Okay?
Conteste, "De acuerdo". Okay.
¿Qué le gustaría hacer? What would you like to do?
Diga en inglés, "Me gustaría comer algo." I'd like to have something to eat.
¿Con quién? With whom?
Now say in English, "Me gustaría comer algo con usted." I'd like to have something to eat with you.
"Bueno" se dice "All right". Repita, "All right". All right.
Repita, "All". All.
All right. All right.
¿Cómo se dice "bueno" en inglés? All right.
Ahora diga "De acuerdo". Okay.
Pero mucho más tarde. But much later.
¿Qué quiere hacer usted? What do you want to do?
Quiero comprar algo. I want to buy something.
"Para mi hijo" se dice "for my son". Repita, "for my son". For my son.

Quiero comprar algo. I want to buy something.
Para mi hijo. For my son.
Say in English, "Quiero comprar algo para mi hijo". I want to buy something for my son.
Me gustaría comprar algo. I'd like to buy something.
Me gustaría comprar algo para mi hijo. I'd like to buy something for my son.
Me gustaría comprar dos cervezas. I'd like to buy two beers.
Bueno. All right.
Para preguntar "¿A qué hora?", diga "At what time?" Repita, "At what time?" At what time?
Ask in English, "¿A qué hora?" At what time?
Para decir, "A la una" se dice "at one o'clock". Repita, "at one o'clock". At one o'clock.
Diga, "Quiero comprar algo para mi hijo." I want to buy something for my son.
¿A qué hora? At what time?
A la una. At one o'clock.
A la una quiero comprar algo para mi hijo. At one o'clock I want to buy something for my son.
¿A qué hora? At what time?
Ask in English, "¿A la una?" At one o'clock?
Answer in English, "No, mucho más tarde." No, much later.
"A las nueve" quiere decir "at nine o'clock". Repita, "At nine o'clock". At nine o'clock.
A las nueve. ¿De acuerdo? At nine o'clock. Okay?
Conteste, "No. A las nueve no". No. Not at nine o'clock.
A la una. At one o'clock.
"A las siete" se dice "At seven o'clock". Repita, "At seven o'clock". At seven o'clock.
Say in English, "A las siete". At seven o'clock.
"A las ocho" se dice "At eight o'clock". Repita, "At eight o'clock". At eight o'clock.
A las siete. At seven o'clock.
A las ocho. At eight o'clock.
No, a las ocho no. A las nueve, por favor. No, not at eight o'clock. At nine o'clock, please.
De acuerdo. A las nueve. Okay. At nine o'clock.
La palabra "entonces" se dice "then". Repita, "then". Then.
¿Cómo se dice, "A las nueve, entonces"? At nine o'clock, then?

Sí, a las nueve. Yes, at nine o'clock.
Ask in English, "¿A las ocho, entonces?" At eight o'clock then?
Para decir "a las dos" se dice "at two o'clock". Repita, "At two o'clock." At two o'clock.
¿A las dos, entonces? At two o'clock, then?
No, mucho más tarde. No, much later.
Mucho más tarde, por favor. Much later, please.
¿A qué hora entonces? At what time then?
No. A las siete, por favor. No. At seven o'clock, please.
¿A las siete? No. Usted no entiende. At seven o'clock? No. You don´t understand.
Repita "What". What.
Ahora repita "What don't I". What don't I.
Ahora diga "What don't I understand?" What don't I understand?
Otra vez, diga "What don't I understand?" What don't I understand?
Así se dice, "¿Qué es lo que no entiendo?" Repita, "What don't I understand?" What don't I understand?
¿Cómo se dice en inglés, "¿Qué es lo que no entiendo?" What don't I understand?
Ask in English again, "¿Qué es lo que no entiendo?" What don't I understand?
Answer in English, "Usted no entiende inglés." You don't understand English.
Now say in English, "Usted no entiende inglés muy bien." You don't understand English very well.
¿Le gustaría beber algo? Would you like something to drink?
No. Se lo agradezco. No thank you.
Pero me gustaría comer algo. But I'd like something to eat.
Me gustaría comer algo, entonces. I'd like something to eat, then.
Lo siento. No entiendo. I'm sorry. I don't understand.
Perdón. Usted no entiende. Excuse me. You don't understand.
¿Qué es lo que no entiendo? What don't I understand?
Me gustaría comer algo. I would like something to eat.
Bueno. All right.
¿Qué le gustaría hacer? What would you like to do?
¿Le gustaría beber algo? Would you like something to drink?
¿O le gustaría comer algo? Or would you like something to eat?
No sé. I don't know.
"¿Usted no sabe?" se dice en inglés, "You don't know?" Repeat, "You don't know?" You don't know?
Say in English, "Me gustaría comer algo." I'd like something to eat.

¿Con quién? With whom?
¿Usted no sabe? You don't know?
¿Con quién? With whom?
¿Conmigo? With me?
Pregunte otra vez, "¿Conmigo?" With me?
Sí. Yes.
"Mi hijo" se dice "My son" en inglés. Repita, "My son". My son.
Pregunte, "¿Conmigo?" With me?
Conteste, "No. Con mi hijo". No. With my son.
Pregunte esto como si fuera a salir, "¿Le gustaría comer algo? Would you like to have something to eat?"
Sí. En un restaurante. Yes. At a restaurant.
Sí. En el Restaurante Avenida Parque. Yes. At the Park Avenue Restaurant.
¿Con quién? With whom?
Con mi hijo. With my son.
¿Sabe usted dónde está el restaurante? Do you know where the restaurant is?
¿Queda aquí? Is it here?
No. No está aquí. No. It's not here.
Está por allá. It's over there.
Pregunte en inglés, "¿A qué hora?" At what time?
Para preguntar "¿Qué hora es?", diga "What time is it?" What time is it?
Pregúnteme en inglés que hora es. What time is it?
Para decir, "Son las cinco", se dice "It's five o'clock." Repita, "It's five o'clock". It's five o'clock.
Otra vez diga "It's five o'clock". It's five o'clock.
¿Cómo cree que se dice "Son las nueve" en inglés? It's nine o'clock.
Ahora diga "Son las ocho". It's eight o'clock.
¿Qué hora es? What time is it?
Conteste que son las dos. It's two o'clock.
Son las cinco. It's five o'clock.
"Son las tres" se dice "It's three o'clock". Repita, "It's three o'clock." It's three o'clock.
¿Qué hora es? What time is it?
"Son las cuatro" se dice "It's four o'clock. Repita "It's four o'clock. It's four o'clock.
Repita, "It's". It's.
Repeat, "It's four." It's four.

Repeat after me, "It's four o'clock." It's four o'clock.
Diga que son las dos. It's two o'clock.
Ahora diga que son las tres. It's three o'clock.
Trate de preguntar si son las cuatro. Is it four o'clock?
Ahora pregunte si son las tres. Is it three o'clock?

End of the speaking/listening lesson. Continue with the reading for Lesson 11.

Reading for Lesson 11

Listen to your student read the following sentences to you. Then read the numbers below. Work especially on the long and short o sound in the words "o'clock" so the student won't pronounce both of them with a Spanish o.

Reading Practice

I'd like to do something later.

Like what? What would you like to do?

Oh, I don't know. Maybe buy something or have something to drink.

When? *In an hour (En una hora)?*

No, not in an hour. Much later. I would like to do something much later.

At what time?

At three o'clock or four o'clock. Is that okay?

No. Much later. I would like to do something too, but much later.

At five o'clock?

No, not at five o'clock. At six or seven o'clock.

Okay. At six o'clock, then.

Yes, at six o'clock *we can (nosotros podemos)* have something to drink and at seven o'clock we can buy something.

Numbers

1	2	3	4	5	6	7	8	9	10
One	Two	Three	Four	Five	Six	Seven	Eight	Nine	Ten

Now review any past reading assignments that may have been difficult for your student.

LEVEL 1: LESSON 12

Remember to help your student with the "th" sound. Don't let them replace it with a "t" sound. Also, a common mistake in practicing telling time in English is that students often initially say, "What time it is?" instead of "What time is it?" Be careful to correct them right away so it doesn't become a habit.

Para decir "Yo creo" se dice "I think". Repita "I think". I think.

Diga "I". I.

Ahora "I think". I think.

Yo creo. I think.

Repita "I think it's four o'clock". I think it's four o'clock.

Say in English, "Yo creo que son las cuatro". I think it's four o'clock.

Now say, "Yo creo que son las dos." I think it's two o'clock.

Ask in English, "¿Son las dos?" Is it two o'clock?

Answer, "No. Yo creo que son las tres". No. I think it's three o'clock.

Pregunte en inglés, "¿Qué hora es?" What time is it?

Son las cuatro. It's four o'clock.

Count with me, "One, two, three, four". One, two, three, four.

Now count, "One, two, three, four, five". One, two, three, four, five.

Say, "Son las cinco" in English. It's five o'clock.

Ahora diga simplemente "Las cinco". Five o'clock.

Las nueve. Nine o'clock.

Las tres. Three o'clock.

Las cinco. Five o'clock.

Las cuatro. Four o'clock.

Yo creo. I think.

Yo creo que son las cuatro. I think it's four o'clock.

Ask me what time it is in English. What time is it?

¿Qué hora es, por favor? What time is it, please?

Answer in English, "No sé. Pero me gustaría comer algo". I don't know. But I'd like to have something to eat.
Ahora no. Más tarde. Not now. Later.
Acuérdese que "Mucho más tarde"se dice "Much later". Diga "Much later". Much later.
¿Cómo se dice "Mucho más tarde" en inglés? Much later.
Diga "Ahora no. Mucho más tarde". Not now. Much later.
Repita "Not now. Much later". Not now. Much later.
Diga "mucho más tarde" en inglés. Much later.
"No. Yo voy a comer ahora" se dice, "No. I´m going to eat now". Diga "No. I´m going to eat now". No. I'm going to eat now.
Ahora diga en partes, primero con "No. I'm going". No. I'm going.
Ahora diga, "No. I'm going to eat now". No. I'm going to eat now.
Repita "I'm going to eat now". I'm going to eat now.
Repita "No. I'm going to eat now". No. I'm going to eat now.
Say in English, "No. Yo voy a comer ahora". No. I'm going to eat now.
Now say in English, "Usted va". You're going.
Usted va a comer. You're going to eat.
Usted va a comer, entonces. You're going to eat, then.
Ask in English, "¿Va a comer usted?" Are you going to eat?
¿Va a comer usted entonces? Are you going to eat then?
Sí. Yo voy a comer. Yes. I'm going to eat.
Yo voy a comer. Pero mucho más tarde. I'm going to eat. But much later.
¿Cómo se dice "Yo voy a almorzar"? I'm going to have lunch.
Ahora. Now.
Voy a almorzar ahora. I'm going to have lunch now.
Voy a comer. I'm going to eat.
Voy a comer mucho más tarde. I'm going to eat much later.
A las cinco. At five o'clock.
How does one say in English, "Voy a comer a las cinco"? I'm going to eat at five o'clock.
How does one ask in English, "¿Va a comer a las cinco?" Are you going to eat at five o'clock?
Answer in English, "No. A las ocho. ¿De acuerdo?" No. At eight o'clock. Okay?
Count with me in English, "One, two, three, four, five, six, seven, eight, nine". One, two, three, four, five, six, seven, eight, nine.
Now repeat, "six, seven, eight, nine". Six, seven, eight, nine.

Ask in English, "¿Va a comer a las cinco?" Are you going to eat at five o'clock?
Now ask, "¿Va a comer a las seis?" Are you going to eat at six o'clock?
Answer, "No. A las siete. Voy a comer a las siete". No. At seven o'clock. I'm going to eat seven o'clock."
Pero yo voy a beber algo. But I'm going to have something to drink.
¿Cuándo? When?
Say in English, "A las tres o a las cuatro". At three o'clock or at four o'clock.
Yo voy a beber algo a las nueve. I'm going to have something to drink at nine o'clock.
¿Qué hora es ahora? What time is it now?
Es la una ahora. It's one o'clock now.
Creo que es la una ahora. I think it's one o'clock now.
Se lo agradezco. Voy a almorzar. Thank you. I'm going to have lunch.
Pero mucho más tarde. But much later.
Y me gustarían dos cervezas. And I'd like two beers.
Hola. Hello.
¿Cómo está? How are you?
Estoy bien, gracias. I'm fine, thanks.
¿Y usted? And you?
¿Cómo le va? How's it going?
Todo bien, gracias. It's going well, thanks.
Perdon. ¿Le gustaría almorzar conmigo? Excuse me. Would you like to have lunch with me?
Claro. Sure.
¿A qué hora le gustaría comer? At what time would you like to eat?
¿A la una? At one o'clock?
No, a la una no. No, not at one o'clock.
¿A las dos? At two o'clock?
No, a las dos no. No, not at two o'clock.
¿A las tres, entonces? At three o'clock, then?
No a las tres, no. A las cuatro. ¿De acuerdo? No, not at three o'clock. At four o'clock. Okay?
No, a las cuatro no. A las cinco. No, not at four o'clock. At five o'clock.
¿Cuándo le gustaría almorzar? When would you like to have lunch?
¿Quiere almorzar? Do you want to have lunch?
Sí, ¿pero cuándo? Yes, but when?
Voy a almorzar ahora. I'm going to have lunch now.
¿Va a almorzar conmigo? Are you going to have lunch with me?

Sí. Voy a almorzar con usted. Yes. I´m going to have lunch with you.
¿Pero cuándo? But when?
"En un rato" se dice, "In a while". Repita, "In a while". In a while.
¿Va a almorzar? Are you going to have lunch?
Answer, "En un rato." In a while.
¿Ahora? Now?
Ahora no. Not now.
En un rato. In a while.
Count with me, "one, two, three, four, five, six, seven, eight, nine". One, two, three, four, five, six, seven, eight, nine."
¿Cómo se dice "en un rato" en inglés? In a while.
Pregúnteme en inglés cuándo me gustaría comer. When would you like to eat?
Answer in English, "En un rato". In a while.
"Demasiado tarde" se dice "Too late" en inglés. Repita, "Too late". Too late.
Diga, "En un rato" en inglés. In a while.
Ahora diga en inglés, "Demasiado tarde". Too late.
¿Se acuerda cómo se dice "Esa calle" en inglés? That street.
"Eso es" se dice "That is" en inglés. Diga, "That is". That is.
Repeat, "That is". That is.
¿Cómo se dice "eso es" en inglés? That is.
Ahora lo decimos utilizando la contracción. Repita, "That's". That's.
Utilizando la contracción, diga en inglés, "Eso es demasiado tarde". That's too late.
Repeat again, "That's too late". That's too late.
Ask in English, "¿Qué hora es?" What time is it?
Answer in English, "No sé". I don't know.
Oh, sí. Yo sé. Oh, yes. I know.
Say in English, "Son las tres". It's three o'clock.
Son las cinco. It's five o'clock.
Ask in English, "¿Sabe usted?" Do you know?
¿Sabe usted que hora es? Do you know what time it is?
Answer in English, "Son las cuatro". It's four o'clock.
Ask again, "¿Sabe usted que hora es?" Do you know what time it is?
Ask in English, "¿Va a almorzar ahora?" Are you going to have lunch now?
En un rato. In a while.
No, voy a comer más tarde. No, I'm going to eat later.
¿Cuándo? When?
En un rato. In a while.

A las ocho. At eight o'clock.
Eso es demasiado tarde. That's too late.

End of the speaking/listening lesson. Continue with the reading for Lesson 12.

Reading for Lesson 12

Listen to your student read the following sentences to you. Have them stop at any mistake and help them correct it before continuing to read.

Reading Practice
I'm going to have something to eat. How about you?
Me? No, thank you. But I'd like to have something to drink.
Where is the Park Avenue Restaurant?
It's over there.
Where is the restaurant?
On Park Avenue.
What would you like to eat?
I don't know.
You don't know? Okay. What would you like to drink?
I don't know yet. And you?
I'm not sure. Maybe some wine or some beer.
Would you like some wine? Some beer?
No, thank you. Not now.
Would you like to have something to eat?
No, thanks.
You don't want to eat?
Not now, thanks.
I'd like some wine. But later.
 I work at the hotel on Park Avenue.
You do? *Since when? (¿Desde cuando?)*
Since last week.
Are you thirsty? (¿Tiene sed?)
Yes.
You can have something to drink later.
But I'd like to have something to drink now.
I'd like to have something to drink now, okay?
Okay. What would you like to eat?
I don't know.
What would you like to drink then?
I don't know. And you? Would you like some wine? Some beer?
No, thanks.

LEVEL 1: LESSON 13

Teaching tip: Watch for the student trying to say "thas" instead of "that's". Also help them relax the jawline so the short "I" doesn't sound like "ee".

"Para mí" se dice, "For me". Repita, "For me". For me.
¿Cómo se dice "Para mí" en inglés? For me.
Say in English, "Eso es demasiado tarde para mí". That's too late for me.
Repeat, "That's too late for me." That's too late for me.
Now say, "Voy a tomar algo de vino". I'm going to have some wine.
Voy a tomar algo de vino más tarde. I'm going to have some wine later.
A las nueve. At nine o'clock.
Ask in English, "¿A que hora?" At what time?
Answer in English, "A las nueve". At nine o'clock.
Now say in English, "Eso es demasiado tarde". That's too late.
¿Qué hora es ahora? What time is it now?
Son las tres ahora. It's three o'clock now.
No, son las cinco. No, it's five o'clock.
Voy a almorzar a las dos. I'm going to have lunch at two o'clock.
¿Cuándo? When?
En un rato. In a while.
¿Le gustaría almorzar conmigo? Would you like to have lunch with me?
¿Le gustaría tomar algo de vino? Would you like to have some wine?
¿Le gustaría tomar algo de vino también? Would you like to have some wine too?
Bueno. All right.
¿Cuándo? When?
¿Dónde? Where?
¿Cuándo? ¿Ahora? When? Now?
Ahora, no. Más tarde, por favor. Not now. Later, please.
"A las seis" se dice "At six o'clock". Repita "At six o'clock". At six o'clock.

Seis. Six.
A las seis. At six o'clock.
A las seis, señorita. At six o'clock, miss.
Bueno. All right.
O a las siete. Or at seven o'clock.
Siete. Seven.
A las siete. At seven o'clock.
A las seis o a las siete. At six o'clock or at seven o'clock.
A las seis no. Not at six o'clock.
Más tarde. Later.
En un rato. In a while.
¿De acuerdo? Okay?
Entonces, a las siete. Then at seven o'clock.
How does one say, "Entonces" in English? Then.
Entonces, a las ocho. Then at eight o'clock.
"Esta noche" se dice "tonight". Repita "tonight". Tonight.
¿Cómo se dice, "esta noche" en inglés? Tonight.
A las ocho esta noche. At eight o'clock tonight.
Cenar se dice "to have dinner" en inglés. Repita, "To have dinner". To have dinner.
Acuérdese que "Yo voy" se dice "I´m going". Repita, "I'm going". I'm going.
How does one say, "Yo voy a cenar" in English? I'm going to have dinner.
Say in English, "Yo voy a almorzar". I'm going to have lunch.
Voy a cenar. I'm going to have dinner.
Voy a cenar esta noche. I'm going to have dinner tonight.
Me gustaría cenar esta noche. I'd like to have dinner tonight.
Voy a. I'm going to.
Me gustaría. I'd like to.
Me gustaría cenar con mi hijo esta noche. I'd like to have dinner with my son tonight.
"A las diez" se dice "At ten o'clock". Repita, "At ten o'clock". At ten o'clock.
A las diez esta noche. At ten o'clock tonight.
¿Cómo se dice "A las diez" en inglés? At ten o'clock.
Ahora diga, "Esta noche voy a cenar a las diez". Tonight I'm going to have dinner at ten o'clock.
¿Esta noche a las diez? Tonight at ten o'clock?
Eso es demasiado tarde. That's too late.
Eso es demasiado tarde para mí. That's too late for me.
A las nueve. At nine o'clock.

A las nueve, entonces. At nine o'clock, then.
"Mañana" se dice "tomorrow" en inglés. Repita, "tomorrow". Tomorrow.
Ahora repita en sílabas. To. To.
Mor. Mor.
Row. Row.
Repita, "tomorrow". Tomorrow.
How do you say "mañana" in English? Tomorrow.
Ahora diga "Esta noche a las siete". Tonight at seven o'clock.
¿Y mañana? And tomorrow?
Mañana voy a cenar con usted. Tomorrow I'm going to have dinner with you.
A las cuatro. At four o'clock.
¿A las cuatro? No. Mucho más tarde, por favor. At four o'clock? No. Much later please.
De acuerdo. ¿A qué hora entonces? Okay. At what time then?
A las seis o a las siete. At six o'clock or at seven o'clock.
A las nueve no. Not at nine o'clock.
Entonces, a las diez. ¿De acuerdo? Then, at ten o'clock. Okay?
Bueno. All right.
Say "Mañana" in English. Tomorrow.
How does one say, "Esta noche" in English? Tonight.
Mañana por la noche. Tomorrow night.
Mañana por la noche a las siete. Tomorrow night at seven o'clock.
¿A las siete? No. Mucho más tarde por favor. At seven o'clock? No. Much later please.
¿A las nueve? At nine o'clock?
No a las nueve. A las diez. Not at nine o'clock. At ten o'clock.
De acuerdo. A las diez entonces. Okay. At ten o'clock then.
"Hoy" se dice "Today" en inglés. Repita, "Today". Today.
How does one say "hoy" in English? Today.
Now say in English, "Hoy a las tres". Today at three o'clock.
Mañana. Tomorrow.
Mañana por la noche. Tomorrow night.
Esta noche. Tonight.
Hoy. Today.
¿Le gustaría cenar conmigo hoy? Would you like to have dinner with me today?
Hoy no. Mañana. ¿De acuerdo? Not today. Tomorrow. Okay?
Bueno. ¿A qué hora? All right. At what time?

A las seis o a las siete. At six o'clock or at seven o'clock.
Voy a cenar ahora. I'm going to have dinner now.
Hoy y mañana también. Today and tomorrow too.
¿Qué hora es ahora? What time is it now?
¿Sabe usted que hora es? Do you know what time it is?
Son las diez, señorita. It's ten o'clock, miss.
Me gustaría cenar con usted esta noche. I'd like to have dinner with you tonight.
Esta noche no. Pero mañana por la noche. Not tonight. But tomorrow night.
Entonces a las ocho. En el Restaurante Avenida Parque. Then at eight o'clock. At the Park Avenue Restaurant.
De acuerdo. Okay.
¿Y esta noche? ¿Qué quiere hacer? And tonight? What do you want to do?
Esta noche voy a tomar algo de cerveza. Tonight I'm going to have some beer.
Bueno. All right.
¿Cómo está hoy? How are you today?
Muy bien. ¿Y usted? Very well. And you?
¿Cómo le va? How's it going?
Todo bien, gracias. It's going well, thanks.
¿Qué quiere hacer? What do you want to do?
¿Qué quiere hacer esta noche? What do you want to do tonight?
¿Le gustaría beber algo en el hotel? Would you like to have something to drink at the hotel?
Sí me gustaría, pero no esta noche. Yes, I would, but not tonight.
Entonces, ¿mañana por la noche? Then tomorrow night?
Bueno. Mañana por la noche. All right. Tomorrow night.
Say in English, "Voy a cenar a las seis". I'm going to have dinner at six o'clock.
Now say in English, "Mañana voy a cenar a las siete". Tomorrow I'm going to have dinner at seven o'clock.
To say, "Tengo hambre", in English say "I'm hungry". Repeat, "I'm hungry". I'm hungry.
Diga en inglés que usted tiene hambre. I'm hungry.
Try to say in English, "Tengo hambre. Quiero comer algo." I'm hungry. I want to eat something.
Say again, "I'm hungry." I'm hungry.
To say, "Tengo sed" in English say "I'm thirsty". Repeat, "I'm thirsty". I'm thirsty.
¿Cómo se dice "Tengo hambre"? I'm hungry.
Ahora diga que usted tiene sed. I'm thirsty.

How does one say in English, "Tengo sed. Quiero beber algo"? I'm thirsty. I want to drink something.

Tell me that you are hungry in English. I am hungry.

Now tell me that you are thirsty in English. I am thirsty.

Si quiere decir en inglés, "Tengo mucha hambre", diga, "I'm very hungry". Repita, "I'm very hungry." I'm very hungry.

Tell me that you're very hungry. I'm very hungry.

Ahora diga que usted tiene mucha sed. I'm very thirsty.

Say "Tengo hambre" in English. I'm hungry.

Say "Tengo sed" in English. I'm thirsty.

Tengo mucha hambre. I'm very hungry.

Tengo mucha sed. I'm very thirsty.

How does one say, "Lo siento" in English? I'm sorry.

Say "Se lo agradezco" in English. Thank you.

Adiós. Goodbye.

"Cuídate" se dice "Take care" en inglés. Repita, "Take care". Take care.

¿Cómo se dice "cuídate" en inglés? Take care.

Say in English, "Te veré más tarde". See you later.

Cuídate. Take care.

Diga que usted tiene hambre. I'm hungry.

Ahora diga que usted tiene mucha hambre. I'm very hungry.

Tengo sed. I'm thirsty.

Tengo mucha sed. I'm very thirsty.

Tell me you want to have some water. I want to have some water.

Te veré más tarde. See you later.

Te veré más tarde hoy. See you later today.

Cuídate. Take care.

Usted también. You too.

End of the speaking/listening lesson. Continue with the reading for lesson 13.

Reading for Lesson 13

Have the student read the following sentences and listen carefully to his/her pronunciation, especially with the contraction "I'd". The "d" sound should be heard clearly.

<u>Reading Practice</u>

What do you want to do?
I'm hungry. I'd like to have something to eat. And you?
Well, I'm hungry too, but I'd like to have something to drink at a restaurant first.
I'd like to have lunch too.
At what time?
How about at one o'clock?
That's in two hours. Okay. Where?
There is a good restaurant on Park Avenue. We can have lunch there.
That sounds good. And we can have something to drink afterwards.
Would you like to have dinner later?
Sure. At what time?
At nine o'clock.
No. At eight o'clock. *Eight o'clock is better (A las ocho es mejor).*
Excuse me, Miss. Would you like to have lunch with me?
What?
Would you like to have lunch with me today?
No, thanks.
I'm sorry, miss. But would you like to have something to drink with me?
No thank you sir.
Later, perhaps?
No. Not now. And not later.
But at one o'clock. Okay?
No, sir. I don't want to have something to drink with you.
Oh, I understand now.
Finally.
Yes. You don't want to have something to drink with me, but you would like to have something to eat with me. At a restaurant.
You don't understand, sir.
What don't I understand?
You don't understand English, sir.

LEVEL 1: LESSON 14

Teaching tip: Encourage your student when he responds correctly. Say English praise words such as "excellent" or "great job" or "very good" and any others you can think of.

¿Cómo se dice "esta noche" en inglés? Tonight.
Ahora diga en inglés, "mañana por la noche". Tomorrow night,
Say in English, "A las seis". At six o'clock.
Now say in English, "Hoy a las seis". Today at six o'clock.
Voy a cenar. I'm going to have dinner.
Voy a cenar en un rato. I'm going to have dinner in a while.
Ask me at what time. At what time?
A las seis. At six o'clock.
No, a las seis no. No, not at six o'clock.
Pregúnteme en inglés qué hora es ahora. What time is it now?
Ask me in English, "¿Sabe que hora es? Do you know what time it is?
Son las diez ahora. It's ten o'clock now.
No, son las cuatro. No, it's four o'clock.
Ask me in English, "¿Qué hora es ahora? What time is it now?
Tell me it's five o'clock. It's five o'clock.
Say in English, "Hola, Señor Lopez. ¿Cómo le va?" Hello, Mr. Lopez. How's it going?
Todo bien, gracias. It's going well, thanks.
¿Cómo se dice, "Cuídate" en inglés? Take care.
Ahora diga, "Te veré más tarde". See you later.
Te veré más tarde hoy. See you later today.
De acuerdo. Okay.
Tell me you´re going to have dinner with your son later. I'm going to have dinner with my son later.

"Hija" se dice "daughter" en inglés. Repita, "daughter". Daughter.
¿Cómo se dice "hija" en inglés? Daughter.
Para decir en inglés, "Mi hija", diga "My daughter". Repita, "My daughter". My daughter.
Voy a cenar con mi hija a las siete. I'm going to have dinner with my daughter at seven o'clock.
¿Con quién? With whom?
Con mi hija. With my daughter.
Voy a cenar con mi hija. I'm going to have dinner with my daughter.
Voy a comer con usted. I'm going to eat with you.
¿Con quién? With whom?
Con usted. Voy a cenar con usted. With you. I'm going to have dinner with you.
Gracias. A mí me gustaría comer también. Thanks. I'd like to eat too.
Tell me you're going to have dinner with your daughter later. I'm going to have dinner with my daughter later.
Tengo hambre. I'm hungry.
Now tell me you're very hungry. I'm very hungry.
Say in English, "Me gustaría cenar con usted". I'd like to have dinner with you.
Now say in English, "Me gustaría cenar con usted hoy en la noche". I'd like to have dinner with you tonight.
En el hotel. At the hotel.
En el hotel en la Avenida Parque. At the hotel on Park Avenue.
Bueno. All right.
¿Va a tomar algo de vino? Are you going to have some wine?
No. Voy a tomar algo de cerveza. No, I'm going to have some beer.
¿Cómo se dice en "hoy" en inglés? Today.
No soy norteamericano. I'm not American.
Tell me in English, "No voy a cenar hoy". I'm not going to have dinner today.
¿Usted no va a cenar? You're not going to have dinner?
No, hoy no. No, not today.
No voy a cenar hoy. I'm not going to have dinner today.
¿Por qué no? Why not?
Porque no tengo hambre. Because I'm not hungry.
Pero tengo sed. But I'm thirsty.
Tell me you're not hungry. I'm not hungry.
Say "hija" in English. Daughter.
Hoy voy a comer a las tres. Today I'm going to eat at three o'clock.

Con mi hija. With my daughter.

¿Con quién? With whom?

"¿Cuánto?" se dice "How much?" en inglés. Repita "How much?" How much?

"¿Cuánto le debo?" se dice "How much do I owe you?" Repita, "How much do I owe you?" How much do I owe you?

Repita en partes. How much. How much.

Do I owe you? Do I owe you?

Now repeat it all, "How much do I owe you?" How much do I owe you?

Again, "How much do I owe you?" How much do I owe you?

Pregunte en inglés, "¿Cuánto le debo?" How much do I owe you?

"Yo le debo" se dice "I owe you". Repita, "I owe you." I owe you.

Ask in English, "¿Cuánto le debo?" How much do I owe you?

"Dólares" es "dollars" en inglés. Diga, "dollars". Dollars.

Say in English, "Cinco dólares". Five dollars.

Say in English, "Yo le debo cinco dólares". I owe you five dollars.

Now say, "Usted me debe cinco dólares". You owe me five dollars.

En inglés, "Usted me debe" se dice, "You owe me". Repita, "You owe me". You owe me.

How does one say, "Usted me debe"? You owe me.

Say in English, "Usted me debe cinco dólares". You owe me five dollars.

Now say in English, "Yo le debo cinco dólares". I owe you five dollars.

Ask again in English, "¿Cuánto le debo?" How much do I owe you?

Answer in English, "Usted me debe cinco dólares". You owe me five dollars.

"One dollar" means "Un dólar" in English. Repeat, "One dollar". One dollar.

How does one say "Un dólar" in English? One dollar.

Ask in English, "¿Cuánto le debo? How much do I owe you?

Answer in English, "Usted me debe un dólar". You owe me a dollar.

Diga en inglés, "No, yo le debo cinco dólares". No, I owe you five dollars.

Para decir "solo", diga "only". Repita, "only". Only.

"Solo un dólar" se dice "Only a dollar" in English. Only a dollar.

Repeat, "You owe me only a dollar". You owe me only a dollar.

Diga en inglés, "Usted me debe solo un dólar". You owe me only a dollar.

Ask in English, "¿Cuánto le debo hoy?" How much do I owe you today?

Solo ocho dólares. Only eight dollars.

"Once dólares" se dice "Eleven dollars". Repita, "Eleven dollars". Eleven dollars.

Say in English, "Solo once dólares". Only eleven dollars.

¿Cuánto? How much?

¿Cuánto le debo? How much do I owe you?
Once dólares. Eleven dollars.
"Doce dólares" se dice "Twelve dollars". Repita, "Twelve dollars". Twelve dollars.
Usted me debe doce dólares. You owe me twelve dollars.
Solo dos dólares. Only two dollars.
Solo doce dólares. Only twelve dollars.
tres dólares. Three dollars.
Once dólares. Eleven dollars.
Utilizando el número, diga "Un dólar". One dollar.
"Trece dólares" se dice "Thirteen dollars". Repita, "Thirteen dollars". Thirteen dollars.
Yo le debo trece dólares. I owe you thirteen dollars.
¿Cuánto le debo a usted? How much do I owe you?
Trece dólares. Thirteen dollars.
Doce dólares. Twelve dollars.
Trece dólares. Thirteen dollars.
Ocho dólares. Eight dollars.
Once dólares. Eleven dollars.
Diez dólares. Ten dollars.
Yo le debo diez dólares. I owe you ten dollars.
Dos dólares. Two dollars.
Seis dólares. Six dollars
¿Cuánto? How much?
Siete. Seven.
"Please repeat" quiere decir "Por favor repita". Diga, "Please repeat". Please repeat.
Lo siento. Por favor repita. I'm sorry. Please repeat.
Say this in English, "Do I owe you five dollars?" Do I owe you five dollars?
Diga que sí en inglés. Yes.
Pregunte otra vez en inglés, "¿Le debo yo cinco dólares?" Do I owe you five dollars?
¿Quiere cinco dólares? Do you want five dollars?
¿Le debo yo cinco dólares? Do I owe you five dollars?
No, señora. Cuatro dólares. No, ma'am. Four dollars.
Y usted, siete dólares. And you, seven dollars.
Yo le debo trece dólares. I owe you thirteen dollars.
No, trece no. No, not thirteen.
Solo doce. Only twelve.

Hola Ramón. ¿Cómo está? Hello Ramón. How are you?
Muy bien, gracias. Very well, thanks.
¿Y usted? ¿Cómo le va? And you? How's it going?
Todo bien, gracias. It's going well, thanks.
Nos vemos más tarde. See you later.
Cuídate. Take care.
Adiós. Goodbye.

End of speaking/listening Lesson. Continue with the reading for lesson 14.

Reading for Lesson 14

As in previous lessons, have your student read the following sentences and phrases to you, correcting as necessary, and answering any questions about meaning. Make sure the student pronounces the last "s" in the word "Starbucks." Enjoy.

<u>Reading Practice</u>
How's it going?
It's going well, thanks. And you? How are you?
I'm fine, thank you.
Hey, do you know what time it is?
Yes, it's three o'clock.
Are you going to have lunch now?
No, not now. It's too late.
Would you like to have some wine?
No, thank you. I don't drink alcohol.
You don't? I didn't know that. Would you like to have some coffee then?
Sure. But where?
There is a Starbucks nearby.
There is? I thought that one closed.
No, it is still open.
The Starbucks on East Fifty Second Street closed. Not the Starbucks on First Street.
Oh, that's good. Let's go there then.
Yes, and maybe we can have dinner afterwards.
Yes, I would like to have dinner at the Park Avenue Restaurant.
What would you like to do tomorrow?
I don't know. Maybe we can go to the park or *the movies (el cine)*.
Maybe. Well we can talk about it at Starbucks.
Okay. *Let's go (Vámonos)*.

LEVEL 1: LESSON 15 (LESSONS 11 – 14 REVIEW)

Teacher note: The student has learned a lot of material at this point. Encourage him on his progress and if there is some word or phrase he is weak at, you can have him practice it a few more times when you can.

Diga en inglés "Hola Mary. Es Jack." Hello Mary. It's Jack.
Hola, Jack. ¿Cómo está? Hello, Jack. How are you?
Muy bien. ¿Y usted, Mary? ¿Cómo le va? Very well. And you, Mary? How's it going?
Todo bien, gracias. Todo bien. It's going well, thanks. It's going well.
Pregunte en inglés, "¿Qué hora es?" What time is it?
Answer me in English, "Son las once". It's eleven o'clock.
Say in English, "No, son las ocho". No, it's eight o'clock.
Ask in English, "¿Cuánto le debo?" How much do I owe you?
Answer in English, "Un dólar". A dollar.
Say in English, "Usted me debe un dólar." You owe me one dollar.
Seis dólares. Six dollars.
Say "trece dólares" in English. Thirteen dollars.
Pregunte "¿Once dólares?" Eleven dollars?
Conteste en inglés, "No, doce". No, twelve.
¿Dos o doce? No entiendo. Two or twelve? I don't understand.
Doce. Twelve.
Diga en inglés "La entiendo". I understand you.
"Ahora" se dice "now" en inglés. Repita "now". Now.
Say in English, "Ahora la entiendo". Now I understand you.
Tell me you don't understand me. I don't understand you.
Again tell me in English, "No lo entiendo". I don't understand you.
Usted. You.
¿Cómo se dice a una persona en inglés, "Lo siento. No la entiendo." I'm sorry. I don't understand you.

"**Por favor escuche" se dice, "Please listen". Repita, "Please listen".** Please, listen.
Cómo se dice "Por favor escuche" en inglés? Please listen.
Acuérdese que "Please repeat" quiere decir, "Por favor, repita". Repita, "Please repeat". Please repeat.
¿Cómo se dice, "Por favor repita" en inglés? Please repeat.
Count in English, "diez, once, doce, trece". Ten, eleven, twelve, thirteen.
Now say in English, "diez u once". Ten or eleven.
Doce o trece. Twelve or thirteen.
Diga en inglés, "Ahora la entiendo". Now I understand you.
Ask in English, "¿Le gustaría cenar conmigo? Would you like to have dinner with me?
¿Le gustaría tomar algo de vino? Would you like to have some wine?
¿Cuándo? ¿Hoy? When? Today?
¿O mañana? Or tomorrow?
Esta noche. Tonight.
Mañana por la noche. Tomorrow night.
¿A qué hora? At what time?
A las seis o a las siete. At six o'clock or at seven o'clock.
¿Hoy? Today?
Sí, hoy. Yes, today.
Mañana por la noche no. Not tomorrow night.
Por favor, escuche. Please listen.
Say in English, "Yo no voy a comer." I'm not going to eat.
Yo no voy a comer con usted. I'm not going to eat with you.
Yo no voy a comer con usted mañana por la noche. I'm not going to eat with you tomorrow night.
Pero me gustaría cenar con usted esta noche. But I would like to have dinner with you tonight.
How does one say, "Me gustaría" in English? I would.
Now say in English, "Me gustaría cenar con usted." I would like to have dinner with you.
Ask in English, "¿Cuántos dólares? How many dollars?
¿Cuántos dólares tiene usted? How many dollars do you have?
¿Cuántos dólares? How many dollars?
Usted tiene. You have.
¿Cuántos dólares tiene usted? How many dollars do you have?
Repeat, "How many dollars do you have?" How many dollars do you have?

Ask in English, "¿Cuántos dólares tengo yo? How many dollars do I have?
Ask again, "How many dollars do I have?" How many dollars do I have?
"Catorce" se dice "Fourteen" en inglés. Repita, "Fourteen". Fourteen.
Catorce dólares. Fourteen dollars.
Yo tengo catorce dólares. I have fourteen dollars.
Yo tengo. I have.
Para decir "hermanos y hermanas" en inglés se dice "brothers and sisters". Repita, "brothers and sisters". Brothers and sisters.
Repita en partes. "Brothers". Brothers.
And sisters. And sisters.
Repita, "Brothers and sisters". Brothers and sisters.
¿Cómo se dice "hermanos y hermanas" en inglés? Brothers and sisters.
¿Cómo cree que se dice "Mis hermanos y hermanas" en inglés? My brothers and sisters.
Pregunte, "¿Cuántos hermanos y hermanas tiene?" How many brothers and sisters do you have?
Answer in English, "Tengo tres hermanos y dos hermanas". I have three brothers and two sisters.
Ask in English, "¿Cuántos dólares tiene? How many dollars do you have?
Quince se dice "fifteen" en inglés. Repita, "Fifteen". Fifteen.
Diga "Tengo quince dólares". I have fifteen dollars.
Tengo quince dólares conmigo. I have fifteen dollars with me.
Tengo catorce dólares. I have fourteen dollars.
Treinta se dice "Thirty". Repita, "Thirty". Thirty.
Tengo treinta dólares en el hotel. I have thirty dollars at the hotel.
Tengo treinta dólares conmigo. I have thirty dollars with me.
Para decir "otros treinta dólares" se dice "Another thirty dollars". Repita, "Another thirty dollars". Another thirty dollars.
¿Cómo se dice "Otros treinta dólares"? Another thirty dollars.
Otros quince dólares. Another fifteen dollars.
Otros catorce dólares. Another fourteen dollars.
Trece, catorce, quince. Thirteen, fourteen, fifteen.
Uno, dos, tres, cuatro, cinco. One, two, three, four, five.
Tengo otros treinta dólares en el hotel. I have another thirty dollars at the hotel.
Tengo quince dólares conmigo y otros treinta dólares en el hotel. I have fifteen dollars with me and another thirty dollars at the hotel.

¿Cuántos hermanos y hermanas tiene usted? How many brothers and sisters do you have?
Tengo dos hermanos aquí. I have two brothers here.
Y otros dos en Los Ángeles. And another two in Los Angeles.
Tengo dos hermanos aquí y otros dos en Los Ángeles. I have two brothers here and another two in Los Angeles.
Tell me you have two sisters here. I have two sisters here.
Now tell me you have two sisters here and another two in Los Angeles. I have two sisters here and another two in Los Angeles.
"Dieciséis dólares" se dice "sixteen dollars". Repita, "sixteen dollars". Sixteen dollars.
Tengo dieciséis dólares. I have sixteen dollars.
Pregunte "¿Tiene usted dieciséis dólares?" Do you have sixteen dollars?
No, yo tengo trece dólares. No, I have thirteen dollars.
Pero tengo otros dieciséis dólares en el hotel. But I have another sixteen dollars at the hotel.
Tengo doce dólares. I have twelve dollars.
Pero tengo quince pesos también. But I have fifteen pesos too.
No tengo dieciséis dólares. I don't have sixteen dollars.
Tengo sólo un dólar. I have only one dollar.
"Qué triste" se dice "How sad". Repita, "How sad". How sad.
¿Cómo se dice "Qué triste" en inglés? How sad.
¿Cuánto le debo, señora? How much do I owe you, ma'am?
Me debe catorce dólares, señor. You owe me fourteen dollars, sir.
¿Y en pesos? ¿Cuánto le debo? And in pesos? How much do I owe you?
Usted me debe catorce pesos. You owe me fourteen pesos.
Yo solo tengo trece pesos. I only have thirteen pesos.
Qué triste. How sad.
Sí. Muy triste. Yes. Very sad.
En dólares son dos dólares In dollars it's two dollars.
Son quince pesos, señor. It's fifteen pesos, sir.
No tengo dieciséis dólares. I don't have sixteen dollars.
Quince dólares, no dieciséis. Fifteen dollars, not sixteen.
Tengo catorce dólares. I have fourteen dollars.
Pero quince no. But not fifteen.
Bueno, entonces. catorce dólares. All right, then. Fourteen dollars.
Bueno, entonces. Son catorce dólares, señor. All right, then. It's fourteen dollars, sir.

Se lo agradezco, señora. Thank you, ma'am.
Adiós. Goodbye.
Ask me in English, "¿Cuánto le debo? How much do I owe you?
Answer me in English, "Otros dos dólares". Another two dollars.
Tell me, "Otros dos dólares, por favor". Another two dollars, please.
Say in English, "Once dólares". Eleven dollars.
Usted me debe once dólares. You owe me eleven dollars.
"Eso es demasiado" se dice "that's too much" en inglés. Repita "that's too much". That's too much.
Diga en inglés, "Eso es demasiado". That's too much.
¿Once dólares? Eso es demasiado. Eleven dollars? That's too much.
Usted me debe. You owe me.
Usted me debe eso. You owe me that.
Pero usted me debe eso. But you owe me that.
¿Cuánto le debo? How much do I owe you?
Usted me debe once dólares. You owe me eleven dollars.
"¿Es todo?" se dice "That's all?" Repita, "That's all?" That's all?
Sí, es todo. Yes, that's all.
"Barato" se dice "Cheap" en inglés. Repita, "Cheap". Cheap.
Eso es barato. That's cheap.
Sí, eso es barato. Yes, that's cheap.
Usted me debe doce dólares. You owe me twelve dollars.
¿Doce dólares? ¿Es todo? Twelve dollars? That's all?
Sí, es todo. Yes, that's all.
Eso es barato. That's cheap.
Sí, es barato. Yo sé. Yes, that's cheap. I know.
Once dólares es barato. Eleven dollars is cheap.
Tiene dieciséis dólares? Do you have sixteen dollars?
¿Y pesos? And pesos?
¿Cuántos pesos tiene? How many pesos do you have?
Tengo quince pesos. I have fifteen pesos.
¿Cuántos pesos quiere? How many pesos do you want?
Quiero diez pesos. I want ten pesos.
Usted me debe diez pesos. You owe me ten pesos.
Aquí están diez pesos. Here are ten pesos.
Otros cinco pesos, por favor. Another five pesos, please.
Lo siento. No entiendo. I'm sorry. I don't understand.

Otros cinco pesos, por favor. Another five pesos, please.

Lo siento. No lo entiendo. I'm sorry. I don't understand you.

Hola. ¿Qué le gustaría beber? Hello. What would you like to drink?

Me gustaría algo de cerveza, por favor. I would like some beer, please.

¿Cuántas cervezas le gustaría? How many beers would you like?

Solo una por favor. Only one please.

¿Solo una? Qué triste. Only one? How sad.

Sí. Muy triste. Yes. Very sad.

Aquí esta su cerveza. Here's your beer.

¿Cuánto le debo? How much do I owe you?

Me debe dos dólares. You owe me two dollars.

End of speaking/listening Lesson. Continue with the reading for Lesson 15.

Reading for Lesson 15

Read the following sentences and phrases with your student. Please make sure that proper intonation is used for all questions.

Reading Practice

Hello, how are you?

Fine, thanks. And you?

Not too bad. What would you like to drink?

I would like some beer, please.

A glass of beer, then?

Two glasses, please. *I'm waiting for my brother (Estoy esperando a mi hermano).*

I think I met your brother yesterday (Creo que conocí a tu hermano ayer).

He looks just like you (Se ve igualito a usted).

Yes, he is here from Los Angeles.

I live in Los Gatos.

I owe you five dollars.

No, you don't.

No? Then how much do I owe you for the beer?

You owe me three dollars, please.

Three dollars? That's all?

Yes. Three dollars is cheap, I know.

Well in that case, I would like four beers.

Two for you and two for your brother?

No. Three beers for me and one beer for my brother.

Well, you owe me six dollars, then.

I only have five dollars. But I have more money at the hotel.

Don't worry about it (No se preocupe por eso). You can pay me the dollar you owe me later.

Or my brother can pay you the dollar. He will be here soon.

Okay.

Here are your beers.

Thanks.

You're welcome.

LEVEL 1: LESSON 16

You can spend 1 – 2 days or more on this review, depending on how well the student has mastered the material. Reviewing the reading lessons that went with lessons 11 – 15 can be of help also. Remember, a student should not move ahead until he or she responds correctly at least 85% of the time.

Repita, "Much later". Much later.
¿Cómo se dice "Mucho más tarde" en inglés? Much later.
Say in English, "Me gustaría hacer algo". I'd like to do something.
Ask in English, "¿Qué le gustaría hacer?" What would you like to do?
Conteste en inglés, "Me gustaría comer algo." I'd like to have something to eat.
Ask in English, "¿Con quién?" With whom?
Answer in English, "Me gustaría comer algo con usted". I'd like to have something to eat with you.
Now say in English, "De acuerdo". Okay.
Ahora diga en inglés "Pero mucho más tarde". But much later.
Ask in English, "Qué quiere hacer usted?" What do you want to do?
Answer in English, "Quiero comprar algo para mi hijo". I want to buy something for my son.
Tell me you'd like to buy something for your son. I'd like to buy something for my son.
A la una quiero comprar algo para mi hijo. At one o'clock I want to buy something for my son.
Conteste, "No. A la una no". No. Not at one o'clock.
A las dos. At two o'clock.
De acuerdo. A las dos. Okay. At two o'clock.
¿A las dos entonces? At two o'clock, then?
Lo siento. No entiendo. I'm sorry. I don't understand.
Perdón. Usted no entiende. Excuse me. You don't understand.

Ask in English, "Qué es lo que no entiendo?" What don't I understand?
¿Sabe usted donde está el restaurante? Do you know where the restaurant is?
¿Queda aquí? Is it here?
No. No está aquí. No. It's not here.
Está por allá. It's over there.
Pregunte, "¿A qué hora?" At what time?
Pregúnteme que hora es. What time is it?
¿Cómo se dice "Son las nueve"? It's nine o'clock.
Ahora diga "Son las ocho". It's eight o'clock.
¿Qué hora es? What time is it?
Son las cinco. It's five o'clock.
Pregunte si son las cuatro. Is it four o'clock?
Ahora pregunte si son las tres. Is it three o'clock?
Yo creo. I think.
¿Cómo se dice "Yo creo que son las cuatro"? I think it's four o'clock.
Ahora diga "Yo creo que son las dos." I think it's two o'clock.
Pregunte "¿Son las dos?" Is it two o'clock?
Conteste, "No. Yo creo que son las tres." No. I think it's three o'clock.
Diga "Usted va". You're going.
Usted va a comer. You're going to eat.
¿Va a comer usted? Are you going to eat?
Si. Yo voy a comer. Yes. I'm going to eat.
Pero más tarde. But later.
Mucho más tarde. Much later.
¿Cómo se dice "Yo voy a almorzar"? I'm going to have lunch.
Tengo hambre. I'm hungry.
Voy a almorzar ahora. I'm going to have lunch now.
Voy a comer mucho más tarde. I'm going to eat much later.
Voy a comer a las cinco. I'm going to eat at five o'clock.
¿A las cinco? Es tarde. At five o'clock? That's late.
¿Va a comer a las cinco? Are you going to eat at five o'clock?
¿Cómo le va? How's it going?
Todo bien, gracias. It's going well, thanks.
Perdón. ¿Le gustaría almorzar conmigo? Excuse me. Would you like to have lunch with me?
Claro. Sure.
¿Cuándo le gustaría almorzar? When would you like to have lunch?

A las dos. At two o'clock.

¿Quiere almorzar? Do you want to have lunch?

Sí, ¿pero cuándo? Yes, but when?

En un rato. In a while.

¿A las tres? At three o'clock?

Say in English, "Demasiado tarde". Too late.

Eso es. That is

Say in English, "Eso es demasiado tarde". That's too late.

Ask in English, "¿Sabe usted que hora es? Do you know what time it is?

Answer in English, "Son las cuatro". It's four o'clock.

¿Va a almorzar ahora? Are you going to have lunch now?

En un rato. In a while.

A las seis. At six o'clock.

Eso es demasiado tarde. That's too late.

Eso es demasiado tarde para mí. That's too late for me.

Pero tengo sed. But I'm thirsty.

Voy a tomar algo de vino. I'm going to have some wine.

¿Le gustaría almorzar conmigo? Would you like to have lunch with me?

Le gustaría tomar algo de vino? Would you like to have some wine?

Claro. Sure.

¿Le gustaría tomar algo de vino también? Would you like to have some wine too?

Bueno. All right.

¿Dónde? Where?

¿Cuándo? ¿Ahora? When? Now?

A las seis, señorita. At six o'clock, miss.

O a las siete. Or at seven o'clock.

A las siete no. Not at seven o'clock.

Más tarde. Later.

En un rato. In a while.

Entonces, a las ocho. Then at eight o'clock.

A las ocho esta noche. At eight o'clock tonight.

Yo voy a cenar. I'm going to have dinner.

Voy a cenar esta noche. I'm going to have dinner tonight.

Me gustaría cenar esta noche. I'd like to have dinner tonight.

Me gustaría cenar con mi hijo esta noche. I'd like to have dinner with my son tonight.

Esta noche voy a cenar a las diez. Tonight I'm going to have dinner at ten o'clock.

Eso es demasiado tarde. That's too late.

¿Y mañana? And tomorrow?
Mañana voy a cenar con usted. Tomorrow I'm going to have dinner with you.
Mañana por la noche a las siete. Tomorrow night at seven o'clock.
No, a las ocho. No, at eight o'clock.
Hoy. Today.
Hoy a las tres. Today at three o'clock.
Mañana. Tomorrow.
Mañana por la noche. Tomorrow night.
Esta noche. Tonight.
Hoy. Today.
¿Le gustaría cenar conmigo hoy? Would you like to have dinner with me today?
Hoy no. Mañana. ¿De acuerdo? Not today. Tomorrow. Okay?
Bueno. ¿A qué hora? All right. At what time?
A las seis o a las siete. At six o'clock or at seven o'clock.
Me gustaría cenar con usted esta noche. I'd like to have dinner with you tonight.
Esta noche no. Pero mañana por la noche. Not tonight. But tomorrow night.
Entonces a las ocho. En el Restaurante Avenida Parque. Then at eight o'clock. At the Park Avenue Restaurant.
Mañana por la noche. Tomorrow night.
Esta noche voy a tomar algo de cerveza. Tonight I'm going to have some beer.
¿Cómo está hoy? How are you today?
¿Qué quiere hacer? What do you want to do?
¿Qué quiere hacer esta noche? What do you want to do tonight?
¿Le gustaría beber algo en el hotel? Would you like to have something to drink at the hotel?
Sí me gustaría, pero no esta noche. Yes, I would, but not tonight.
Entonces, ¿mañana por la noche? Then tomorrow night?
Bueno. Mañana en la noche. All right. Tomorrow night.
Tengo hambre. I'm hungry.
Tengo mucha hambre. I'm very hungry.
Tengo sed. I'm thirsty.
Tengo mucha sed. I'm very thirsty.
Adiós. Good bye.
"Be careful" means "Ten cuidado" in English. Repeat, "Be careful". Be careful.
Cuídate. Take care.
¿Qué hora es ahora? What time is it now?
Son las cinco. It's five o'clock.

¿Va a tomar algo de vino? Are you going to have some wine?
No. Voy a tomar algo de cerveza. No, I'm going to have some beer.
Ten cuidado. Be careful.
No soy norteamericano. I'm not American.
Y no soy mexicano. And I'm not Mexican.
No tengo hambre. I'm not hungry.
No voy a cenar hoy. I'm not going to have dinner today.
¿Usted no va a cenar? You're not going to have dinner?
No, hoy no. No, not today.
No voy a cenar hoy. I'm not going to have dinner today.
¿Por qué no? Why not?
Porque no tengo hambre. Because I'm not hungry.
Ahora pregunte "¿Cuánto le debo? How much do I owe you?
Yo le debo cinco dólares. I owe you five dollars.
Usted me debe cinco dólares. You owe me five dollars.
Usted me debe un dólar. You owe me one dollar.
¿Cuánto le debo hoy? How much do I owe you today?
Solo ocho dólares. Only eight dollars.
Solo once dólares. Only eleven dollars.
¿Cuánto? How much?
Usted me debe doce dólares. You owe me twelve dollars.
Solo dos dólares. Only two dollars.
tres dólares. Three dollars.
Un dólar. One dollar.
Trece dólares. Thirteen dollars.
Yo le debo trece dólares. I owe you thirteen dollars.
Yo le debo diez dólares. I owe you ten dollars.
Seis dólares. Six dollars.
Siete. Seven.
¿Quiere cinco dólares? Do you want five dollars?
¿Le debo yo cinco dólares? Do I owe you five dollars?
No, Señora. Cuatro dólares. No, ma'am. Four dollars.
Usted me debe cuatro dólares. You owe me four dollars.
Usted me debe doce. You owe me twelve.
¿Dos o doce? No entiendo. Two or twelve? I don't understand.
Doce. Twelve.
Ahora la entiendo. Now I understand you.

Say "Ten cuidado" in English. Be careful.
No la entiendo. I don't understand you.
¿How does one say in English, "Usted"? You.
¿Le gustaría cenar conmigo? Would you like to have dinner with me?
¿Le gustaría tomar algo de vino? Would you like to have some wine?
¿A qué hora? At what time?
A las seis o a las siete. At six o'clock or at seven o'clock.
¿Hoy? No puedo. Lo siento. Today? I can't. I'm sorry.
Yo no voy a comer. I'm not going to eat.
Yo no voy a comer con usted. I'm not going to eat with you.
Yo no voy a comer con usted mañana por la noche. I'm not going to eat with you tomorrow night.
Pero me gustaría cenar con usted esta noche. But I would like to have dinner with you tonight.
Me gustaría. I would.
Me gustaría cenar con usted. I would like to have dinner with you.
¿Cuántos dólares tiene usted? How many dollars do you have?
¿Cuántos dólares? How many dollars?
¿Cuántos dólares tengo yo? How many dollars do I have?
Repeat in English, "How many dollars do I have?" How many dollars do I have?
Say in English, "Yo tengo catorce dólares." I have fourteen dollars.
Tengo quince dólares conmigo. I have fifteen dollars with me.
Tengo otros treinta dólares en el hotel. I have another thirty dollars at the hotel.
¿Tiene usted dieciséis dólares? Do you have sixteen dollars?
No, tengo trece dólares. No, I have thirteen dollars.
Pero tengo quince pesos también. But I have fifteen pesos also.
No tengo dieciséis dólares. I don't have sixteen dollars.
Tengo sólo un dólar. I have only one dollar.
Qué triste. How sad.
Yo sé. I know.
¿Cuánto le debo, señora? How much do I owe you, ma'am?
Me debe catorce dólares, señor. You owe me fourteen dollars, sir.
¿Y en pesos? ¿Cuánto le debo? And in pesos? How much do I owe you?
Usted me debe cuarenta pesos. You owe me forty pesos.
Yo sólo tengo veinte pesos. I only have twenty pesos.
Qué triste. How sad.
Yo sé. I know.

En dólares son dos dólares. In dollars it's two dollars.

Usted me debe once dólares. You owe me eleven dollars.

¿Once dólares? Eso es demasiado. Eleven dollars? That's too much.

Pero usted me debe eso. But you owe me that.

Usted me debe once dólares. You owe me eleven dollars.

¿Es todo? That's all?

Es barato. That's cheap.

Once dólares es barato. Eleven dollars is cheap.

End of speaking/listening lesson. Continue with the reading for Lesson 16.

Reading for Lesson 16

Have the student attempt to read all of these by himself. Correct him as necessary. He should be able to understand most of the text. You can explain to him anything in it he may not understand.

Reading Practice
I'd like to do something today.
Like what?
I don't know. I'm very hungry.
Would you like to eat something at a restaurant?
I am hungry for *Chinese food* (*comida China*).
I am hungry for *Italian food* (*comida Italiana*).
I want to eat at a Chinese restaurant.
Now?
No. In a while. At two o'clock.
Not at two o'clock. At four o'clock.
Four o'clock is too late.
Three o'clock then?
Okay. Three o'clock.
How much money do I owe you?
You owe me five dollars.
No, I owe you ten dollars.
Right. You owe me ten.
How is your son?
He is well. How is your daughter?
She is fine, thanks.
See you later.
Good bye.

LEVEL 1: LESSON 17

Teaching tip: Make sure the student pronounces the "t" sound in "cents". Also make sure he pronounces the "t" sound in words like "don't" and any words that have the "t" at the end.

"Centavos" se dice "Cents" en inglés. Repita, "Cents". Cents.
Treinta centavos, por favor. Thirty cents, please.
Lo siento. Otros diez centavos, por favor. I'm sorry. Another ten cents, please.
Lo siento. No entiendo. I'm sorry. I don't understand.
No entiendo inglés muy bien. I don't understand English very well.
Lo siento. Por favor repita. I'm sorry. Please repeat.
¿Tiene dólares? Do you have any dollars?
Ask me if I have any money. Do you have any money?
Ask again in English, "¿Tiene dinero? Do you have any money?
Para preguntar, "¿Tiene dinero consigo?" se dice, "Do you have any money on you?" Repita, "Do you have any money on you?" Do you have any money on you?
Creo que sí. I think so.
¿Cree que sí? ¿No está seguro? You think so? You're not sure?
No, no estoy seguro. No, I'm not sure.
Ahora cómo se dice en inglés, "Estoy seguro". I'm sure.
No estoy seguro. I'm not sure.
Ask me if I have any wine. Do you have any wine?
Answer in English, "No tengo vino". I don't have any wine.
Pero tengo algo de cerveza. But I have some beer.
Entonces, deme una cerveza. Then give me a beer.
¿Tiene dinero consigo? Do you have any money on you?
En inglés, "diecinueve" se dice "Nineteen". Repita, "Nineteen". Nineteen.
Say in English, "Diecinueve dólares". Nineteen dollars.
Aquí están cinco pesos. Here are five pesos.

¿Usted no tiene dólares? You don't have any dollars?
También tengo unos dólares. I have some dollars too.
Diecisiete se dice "Seventeen". Repita, "Seventeen". Seventeen.
"Deme" se dice "Give me" en inglés. Repita, "Give me". Give me.
Deme diecisiete dólares. Give me seventeen dollars.
Deme diecisiete dólares, por favor. Give me seventeen dollars, please.
Para decir en inglés, "¿Qué soy yo, un banco?" diga, "What am I, a bank?" Repita, "What am I, a bank?" What am I, a bank?
Deme diecinueve dólares, por favor. Give me nineteen dollars, please.
Ask in English, "¿Qué soy yo, un banco?" What am I, a bank?
Perdón, diecisiete, no diecinueve. Excuse me, seventeen, not nineteen.
¿Cuántos? ¿Dieciocho? How many? Eighteen?
No, diecisiete. No, seventeen.
Diecisiete, no dieciocho. Seventeen, not eighteen.
Otro dólar, por favor. Another dollar, please.
Deme otro dólar, por favor. Give me another dollar, please.
¿Dieciocho? ¿Está seguro? Eso es mucho. Eighteen? Are you sure? That's a lot.
No señora. Dieciséis. No ma'am. Sixteen.
Dieciséis dólares, por favor. Sixteen dollars, please.
Aquí están quince dólares. Here's fifteen dollars.
Otro dólar, por favor. Another dollar, please.
¿Qué soy yo, un banco? What am I, a bank?
Sí. Usted es un banco. Yes. You are a bank.
How does one say, "Aquí" in English? Here.
Now say in English, "Son catorce, señora". It's fourteen, ma'am.
Utilizando el número, diga, "Entonces, deme un dólar". Then give me one dollar.
¿Tiene dinero consigo? Do you have any money on you?
¿Cuánto le debo? How much do I owe you?
No mucho. Not a lot.
Diecinueve. Nineteen.
¿Sabe usted que hora es? Do you know what time it is?
Diga en inglés, "No I don't". No, I don't.
"No I don't" es como decir "No I don't know" brevemente. Otra vez, diga "No, I don't." No, I don't.
"Yes, I do" es como decir "yes, I do know" brevemente. Diga por favor, "Yes, I do". Yes, I do.
Otra vez diga, "Yes, I do". Yes, I do.

¿Tiene usted vino? Do you have any wine?
Conteste brevemente que no tiene. No, I don't.
¿Tiene cerveza entonces? Do you have any beer, then?
Conteste brevemente que sí tiene. Yes, I do.
Para decir, "¿Por qué pregunta?" se dice "Why do you ask?" Repita, "Why do you ask?" Why do you ask?
Tengo mucha cerveza. I have a lot of beer.
Tengo mucha cerveza. ¿Por qué pregunta? I have a lot of beer. Why do you ask?
Say that you are very thirsty. I am very thirsty.
Aquí está una cerveza. Here's a beer.
La cerveza es para usted. The beer is for you.
Para usted. For you.
La cerveza es para usted. The beer is for you.
"Para mí" se dice, "for me". ¿Cómo se dice "para mí" en inglés? For me.
Otra vez, "para mí". For me.
Ahora diga lo mismo pero con entonación de pregunta. Repita, "¿For me?" For me?
Pregunte "¿Para mí?" en inglés. For me?
¿La cerveza es para mí? Is the beer for me?
Sí, la cerveza es para usted. Yes, the beer is for you.
¿Para mí? For me?
Sí, para usted. Yes, for you.
La cerveza es para mí? Is the beer for me?
Sí, pero el vino es para Charles. Yes, but the wine is for Charles.
¿Tiene vino? Do you have any wine?
Conteste que sí en inglés, brevemente. Yes, I do.
Tengo algo. I have some.
Repita, "Yes, I do. I have some". Yes, I do. I have some.
Ahora diga que no, brevemente. No, I don't.
No tengo nada. I don't have any.
Repita, "No, I don't. I don't have any". No, I don't. I don't have any.
¿Quiere algo de vino? Do you want some wine?
Conteste que no, brevemente. No, I don't.
No gracias. No thanks.
Conteste que sí, brevemente. Yes, I do.
"Un vaso" se dice "A glass". Repita, "A glass". A glass.
Say in English, "Sí. Me gustaría un vaso". Yes, I'd like a glass.

Now say in English, "Sí. Me gustaría un vaso, por favor". Yes, I'd like a glass, please.

De acuerdo. El vino es para usted. Okay. The wine is for you.

Muchas gracias. Thank you very much.

Ask in English, ¿Cuánto cuesta, o cuánto es por una cerveza? How much is a beer?

¿Cuánto es? How much is it?

¿Una cerveza? A beer?

Un dólar. A dollar.

Y el vino, seis dólares. And the wine, six dollars.

¿Cuánto cuesta? How much is it?

Lo siento. ¿Cuánto es? I'm sorry. How much is it?

Aquí están dos dólares. Here are two dollars.

Por favor, deme tres dólares. Please give me three dollars.

Aquí está otro dólar. Here's another dollar.

The words, "yo puedo" mean "I can" in English. Say "yo puedo". I can.

How does one say, "Voy al banco"? I'm going to the bank.

Say in English, "Puedo". I can.

Now say in English, "Puedo darle." I can give you.

Puedo darle tres dólares. I can give you three dollars.

De acuerdo. Puedo darle tres dólares. Okay. I can give you three dollars.

No puedo. I can't.

Yo no puedo. I can't.

Pero yo no puedo. But I can't.

Ask in English, "¿Qué soy yo, un banco?" What am I, a bank?

Voy al banco. I'm going to the bank.

Yo no puedo darle tres dólares. I can't give you three dollars.

No puedo darle dólares. I can't give you any dollars.

Usted puede. You can.

Yo puedo darle solo tres dólares. I can give you only three dollars.

Usted puede. You can.

¿Puede usted? Can you?

¿Puede usted darme unos dólares? Can you give me some dollars?

Yo no puedo. I can't.

¿Por qué no? Why not?

No quiero. I don't want to.

¿Qué soy yo, un banco? What am I, a bank?

Senorita, ¿tiene vino? Do you have any wine, miss?

Sí, tengo algo. Yes, I have some.
Tengo algo. I have some.
¿Tiene cerveza? Do you have any beer?
Sí, tengo algo. Yes, I have some.
Tengo algo de cerveza. I have some beer.
No tengo. I don't have any.
Ask in English, "¿Tiene dólares?" Do you have any dollars?
Answer in English, "Sí, tengo algo". Yes, I have some.
Tell me that you have a lot. I have a lot.
Now tell me you don't have any. No, I don't have any.
No tengo muchos. I don't have a lot.
Yo quiero algunos. I want some.
Yo quiero algunos dólares. I want some dollars.
Usted quiere algunos. You want some.
Usted quiere algunos dólares. You want some dollars.
¿Algunos dólares? Some dollars?
¿Usted quiere algunos dólares? You want some dollars?
¿Qué soy yo, un banco? What am I, a bank?
No puedo. I can't.
¿Usted no puede? You can't?
¿Por qué no? Why not?
No tengo dólares. I don't have any dollars.
No tengo dólares conmigo. I don't have any dollars on me.
No tengo. I don't have any.
Quiero algunos. I want some.
Quiero algunos dólares. I want some dollars.
No tengo. I don't have any.
No tengo muchos. I don't have a lot.
Entonces, deme algunos pesos. Then give me some pesos.
No puedo. I can't.
¿Usted no puede? You can't?
¿Por qué no? Why not?
Puedo. I can.
Pero no quiero. But I don't want to.
Usted tiene pesos. You have pesos.
Pero no quiero. But I don't want any.
Pregunte en inglés, "¿Dos y dos es cuánto?" Two and two is how much?

Repeat in English, "Two and two is how much?" Two and two is how much?
Now answer in English, three and four is how much? Seven.
Nine and one is how much? Ten.
Six and seven is how much? Thirteen.
Thirteen and two is how much? Fifteen.
Eight and four is how much? Twelve.
Thirteen and three is how much? Sixteen.
Fifteen and two is how much? Seventeen.
Seventeen and two is how much? Nineteen.
Ask me in English, "¿Dos y dos es cuánto?" Two and two is how much?
Repeat one more time, "Two and two is how much?" Two and two is how much?
If someone asks you "Hello, how are you?" what do you say? I'm fine thanks, and you?
Answer the following in the affirmative: would you like to have dinner with us? Yes.
Ask me at what time. At what time?
"How about at seven o´clock?" es como decir, "¿Qué le parece a las siete?" Repita, "How about at seven o'clock?" How about at seven o'clock?
How does one ask in English, "¿Qué le parece a las seis?" How about at six o´clock?
Ask in English, "¿Qué le parece a las cinco?" How about at five o´clock?
I don't have any wine. Can you buy some wine? Conteste en inglés, "Sí, puedo. Puedo comprar algo para ti". Yes, I can. I can buy some for you.
Repita, "Yes, I can. I can buy some for you". Yes, I can. I can buy some for you.

End of speaking/listening lesson. Continue with the reading for Lesson 17.

DR. EPHRAIN TRISTAN ORTIZ

Reading for Lesson 17

Have the student read the following sentences and phrases to you out loud. Wait until he or she reads the whole line before making any corrections. If there are any corrections, have the student read the line again.

Reading Practice

All right. Here's sixteen dollars. *Do I owe you anymore? (¿Le debo algo más?)*
No, you don't owe me anymore.
How many pesos do you have?
I don't have any pesos. But I have a lot of dollars.
You don't have any pesos? You're not Mexican.
You're right. I'm not Mexican. I'm Guatemalan.
I have some dollars, but I don't have any pesos, and I need pesos.
Is the beer for me?
Yes, the beer is for you.
Here's eleven pesos. I'm sorry. I don't have any dollars.
Why not?
I spent all my money on the beer (Gasté todo my dinero en la cerveza).
I have seventeen dollars. Excuse me. I have eighteen, not seventeen
Here's a couple (Aquí hay un par) of ones.
I have nineteen pesos and a lot of dollars too.
No, you have seventeen.
I don't have any beer. I'd like to buy some beer.
I have some beer.
You do? I'd like a beer.
Here's a beer. How about you, Joey? Would you like one too?
I think so.
You think so? You're not sure?
Yes, I'm sure.
Now give me seventeen dollars, please. No, give me seven dollars.
I'd like to buy some wine.
Here's the wine and here's a beer.
Do you have any pesos?
No, I don't have any pesos. But I have some dollars.
You do?
Yes. I have a lot.
How many? Twelve?

That's not a lot.

LEVEL 1: LESSON 18

Spanish uses double negatives in sentences, but English only uses one. So watch and make sure the student doesn't say "I don't have no idea" in this lesson.

Ask this question, "do you have any dollars on you?" Do you have any dollars on you?
Conteste que sí, brevemente. Yes, I do.
¿Está seguro? Are you sure?
Sí, estoy seguro. Yes, I'm sure.
¿Tiene mucho? Do you have a lot?
Sí. Tengo muchos dólares y voy a comprar mucho vino. Yes, I have a lot of dollars and I'm going to buy a lot of wine.
"No tengo ninguna idea" se dice, "I have no idea" en inglés. Repita "I have no idea". I have no idea.
¿Por qué no? Why not?
No sé. I don't know.
Repeat in English, "I have no idea". I have no idea.
Ask me in English, "¿Sabe usted qué hora es?" Do you know what time it is?
No tengo ninguna idea. I have no idea.
No tengo ninguna idea. Lo siento. I have no idea. I'm sorry.
Hola Carlos. Es Cynthia. Hello, Carlos. It's Cynthia.
"Aquí" se puede usar en inglés como "tenga". Diga "aquí". Here.
Es para usted. It's for you.
Aquí/tenga. Es para usted. Here. It's for you.
¿Qué es? What is it?
No tengo ningún idea. I have no idea.
Pero es para ti. But it's for you.
¿Para mí? For me?
Se lo agradezco. Thank you.

¿Cuánto le debo? How much do I owe you?
Usted me debe cinco dólares. You owe me five dollars.
Aquí están cuatro dólares. Here are four dollars.
Otro dólar, por favor. Another dollar, please.
Oh, sí. Lo siento. Aquí está otro dólar. Oh, yes. I'm sorry. Here's another dollar.
¿Tiene usted cinco dólares? Do you have five dollars?
Conteste que sí brevemente. Yes, I do.
¿Tiene usted cinco dólares consigo? Do you have five dollars on you?
Diga que sí, brevemente. Yes, I do.
Conteste que no, brevemente. No, I don't.
No tengo dólares. I don't have any dollars.
En pesos, ¿cuánto cuesta? In pesos how much does it cost?
Deme algunos dólares. Give me some dollars.
Deme algunos dólares, por favor. Give me some dollars, please.
No tengo. I don't have any.
"Cajón" se dice "drawer" en inglés. Repita, "Drawer". Drawer.
One more time repeat, "Drawer". Drawer.
How does one say "El cajón" in English? The drawer.
"Del cajón" se dice "From the drawer". Repita, "From the drawer". From the drawer.
Say "Del cajón" in English. From the drawer.
How does one say in English, "Deme algunos dólares del cajón"? Give me some dollars from the drawer.
Now say in English, "Deme algunos dólares del cajón, por favor". Give me some dollars from the drawer, please.
Usted no tiene. You don't have any.
Pero usted no tiene. But you don't have any.
Puedo darle pesos. I can give you pesos.
Puedo. I can.
No quiero. I don't want any.
Pesos no. Not pesos.
No, no puedo. No, I can't.
En el cajón. In the drawer.
Tengo diecisiete dólares en el cajón. I have seventeen dollars in the drawer.
En el cajón. In the drawer.
Tengo diecinueve dólares en el cajón. I have nineteen dollars in the drawer.
¿Dónde? Where?

En el cajón. In the drawer.
Tengo diecinueve dólares en el cajón. I have nineteen dollars in the drawer.
Tengo diez centavos. I have ten cents.
Tengo once centavos. I have eleven cents.
Tengo unos dólares en el cajón. I have some dollars in the drawer.
Aquí están diecisiete dólares. Here are seventeen dollars.
Eso es mucho. That's a lot.
"Dinero" se dice "money" en inglés. Repita, "dinero". Dinero.
Eso es mucho dinero. That's a lot of money.
Mucho dinero. A lot of money.
Eso es mucho dinero. That's a lot of money.
¿Dieciocho dólares? Eso es mucho dinero. Eighteen dollars? That's a lot of money.
"It's too much" quiere decir "Es demasiado". Repita, "It's too much". It's too much.
One more time repeat, "It's too much". It's too much.
Es demasiado. It's too much.
Demasiado. Too much.
Es demasiado. It's too much.
Es demasiado dinero. It's too much money.
Ask me in English, "¿Cuánto dinero tiene?" How much money do you have?
Tengo veinte dólares. I have twenty dollars.
Usted tiene veinte dólares. You have twenty dollars.
No, veinticuatro. No, twenty four.
Usted tiene veinticinco dólares. You have twenty five dollars.
Es mucho dinero. It's a lot of money.
Es demasiado. It's too much.
Veintiocho. Twenty eight.
Usted tiene demasiado dinero. You have too much money.
Tengo treinta dólares. I have thirty dollars.
Yo tengo treinta dólares conmigo. I have thirty dollars on me.
Yo tengo treinta y nueve dólares. I have thirty nine dollars.
No, veintinueve. No, twenty nine.
¿Eso es demasiado? Is that too much?
"Suficiente" se dice "enough" en inglés. Cómo se dice "suficiente" en inglés? Enough.
No, pero es suficiente. No, but it's enough.
Say in English, "Es suficiente". It's enough.
Now ask in English, "¿Es suficiente?" Is it enough?

Answer in English, "No, no es suficiente". No, it's not enough.
How does one say in English, "Treinta y cinco. Eso es suficiente". Thirty five. That's enough.
Es demasiado. It's too much.
¿Es demasiado? Is it too much?
Sí. Es demasiado dinero. Yes, it's too much money.
"Deme cuarenta dólares" se dice, "Give me forty dollars". Repita, "Give me forty dollars". Give me forty dollars.
Cuarenta dólares. Forty dollars.
Catorce. Fourteen.
Deme catorce dólares, por favor. Give me fourteen dollars, please.
Cuarenta. Forty.
Catorce dólares. Fourteen dollars.
Deme cuarenta dólares. Give me forty dollars.
Tell me to give you forty seven dollars. Give me forty seven dollars.
Now tell me to give you forty six dollars. Give me forty six dollars.
Say in English, "Cuarenta y seis. Eso es suficiente." Forty six. That's enough.
Ask in English, "¿Es suficiente? Is it enough?
Tell me that "No, it's not enough". No, it's not enough.
Me gustaría cuarenta y ocho dólares. I'd like forty eight dollars.
No, treinta y ocho. No, thirty eight.
No, veintiocho. No, twenty eight.
¿Cuantos dólares quiere usted? How many dollars do you want?
Deme algunos dólares. Give me some dollars.
No tengo dólares. I don't have any dollars.
Deme algo de dinero. Give me some money.
Por favor deme algo de dinero. Please give me some money.
No tengo. I don't have any.
No tengo dinero. I don't have any money.
¿Tiene usted dinero? Do you have any money?
No, no tengo dinero. No, I don't have any money.
Me gustaría algo de dinero. I'd like some money.
Por favor deme algo de dinero. Please give some money.
No puedo. I can't.
¿Por qué no? Why not?
No tengo. I don't have any.
Sí, usted tiene algo. Yes, you have some.

Usted tiene mucho. You have a lot.
Bueno, aquí están veinticinco dólares. All right. Here are twenty five dollars.
Aquí están veinticinco dólares para usted. Here are twenty five dollars for you.
Gracias. Eso es suficiente. Thanks. That's enough.
Conteste esta pregunta: Two and three is how much? Five.
Answer this question: Five and three is how much? Eight.
Now answer this question: Eight and five is how much? Thirteen.
Now answer this one: Eleven and four is how much? Fifteen.
Thirteen and four is how much? Seventeen.
Sixteen and four is how much? Twenty.
Twenty and six is how much? Twenty six.
Twenty eight and four is how much? Thirty two.
Thirty two and two is how much? Thirty four.
Thirty four and twelve is how much? Forty six.
Thirty three and ten is how much? Forty three.
One more question: Twenty five and eleven is how much? Thirty six.
Diga, "Eso es suficiente". That's enough.
"Basta" también se dice "enough" en inglés. Cómo se dice "basta" en inglés? Enough.
"Enough already" es como decir "basta ya". Diga, "Enough already". Enough already.
Hola. Hello.
Perdón, ¿pero tiene algo de dinero? Excuse me, but do you have some money?
¿Tiene mucho? Do you have a lot?
Voy a tomar una cerveza. I'm going to have a beer.
¿Le gustaría tomar una cerveza conmigo? Would you like to have a beer with me?
No hoy. Pero me gustaría tomar una con usted mañana. Not today. But I'd like to have one with you tomorrow.
Eso es suficiente. That's enough.
Basta ya. Enough already.

End of speaking/listening lesson. Continue with the reading for Lesson 18.

Reading for Lesson 18

Here are a couple of short dialogues. You can have your student read after you and you can also play the parts of the two people speaking as well. Be sure to read these with the fluency of real people talking and not as if you were just reading in some kind of monotone. There are a few new phrases here. They are placed in italicized print with their translation in parenthesis.

Conversation 1

Hey, Ralph.

Hello, Mike. How are you?

Fine, thanks. And you?

Good. Hey, do you know what time it is?

I have no idea. Sorry.

Would you like to have a beer with me later?

Where?

At the restaurant in the hotel.

Sure. At what time?

How about at six o'clock?

Okay. See you then.

Conversation 2

Elena, do you have any money on you? I need twenty dollars for the taxi.

No, but you have forty dollars in the drawer.

No, I don't. I spent those at the restaurant.

Are you sure? *I just looked (Acabo de ver)* in there and I saw forty dollars.

You did?

Yes. There are forty dollars in the drawer.

Let me check.

Do you see?

Yes, I do. You are right. I have forty dollars here.

Good. You can have twenty dollars for the taxi and I can have twenty for some wine.

Okay.

Would you like to have a beer with me and Ralph at the restaurant later?

I'm sorry. I can't.

Why not?

I have to go to the hotel.

Oh yeah. You are going to have lunch with Lydia.

Yes, and *we are going to the movies (vamos al cine)* after lunch.
Have fun (Qué te diviertas).
Thanks. You too.

LEVEL 1: LESSON 19

Teaching tip: Watch out for the student dropping "t" sound at the end of words like "don't. If the student omits them, have him stop and say the word again with the "t" sound pronounced clearly.

Tell me you're going to have lunch. I'm going to have lunch.
En un restaurante o en el hotel. At a restaurant or at the hotel.
Ask me if I have any money. Do you have any money?
Say, "No, I don't". No, I don't.
Now tell me in English, "I don't have any". I don't have any.
Say in English, "Puedo darle algo." I can give you some.
How does one say in English, "Puedo darle algo de dinero". I can give you some money.
Pero no puedo darle mucho. But I can't give you a lot.
¿Usted no puede? You can't?
Me gustaría darle algo de dinero. I'd like to give you some money.
Pero no puedo. But I can't.
Ask in English, "¿Por qué no?" Why not?
Now ask, "¿Tiene usted dólares para mí?" Do you have any dollars for me?
Answer in English, "Sí, tengo." Yes, I do.
Tengo suficientes dólares. I have enough dollars.
Tengo algunos para usted. I have some for you.
Aquí está un dólar. Here's a dollar.
"Here is" se dice "here's" cuando se utiliza la contracción. Repita "here's". Here's.
Utilizando la contracción, diga, "Aquí hay cuarenta y cinco dólares". Here's forty five dollars.
Muchas gracias. Thank you very much.
¿Eso es suficiente? Is that enough?
Eso es demasiado. That's too much.

Eso es demasiado dinero. That's too much money.
Tengo veintiún dólares. I have twenty one dollars.
"Pero necesito" se dice "But I need". Repita, "But I need". But I need.
Yo necesito algo de dinero. I need some money.
¿Tiene usted dólares para mí? Do you have any dollars for me?
Answer in English, "Tengo algunos". I have some.
"Pero los necesito" se dice "But I need them". Repita, "But I need them". But I need them.
Say "Pero los necesito" in English. But I need them.
Pero los necesito para un taxi. But I need them for a taxi.
Cómo se dice "¿Veinticinco" en inglés? Twenty five.
¿Tiene veinticinco dólares? Do you have twenty five dollars?
Los necesito para un taxi. I need them for a taxi.
How does one say "Calle Veintidós Norte" in English? North Twenty Second Street.
Sesenta. Sixty.
Cincuenta. Fifty.
Sesenta y uno. Sixty one.
Calle Veintidós Norte. North Twenty Second Street
Cincuenta y siete. Fifty seven.
Buenos días. Good morning.
¿Cómo está hoy? How are you today?
Bien, gracias. ¿Y usted? Fine, thanks. And you?
Para decir "¿Cómo le fue?" se dice, "How did it go?" Pregunte "How did it go?" How did it go?
¿Cómo le fue? How did it go?
Repeat one more time in English, "How did it go"? How did it go?
"Entrevista" se dice "interview" en inglés. Repita "interview". Interview.
Diga "La entrevista". The interview.
¿Cómo le fue con la entrevista? How did it go with the interview?
"Su entrevista" se dice "Your interview". Repita, "Your interview". Your interview.
¿Cómo le fue con su entrevista? How did it go with your interview?
Ask again, "How did it go with your interview?" How did it go with your interview?
Con su entrevista. With your interview.
¿Cómo le fue con su entrevista? How did it go with your interview?
¿Cómo se dice "Mi entrevista" en inglés? My interview.
How does one say "entrevista" in English? Interview.
¿Cómo le fue con su entrevista? How did it go with your interview?

Muy bien, gracias. Very well, thanks.
¿Mi entrevista? Oh, muy bien, gracias. My interview? Oh, very well, thanks.
Deme seis dólares, por favor. Give me six dollars please.
¿Puede darme sesenta dólares? Can you give me sixty dollars?
¿Cuánto le debo? How much do I owe you?
Usted me debe. You owe me.
Usted me debe treinta y ocho dólares. You owe me thirty eight dollars.
Cincuenta y tres dólares. Fifty three dollars.
¿Es demasiado eso? Is that too much?
No es mucho aquí. It's not much here.
Sí, es demasiado. Yes, it's too much.
"Caro" es "expensive" en inglés. Diga, "expensive". Expensive.
How does one say "Es caro" in English? It's expensive.
Now say in English, "Es muy caro". It's very expensive.
Es demasiado caro. It's too expensive.
No es mucho aquí. It's not much here.
Todo está caro aquí. Everything is expensive here.
"Especialmente" se dice "especially" en inglés. Repita, "especially". Especially.
Es. Es.
Special. Special.
Repeat again, "Especially". Especially.
¿Cómo se dice "especialmente"? en inglés? Especially.
Todo está caro aquí. Especialmente la gasolina. Everything is expensive here. Especially the gasoline.
Diga otra vez en inglés, "Todo está caro aquí. Especialmente la gasolina. Everything is expensive here. Especially the gasoline.
No es demasiado caro. It's not too expensive.
¿Qué no es demasiado caro? What is not too expensive?
Todo está caro. Everything is expensive.
¿Todo? ¿O solo la gasolina? Everything? Or only the gasoline?
"Todo lo demás" se dice "Everything else". Repita, "Everything else". Everything else.
Say in English, "La gasolina y todo lo demás". The gasoline and everything else.
La gasolina y todo lo demás es caro. The gasoline and everything else is expensive.
No es demasiado caro. It's not too expensive.
No es muy caro. It's not very expensive.
Sí, es muy caro. Yes, it is very expensive.

Say "Cincuenta dólares" in English. Fifty dollars.
Now say, "Voy a darle cincuenta dólares". I'm going to give you fifty dollars.
Aquí está cincuenta dólares para usted. Here are fifty dollars for you.
No, deme sesenta dólares. No, give me sixty dollars.
No puedo darle sesenta dólares. I can't give you sixty dollars.
¿Por qué no? Why not?
No tengo suficiente dinero. I don't have enough money.
No es caro. It's not expensive.
En dólares no es caro. Especialmente aquí. In dollars it's not expensive. Especially here.
Es caro. It's expensive.
Sí, es demasiado caro. Yes, it's too expensive.
En pesos es demasiado caro. In pesos it's too expensive.
La gasolina y todo lo demás es caro. The gasoline and everything else is expensive.
"Se acuerda como decir "Usted" en inglés? You.
Do you remember how to say "Usted habla inglés"? You speak English?
Now ask me if I speak English. Do you speak English?
Sí, un poco. Yes, a little.
¿Un poco? No, usted habla muy bien. A little? No, you speak very well.
Tell me I speak very fast. You speak very fast.
Lo siento. Usted habla demasiado rápido. I'm sorry. You speak too fast.
Usted habla demasiado rápido para mí. You speak too fast for me.
How does one say, "Yo no hablo rápido"? I don't speak fast.
Sí, usted habla muy rápido. Yes, you speak very fast.
Usted habla inglés muy rápido. You speak English very fast.
Usted habla inglés demasiado rápido. You speak English too fast.
Usted habla demasiado rápido para mí. You speak too fast for me.
Y no lo entiendo. And I don't understand you.
Lo siento. Usted habla demasiado rápido y no lo entiendo. I'm sorry. You speak too fast and I don't understand you.
Say in English, "Caro". Expensive.
El vino es muy caro. The wine is very expensive.
El vino es muy caro aquí. The wine is very expensive here.
En dólares es muy caro. In dollars it's very expensive.
How does one say, "Es demasiado caro" in English? It's too expensive.
Es demasiado caro para mí. It's too expensive for me.
Y usted habla inglés muy rápido. And you speak English very fast.

Le gustaría cerveza Americana, ¿verdad? You'd like American beer, right?
No, quiero cerveza mexicana. No, I want Mexican beer.
¿Cuánto le debo? How much do I owe you?
¿Treinta dólares? Thirty dollars?
No, cuarenta. No, forty.
Usted me debe cuarenta dólares. You owe me forty dollars.
Le debo cuarenta dólares, ¿verdad? I owe you forty dollars, right?
No, usted me debe cincuenta dólares. No, you owe me fifty dollars.
Son cincuenta que le debo, ¿verdad? It's fifty I owe you, right?
No, son sesenta dólares que usted me debe. No, it's sixty dollars you owe me.
Son cincuenta que le debo, ¿verdad? It's fifty I owe you, right?
Sí, usted me debe cincuenta. Yes, you owe me fifty.
Tell me I don't understand English. You don't understand English.
Sí, entiendo muy bien. Yes, I understand very well.
Tell me you can speak Spanish. I can speak Spanish.
No, yo entiendo inglés. No, I understand English.
Ask in English, "¿Hablo demasiado rápido?" Do I speak too fast?
No, usted no habla demasiado rápido. No, you don't speak too fast.
Usted me debe algo de dinero. You owe me some money.
¿Cuánto le debo? How much do I owe you?
Por favor deme sesenta y uno dólares. Please give me sixty one dollars.
Se lo agradezco. Eso es suficiente. Thank you. That's enough.
¿Cómo le fue con su entrevista? How did it go with your interview?
Muy bien, gracias. Very well, thanks.
Tell me that everything is expensive here. Everything is expensive here.
Yo sé. Especialmente la gasolina. I know. Especially the gasoline.
Sí. La gasolina es cara. Yes. The gasoline is expensive.
Y todo lo demás. And everything else.
"Se acuerda cómo decir "cajón" en inglés? Drawer.
Do you remember how to say, "Tengo treinta dólares en el cajón"? I have thirty dollars in the drawer.

End of speaking/listening lesson. Continue with the reading for Lesson 19.

Reading for Lesson 19

Here are two short conversations. Read each line and have your student read each line after you do. When you finish, have your student read both dialogues by him or herself.

Conversation 1

I'm going to have lunch with Rudy at the hotel later.

Do you have any money?

Only seven or eight dollars.

That's not much. I can give you some but I can't give you a lot.

Can you give me ten dollars?

Okay. Here are ten dollars.

Thank you.

You're welcome. So how did it go with your interview?

Very well, thank you. *I have to go again (tengo que ir otra vez)* for a second interview tomorrow.

Good for you (Qué bueno para usted).

Yes. *I hope I can work there (Espero que pueda trabajar allí).*

Conversation 2

How much do I owe you?

You owe me sixty dollars.

Here are fifty dollars.

I need another (necesito otras) ten.

Excuse me?

It's sixty dollars you owe me. Not fifty.

I'm sorry. I don't understand.

You understand very well. You owe me sixty dollars, not fifty. Please pay me ten more dollars.

Okay. *Take it easy (Tómelo tranquilo).*

I will take it easy (Lo tomaré tranquilo) when you pay me ten more dollars.

All right. Here.

Thank you.

You're welcome.

Now I can take it easy (Ahora lo puedo tomar tranquilo).

LEVEL 1: LESSON 20 (LESSONS 16 – 19 REVIEW)

Teaching Tip: Be sure that the student continues to pronounce the "t" sound at the end of words! Watch this especially in his pronounciation of the word "without" which is used later in this lesson. Also make sure that when the student says the word "ice" that there is no sound after the soft "c" sound (eg. "ice-eh").

Tell me in English, "Todo está caro aquí". Everything is expensive here.
Say in English, "Yo sé. Todo, especialmente la gasolina". I know. Everything, especially the gasoline.
Aquí están treinta dólares. ¿Es suficiente? Here are thirty dollars. Is it enough?
Answer in English, "Sí. Es suficiente". Yes. It's enough.
Para decir en inglés, "Eso es más que suficiente", se dice "That's more than enough". That's more than enough.
¿Cómo se dice en inglés, "Eso es más que suficiente?" That's more than enough.
Repeat, "That's more than enough". That's more than enough.
Say "más que"in English. More than.
Now say in English, "Eso es más que suficiente". That's more than enough.
Cincuenta. Fifty.
Now do you say the number "sesenta" in English? Sixty.
Now say "treinta y cinco" in English. Thirty five.
Veintiocho. Eso es más que suficiente. Twenty eight. That's more than enough.
Do you remember how to say, "Buenos días" in English? Good morning.
¿Cómo le fue con su entrevista? How did it go with your interview?
Muy bien, gracias. Very well, thank you.
Eso es caro. That's expensive.
Eso no es caro. That's not expensive.
Sí, es caro. Yes, it is expensive.
¿Usted cree? Do you think so?
Sí. Creo que sí. Yes. I think so.

Es muy caro. It's very expensive.
¿Usted cree? Do you think so?
Para decir, "No estoy de acuerdo" se dice "I don't agree". Diga "I don't agree". I don't agree.
Repeat, "I don't agree". I don't agree.
Es muy caro. It's very expensive.
No estoy de acuerdo. I don't agree.
Treinta y cinco dólares es demasiado dinero. Thirty five dollars is too much money.
"Para un libro" se dice "For a book". Repita, "For a book". For a book.
Treinta y cinco dólares es demasiado dinero para un libro. Thirty five dollars is too much money for a book.
Repeat, "Thirty five dollars is too much money for a book. Thirty five dollars is too much money for a book.
No es mucho. It's not much.
No estoy de acuerdo. Treinta y cinco dólares es demasiado dinero para un libro. I don't agree. Thirty five dollars is too much money for a book.
¿Se acuerda cómo se dice "especialmente" en inglés? Especially.
Treinta y cinco dólares es demasiado por un libro. Thirty five dollars is too much for a book.
¿No está de acuerdo? You don't agree?
Tell me you don't agree. I don't agree.
Cuarenta y cinco dólares es demasiado dinero para un libro. Forty five dollars is too much money for a book.
No estoy de acuerdo. I don't agree.
¿No está de acuerdo? You don't agree?
Bueno. No voy a comprar el libro entonces. Fine. I'm not going to buy the book, then.
Try to say "En dólares es caro". In dollars it's expensive.
Do you remember how to say, "Usted habla demasiado rápido" in English? You speak too fast.
Lo siento. Usted habla demasiado rápido. No lo entiendo. I'm sorry. You speak too fast. I don't understand you.
Usted habla demasiado rápido para mí. You speak too fast for me.
Ask me if I have enough money. Do you have enough money?
¿Usted tiene suficiente dinero para comprar el libro? Do you have enough money to buy the book?
Tell me you have forty one dollars. I have forty one dollars.

¿Cuarenta y uno? Usted tiene suficiente, entonces. Forty one? You have enough, then.

Eso es demasiado. That's too much.

No, pero es suficiente. No, but it's enough.

Tell me it costs too much. It costs too much.

Now tell me it's not expensive. It's not expensive.

No estoy de acuerdo. I don't agree.

En dólares no es demasiado caro. In dollars it's not too expensive.

Más caro. More expensive.

Aquí es más caro. Here it's more expensive.

Ask me if I have enough money. Do you have enough money?

Say in English, "Usted habla muy rápido". You speak very fast.

Usted habla inglés demasiado rápido. You speak English too fast.

Aquí es más caro. Here it's more expensive.

Buenos días. Good morning.

Para preguntar "¿quién es ese?" se dice "Who is that?" Repita "Who is that?" Who is that?

Otra vez diga en inglés "¿Quién es ese?" Who is that?

Ahora, utilizando la contracción se dice "Who's that?" Pregunte "¿Quién es ese?" usando la contracción. Who's that?

"Mi esposo" se dice "My husband". Repita, "My husband". My husband.

¿Quién es ese? Who is that?

Mi esposo. My husband.

"Mi esposa" se dice "My wife". Repita, "My wife". My wife.

¿Quién es ese? Who is that?

Mi esposa. My wife.

"Ese es mi esposo" se dice "That's my husband". Repita, "That's my husband". That's my husband.

Ask in English, "¿Quién es ese?" Who's that?

Answer in English, "Ese es mi esposo". That's my husband.

¿Cómo cree que se dice en inglés, "Esa es mi esposa"? That's my wife.

Say again in English, "Esa es mi esposa". That's my wife.

Ask in English, "¿Ese es su esposo?" That's your husband?

Now ask in English, "¿Esa es su esposa? That's your wife?

Do you remember how to say "¿Quién es?" in English? Who's that?

How do you say "mi esposa." in English? My wife.

Now say in English, "su esposa". Your wife.

Su esposa está aquí. Your wife is here.
Su esposo. Your husband.
Su esposo está aquí. Your husband is here.
Esa es mi esposa. That's my wife.
Mi esposa está por allá. My wife is over there.
Please say this in English "A mi esposa le gustaría beber algo." My wife would like something to drink.
Now say this: "A mi esposa le gustaría." My wife would like.
Beber algo. Something to drink.
A mí me gustaría beber algo. I'd like something to drink.
A mi esposo le gustaría beber algo. My husband would like something to drink.
A mi esposo le gustaría tomar algo de vino. My husband would like to have some wine.
A mi me gustaría tomar algo de té helado. I'd like to have some iced tea.
"Water" es como se dice "Agua" en inglés. Repita, "Water". Water.
Say "agua" in English. Water.
How do you say "algo de agua"? Some water.
A mi esposo le gustaría tomar algo de agua. My husband would like to have some water.
Algo de agua, por favor. Some water, please.
A mi esposa le gustaría tomar algo de agua. My wife would like to have some water.
Tell me you'd like some coffee. I'd like some coffee.
Algo de café. Some coffee.
Tell me in English, "Café, por favor". Coffee, please.
A mi esposo le gustaría algo de café. My husband would like some coffee.
¿Y qué le gustaría a usted? And what would you like?
Algo de té helado, por favor. Some iced tea, please.
Tell me you'd like some coffee. I'd like some coffee.
¿Y qué le gustaría a usted? And what would you like?
Agua para mí. Water for me.
Su esposa. Your wife.
Su esposa está aquí. Your wife is here.
Su esposo está aquí. Your husband is here.
How does one ask "¿Dónde está mi esposo?" in English? Where is my husband?
¿Dónde está mi esposa? Where's my wife?
Su esposa no está aquí. Your wife is not here.

Utilizando la contracción, diga en inglés, "Su esposa no está aquí". Your wife isn't here.
Use the contraction and say in English, "Su esposo no está aquí." Your husband isn't here.
¿Mi esposo? My husband?
A mi esposa le gustaría algo de café. My wife would like some coffee.
A mi esposo le gustaría algo de agua. My husband would like some water.
Ask me in English if I have any wine. Do you have any wine?
Answer in English, "No, no tengo". No, I don't.
No, Señora. No tengo. No, ma'am. I don't.
Lo siento. No tengo. I'm sorry. I don't.
Aquí el vino es más caro. Here the wine is more expensive.
Tell me that everything is expensive here, especially the wine. Everything is expensive here, especially the wine.
Lo siento. Usted habla demasiado rápido. I'm sorry. You speak too fast.
¿Quién es ese? Who's that?
Para preguntar "¿Me entiende?" se dice "do you understand me? Say "Do you understand me?" Do you understand me?
Lo siento. Usted habla demasiado rápido. I'm sorry. You speak too fast.
Usted habla demasiado rápido para mí. You speak too fast for me.
Ask me if I understand English. Do you understand English?
¿Me entiende? Do you understand me?
Para decir "No. No lo entiendo" brevemente se dice "No I don't". Say in English "No I don't." No I don't.
¿Me entiende? Do you understand me?
Conteste que no brevemente. No I don't.
Say "ahora" in English. Now.
Now say "Lo siento. Usted habla demasiado rápido." I'm sorry. You speak too fast.
Ask in English, "¿Quién está por allá?" Who's over there?
Answer, "Esa es mi esposa". That's my wife.
¿Qué quiere hacer su esposa? What does your wife want to do?
Ask again in English: "¿Qué quiere hacer su esposa?" What does your wife want to do?
A mi esposa le gustaría. My wife would like.
A mi esposa le gustaría comer algo. My wife would like to have something to eat.
¿Su esposa quiere beber algo? Does your wife want to have something to drink?
¿Quiere usted beber algo? Do you want to have something to drink?

Repeat this word: "Do". Do.
Now repeat this word: "does". Does.
¿Su esposa quiere beber algo? Does your wife want to have something to drink?
¿Y usted? ¿Qué le gustaría beber? And you? What would you like to drink?
¿Café o agua? Coffee or water?
Agua, por favor. Water, please.
Para decir "sin hielo" se dice "without ice". Repita "without ice". Without ice.
¿Cómo se dice "hielo"? Ice.
Ahora diga "sin". Without.
Sin hielo. Without ice.
Me gustaría algo de agua. I would like some water.
Pero sin hielo. But without ice.
Agua, por favor, pero sin hielo. Water please, but without ice.
Su esposa puede tomar algo de agua. Your wife can have some water.
Y usted puede tomar algo de café. And you can have some coffee.
Muchas gracias. Thank you very much.
Ask me where my wife is. Where is your wife?
¿Mi esposa? Yo no sé. My wife? I don't know.
Mi esposa no está aquí. My wife isn't here.
¿Le gustaría cenar conmigo? Would you like to have dinner with me?
Answer, "Lo siento. Pero no puedo". I'm sorry, but I can't.
Voy a cenar con mi esposo. I'm going to have dinner with my husband.
Voy a cenar con mi esposo esta noche. I'm going to have dinner with my husband tonight.
Entonces, ¿a usted le gustaría beber algo? Then would you like to have something to drink?
Sí, me gustaría. Yes I would.
¿Qué le gustaría beber? What would you like to drink?
Café. Coffee.
¿Y usted? And you?
Agua, pero sin hielo. Water, but without ice.
Agua, por favor. Pero sin hielo. Water, please. But without ice.
Tell me that I can have some wine. You can have some wine.
No, es demasiado caro. No, it's too expensive.
¿De verdad? Really?
Tell me that here it's more expensive. Here it's more expensive.
¿Una cerveza entonces? A beer then?

Por favor, deme algo de café. Please give me some coffee.
¿Su esposo también quiere café? Does your husband want coffee too?
No sé. Mi esposo no está aquí. I don't know. My husband isn't here.
Use the number one and say, "Un café, por favor". One coffee, please.
Aquí está su café, señora. Here's your coffee, ma'am.
Y allí está mi esposo. And there's my husband.
Y su esposa. And your wife.
Ask in English, "¿Cómo le fue con su entrevista?" How did it go with your interview?
Muy bien, gracias. Very well, thanks.
Say in English, "Treinta centavos, por favor". Thirty cents, please.
Now say in English, "Lo siento. Otros diez centavos, por favor." I'm sorry. Another ten cents, please.
How does one say in English, "Lo siento. No entiendo inglés muy bien"? I don't understand English very well.
Lo siento. Por favor repita. I'm sorry. Please repeat.
¿Tiene dólares? Do you have any dollars?
Ask me in English if I have any money. Do you have any money?
Now ask me in English if I have any money on me. Do you have any money on you?
Answer in English, "Creo que sí". I think so.
Ask in English, "¿Cree que sí? ¿No está seguro?" You think so? You're not sure?
Answer in English, "No, no estoy seguro". No, I'm not sure.
¿Ahora cómo se dice en inglés, "Estoy seguro"? I'm sure.
Ask me if I have any wine. Do you have any wine?
Tell me you don't have any wine but you have some beer. I don't have any wine but I have some beer.
Entonces, deme una cerveza. Then give me a beer.
Aquí están cinco pesos. Here's five pesos.
¿Usted no tiene dólares? You don't have any dollars?
También tengo unos dólares. I have some dollars too.
Deme diecisiete dólares, por favor. Give me seventeen dollars, please.
Deme diecinueve dólares, por favor. Give me nineteen dollars, please.
Perdón, diecisiete, no diecinueve. Excuse me, seventeen, not nineteen.
¿Cuántos? ¿Dieciocho? How many? Eighteen?
No, diecisiete. No, seventeen.
Diecisiete, no dieciocho. Seventeen, not eighteen.
Deme otro dólar, por favor. Give me another dollar, please.
¿Dieciocho? ¿Está seguro? Eso es mucho. Eighteen? Are you sure? That's a lot.

No señora. Dieciséis dólares, por favor. No ma'am. Sixteen dollars, please.
Aquí están quince dólares. Here are fifteen dollars.
Otro dólar, por favor. Another dollar, please.
Aquí. Here.
Son catorce, señora. It's fourteen, ma'am.
Utilizando el número, diga, "Entonces, deme un dólar". Then give me one dollar.
Ask in English, "¿Tiene dinero consigo?" Do you have any money on you?
Now ask me how much do I owe you. How much do I owe you?
No mucho. Not a lot.
¿Sabe usted qué hora es? Do you know what time it is?
Conteste que no, brevemente. No, I don't.
Ahora conteste que sí, brevemente. Yes, I do.
Ask me if I have any wine. Do you have any wine?
Conteste brevemente que no tiene. No, I don't.
¿Tiene cerveza entonces? Do you have any beer, then?
Conteste brevemente que sí tiene. Yes, I do.
Tengo mucha cerveza. ¿Por qué pregunta? I have a lot of beer. Why do you ask?
Aquí está una cerveza. La cerveza es para usted. Here's a beer. The beer is for you.
Pregunte "¿Para mí?" en inglés. For me?
¿La cerveza es para mí? Is the beer for me?
Sí, la cerveza es para usted. Yes, the beer is for you.
Ask again in English, "¿Para mí?" For me?
Answer, "Sí, para usted". Yes, for you.
¿La cerveza es para mí? Is the beer for me?
Sí, pero el vino es para Charles. Yes, but the wine is for Charles.
¿Tiene vino? Do you have any wine?
Conteste que sí, brevemente. Yes, I do.
Tell me you have some. I have some.
Now tell me you don't have any. I don't have any.
Ask me if I want some wine. Do you want some wine?
Conteste en inglés que no, brevemente. No, I don't.
No gracias. No thanks.
En inglés conteste que sí, brevemente. Yes, I do.
Sí. Me gustaría un vaso, por favor. Yes, I'd like a glass, please.
De acuerdo. El vino es para usted. Okay. The wine is for you.
Muchas gracias. Thank you very much.
¿Cuánto cuesta, o cuánto es por una cerveza? How much is a beer?

¿Cuánto es? How much is it?
¿Una cerveza? Un dólar. A beer? A dollar.
Y el vino, seis dólares. And the wine, six dollars.
Lo siento. ¿Cuánto es? I'm sorry. How much is it?
Aquí están dos dólares. Here are two dollars.
Por favor, deme tres dólares. Please give me three dollars.
Aquí está otro dólar. Here's another dollar.
Tell me that you can give me three dollars. I can give you three dollars.
Say in English, "No puedo." I can't.
Pero yo no puedo. But I can't.
Now tell me that you can't give me three dollars. I can't give you three dollars.
No puedo darle dólares. I can't give you any dollars.
Usted puede. You can.
Yo puedo darle solo tres dólares. I can give you only three dollars.
¿Puede usted? Can you?
¿Puede usted darme unos dólares? Can you give me some dollars?
Yo no puedo. I can't.
No quiero. I don't want to.
Senorita, ¿tiene vino? Do you have any wine, miss?
Sí, tengo algo. Yes, I have some.
¿Tiene cerveza? Do you have any beer?
Conteste que sí, brevemente. Yes, I do.
Tengo algo de cerveza. I have some beer.
¿Tiene dólares? Do you have any dollars?
Sí, tengo algo. Yes, I have some.
Tengo muchos. I have a lot.
No, no tengo. No, I don't have any.
Yo quiero algunos. I want some.
Yo quiero algunos dólares. I want some dollars.
¿Usted quiere algunos dólares? Do you want some dollars?
No tengo dólares. I don't have any dollars.
Tell me you don't have any dollars on you. I don't have any dollars on me.
No tengo. I don't have any.
Now tell me that you don't have a lot. I don't have a lot.
Entonces, deme algunos pesos. Then give me some pesos.
No puedo. I can't.
¿Usted no puede? You can't?

Puedo pero no quiero. I can but I don't want to.
Usted tiene pesos. You have pesos.
Pero no quiero. But I don't want any.
Pregunte en inglés, "¿Dos y dos es cuanto?" Two and two is how much?
Now answer these Math problems in English. Three and four is how much? Seven.
Nine and one is how much? Ten.
Six and seven is how much? Thirteen.
Thirteen and two is how much? Fifteen.
Eight and four is how much? Twelve.
Thirteen and three is how much? Sixteen.
Fifteen and two is how much? Seventeen.
Seventeen and two is how much? Nineteen.
How does one say, "Gracias, Señor"? Thanks, sir.
Se lo agradezco, señorita. Thank you, miss.
Respond to this greeting: Hello, how are you? I'm fine thanks, and you?
Answer the following in the affirmative: would you like to have dinner with us? Yes.
Ask me at what time. At what time?
Ask me in English, "¿Qué le parece a las siete?" How about at seven o'clock?
¿Qué le parece a las seis? How about at six o'clock?
I don´t have any wine. Can you buy some wine? Conteste en inglés, "Sí, puedo. Puedo comprar algo para ti". Yes, I can. I can buy some for you.
Repita esta pregunta, "Do you have any dollars on you?" Do you have any dollars on you?
Conteste que sí, brevemente. Yes, I do.
Ask me if I'm sure. Are you sure?
Sí, estoy seguro. Yes, I'm sure.
Ask me if I have a lot. Do you have a lot?
Sí. Tengo muchos dólares y voy a comprar mucho vino. Yes, I have a lot of dollars and I'm going to buy a lot of wine.
¿Sabe usted qué hora es? Do you know what time it is?
No tengo ninguna idea. Lo siento. I have no idea. I'm sorry.
Hola Carlos. Es Cynthia. Hello, Carlos. It's Cynthia.
Aquí. Es para usted. Here. It's for you.
¿Qué es? What is it?
No tengo ninguna idea, but it´s for you. I have no idea, but it's for you.
¿Para mí? Se lo agradezco. For me? Thank you.

¿Cuánto le debo? How much do I owe you?
Usted me debe cinco dólares. You owe me five dollars.
Aquí están cuatro dólares. Here's four dollars.
Otro dólar, por favor. Another dollar, please.
Oh, si. Lo siento. Aquí está otro dólar. Oh, yes. I'm sorry. Here's another dollar.
Ask me if I have five dollars. Do you have five dollars?
Conteste que sí brevemente. Yes, I do.
¿Tiene usted cinco dólares consigo? Do you have five dollars on you?
Conteste que no, brevemente. No, I don´t.
Tell me you don't have any dollars. I don't have any dollars.
¿En pesos, cuánto cuesta? In pesos how much is it?
Deme algunos dólares, por favor. Give me some dollars, please.
Say in English, "No tengo". I don't have any.
Do you remember how to say in English, "Deme algunos dólares del cajón, por favor"? Give me some dollars from the drawer, please.
Do you remember how to say in English, "Pero usted no tiene"? But you don´t have any.
Puedo darle pesos. I can give you pesos.
Puedo. I can.
How does one say "No quiero" in English? I don't want any.
Pesos no. Not pesos.
Tell me that no, you can't. No, I can't.
Tengo diecisiete dólares en el cajón. I have seventeen dollars in the drawer.
¿Dónde? Where?
En el cajón. In the drawer.
Tell me you have nineteeen dollars in the drawer. I have nineteen dollars in the drawer.
Tengo diez centavos. I have ten cents.
Now tell me you have eleven cents. I have eleven cents.
Tengo unos dólares en el cajón. I have some dollars in the drawer.
Aquí están diecisiete dólares. Here are seventeen dollars.
Eso es mucho. That's a lot.
Eso es mucho dinero. That's a lot of money.
¿Dieciocho dólares? Eso es mucho dinero. Eighteen dollars? That's a lot of money.
Es demasiado dinero. It's too much money.

End of speaking/listening lesson. Continue with the reading for Lesson 20.

Reading for Lesson 20

Here are two more short dialogues. As in the reading for lesson 19, read each line and have your student read each line after you do. When you finish, have your student read both dialogues by him or herself. You and the students can also take the parts of the people speaking as well.

Conversation 1

Everything is expensive here.

I know. Everything costs a lot, especially the wine.

Would you like to go to another restaurant?

No, it's okay. We can have lunch here.

Are you sure? We can go to another restaurant.

No. We can eat here. I can have a salad and some water.

A salad and water? *That isn't a lunch (Eso no es un almuerzo).*

Well I'm not very hungry.

You only want a salad and water? Are you sure?

Yes. I am going to have dinner with my husband later. I can eat a lot then.

All right. We can have lunch here if you want.

Yes, please.

Conversation 2

What would you like to drink?

I'd like a glass of water, but without ice.

And your husband? Would he like something to drink too?

Yes. He would like a beer.

And you miss?

Some coffee for me, please.

Okay.

Thank you.

Who is that over there (Quién es ese de allá)?

That is my husband.

Is he going to have dinner with us?

I think so.

LEVEL 1: LESSON 21

Teaching tip: You can spend 1 – 3 days or more on this review, depending on how well the student has mastered the material. Reviewing the reading lessons that went with lessons 17 – 20 can be of help also. Remember, a student should not move ahead until he or she responds correctly at least 85% of the time.

Ask me how much money I have. How much money do you have?

Tengo veinte dólares. I have twenty dollars.

Usted tiene veinte dólares. You have twenty dollars.

No, veinticuatro. No, twenty four.

Usted tiene veinticinco dólares. You have twenty five dollars.

Es mucho dinero. It's a lot of money.

Es demasiado. It´s too much.

Say "Veintiocho" in English. Twenty eight.

How does one say in English, "Usted tiene demasiado dinero". You have too much money.

Now say in English, "Tengo treinta dólares". I have thirty dollars.

Do you remember how to say, "Yo tengo treinta dólares conmigo" in English? I have thirty dollars on me.

Yo tengo treinta y nueve dólares. I have thirty nine dollars.

No, veintinueve. No, twenty nine.

Ask in English, "¿Eso es demasiado?" Is that too much?

Answer in English, "No, pero es suficiente". No, but it's enough.

¿Es suficiente? Is it enough?

No, no es suficiente. No, it's not enough.

Treinta y cinco. Eso es suficiente. Thirty five. That's enough.

¿Es demasiado? Is it too much?

Sí. Es demasiado dinero. Yes, it's too much money.

Tell me to give you forty dollars. Give me forty dollars.

Deme catorce dólares, por favor. Give me fourteen dollars, please.
Deme cuarenta y siete dólares. Give me forty seven dollars.
Cuarenta y seis. Eso es suficiente. Forty six. That's enough.
¿Es suficiente? Is it enough?
Tell me no, it's not enough. No, it's not enough.
Me gustaría cuarenta y ocho dólares. I'd like forty-eight dollars.
No, treinta y ocho. No, thirty eight.
No, veintiocho. No, twenty eight.
Ask me how many dollars do I want. How many dollars do you want?
Deme algunos dólares. Give me some dollars.
¿Qué soy yo, un banco? What am I, a bank?
Sí, usted es un banco. Yes, you are a bank.
Tell me you don't have any dollars. I don't have any dollars.
Deme algo de dinero. Give me some money.
Por favor deme algo de dinero. Please give me some money.
Tell me you don't have any. I don't have any.
¿Tiene usted dinero? Do you have any money?
No, no tengo dinero. No, I don't have any money.
Me gustaría algo de dinero. I'd like some money.
Por favor deme algo de dinero. Please give some money.
No puedo. No tengo. I can't. I don't have any.
Sí, usted tiene algo. Usted tiene mucho. Yes, you have some. You have a lot.
Bueno, aquí están veinticinco dólares. All right. Here are twenty five dollars.
Aquí están veinticinco dólares para usted. Here are twenty five dollars for you.
Gracias. Eso es suficiente. Thanks. That's enough.
Answer these math problems: Two and three is how much? Five.
Five and three is how much? Eight.
Eight and five is how much? Thirteen.
Eleven and four is how much? Fifteen.
Thirteen and four is how much? Seventeen.
Sixteen and four is how much? Twenty.
Twenty and six is how much? Twenty six.
Twenty eight and four is how much? Thirty two.
Thirty two and two is how much? Thirty four.
Thirty four and twelve is how much? Forty six.
Thirty three and ten is how much? Forty three.
One more question: Twenty five and eleven is how much? Thirty six.

Diga, "Eso es suficiente". That's enough.
Now say, "Basta" in English. Enough.
Do you remember how to say "Basta ya" in English? Enough already.
Hola. Hello.
Perdón, ¿pero tiene algo de dinero? Excuse me, but do you have some money?
¿Tiene mucho? Do you have a lot?
¿Por qué pregunta? Why do you ask?
Voy a tomar una cerveza. I'm going to have a beer.
¿Le gustaría tomar una cerveza conmigo? Would you like to have a beer with me?
No hoy. Pero me gustaría tomar una con usted mañana. Not today. But I'd like to have one with you tomorrow.
Diga "Voy a almorzar". I'm going to have lunch.
En un restaurante o en el hotel. At a restaurant or at the hotel.
¿Tiene dinero? Do you have any money?
Say, "No, I don't". No, I don't.
Say in English, "Puedo darle algo de dinero". I can give you some money.
Pero no puedo darle mucho. But I can't give you a lot.
¿Usted no puede? You can't?
Tell me that you'd like to give me some money but you can't. I'd like to give you some money, but I can´t.
Ask in English, "¿Por qué no?" Why not?
Now ask, "¿Tiene usted dólares para mí?" Do you have any dollars for me?
Answer in English, "Sí, tengo." Yes, I do.
Tengo suficiente dólares. I have enough dollars.
Tengo algunos para usted. I have some for you.
Aquí esta un dólar. Here's a dollar.
"Aquí hay cuarenta y cinco dólares". Here are forty five dollars.
Muchas gracias. Thank you very much.
¿Eso es suficiente? Is that enough?
Eso es demasiado. That's too much.
Eso es demasiado dinero. That's too much money.
Tengo veintiún dólares. I have twenty one dollars.
Yo necesito algo de dinero. I need some money.
Tengo algunos, pero los necesito para un taxi. I have some, but I need them for a taxi.
Do you remember how to say, "Veinticinco" in English? Twenty five.
¿Tiene veinticinco dólares? Do you have twenty five dollars?
Sí, pero los necesito para un taxi. Yes, but I need them for a taxi.

Say "Sesenta" in English. Sixty.
Now say "Cincuenta". Fifty.
Sesenta y uno. Sixty one.
Cincuenta y siete. Fifty seven.
Say "Buenos días" in English. Good morning.
Ask me how I am today. How are you today?
Bien, gracias. ¿Y usted? Fine, thanks. And you?
¿Cómo le fue? How did it go?
¿Cómo le fue con la entrevista? How did it go with the interview?
¿Cómo le fue con su entrevista? How did it go with your interview?
¿Cómo se dice "Mi entrevista" en inglés? My interview.
¿Cómo le fue con su entrevista? How did it go with your interview?
Muy bien, gracias. Very well, thanks.
¿Mi entrevista? O, muy bien, gracias. My interview? Oh, very well, thanks.
Tell me to give you six dollars please. Give me six dollars please.
¿Puede darme sesenta dólares? Can you give me sixty dollars?
¿Cuánto le debo? How much do I owe you?
Usted me debe treinta y ocho dólares. You owe me thirty eight dollars.
Cincuenta y tres dólares. Fifty three dollars.
¿Eso es demasiado? Is that too much?
No es mucho aquí. It's not much here.
Say that yes, it's too much. Yes, it's too much.
Es caro. It's expensive.
Es muy caro. It's very expensive.
Es demasiado caro. It's too expensive.
Tell me that everything is expensive here. Everything is expensive here.
Do you remember how to say in English, "Todo está caro aquí. Especialmente la gasolina"? Everything is expensive here. Especially the gasoline.
Now say in English, "No es demasiado caro". It's not too expensive.
Ask in English, "¿Qué no es demasiado caro? What is not too expensive?
¿Todo? ¿O solo la gasolina? Everything? Or only the gasoline?
"Todo lo demás" se dice "Everything else". Repita, "Everything else". Everything else.
Say in English, "La gasolina y todo lo demás". The gasoline and everything else.
La gasolina y todo lo demás es caro. The gasoline and everything else is expensive.
No es demasiado caro. It's not too expensive.
Say it's not very expensive. It's not very expensive.

Sí, es muy caro. Yes, it is very expensive.
Voy a darle cincuenta dólares. I'm going to give you fifty dollars.
Aquí está cincuenta dólares para usted. Here are fifty dollars for you.
No, deme sesenta dólares. No, give me sixty dollars.
Proteste en inglés. Protest in English, "No puedo darle sesenta dólares". I can't give you sixty dollars.
Tell me you don't have enough money. I don't have enough money.
No es caro. It's not expensive.
En dólares no es caro. Especialmente aquí. In dollars it's not expensive. Especially here.
Sí, es demasiado caro. Yes, it's too expensive.
En pesos es demasiado caro. In pesos it's too expensive.
Protest in English, "La gasolina y todo lo demás es caro". The gasoline and everything else is expensive.
Ask me if I speak English. Do you speak English?
Answer in English, "Sí, un poco." Yes, a little.
¿Un poco? No, usted habla muy bien. A little? No, you speak very well.
Usted habla muy rápido. You speak very fast.
Lo siento. Usted habla demasiado rápido. I'm sorry. You speak too fast.
Yo no hablo rápido. I don't speak fast.
Sí, usted habla muy rápido. Yes, you speak very fast.
Tell me that I speak English very fast. You speak English very fast.
Usted habla inglés demasiado rápido. You speak English too fast.
Usted habla inglés demasiado rápido para mí. You speak English too fast for me.
Lo siento. Usted habla demasiado rápido y no lo entiendo. I'm sorry. You speak too fast and I don't understand you.
El vino es muy caro. The wine is very expensive.
Tell me that the wine is very expensive here. The wine is very expensive here.
En dólares es muy caro. In dollars it's very expensive.
Y usted habla inglés muy rápido. And you speak English very fast.
Le gustaría cerveza Americana, ¿verdad? You'd like American beer, right?
No, yo quiero cerveza mexicana. No, I want Mexican beer.
¿Cuánto le debo? ¿Treinta dólares? How much do I owe you? Thirty dollars?
No, cuarenta. No, forty.
Tell me that I owe you forty dollars. You owe me forty dollars.
Le debo cuarenta dólares, ¿verdad? I owe you forty dollars, right?
No, usted me debe treinta dólares. No, you owe me thirty dollars.

Son treinta que le debo, ¿verdad? It's thirty I owe you, right?
No, son sesenta dólares que usted me debe. No, it's sixty dollars you owe me.
Son treinta y cinco que le debo, ¿verdad? It's thirty five I owe you, right?
Sí, usted me debe treinta y cinco. Yes, you owe me thirty five.
Usted no entiende inglés. You don't understand English.
Sí, entiendo muy bien. Yes, I understand very well.
Tell me you can speak Spanish. I can speak Spanish.
No, yo entiendo inglés. No, I understand English.
Ask in English, "¿Hablo demasiado rápido?" Do I speak too fast?
Answer in English, "No, usted no habla demasiado rápido". No, you don't speak too fast.
Usted me debe algo de dinero. You owe me some money.
¿Cuánto le debo? How much do I owe you?
Tell me to please give you sixty one dollars. Please give me sixty one dollars.
Se lo agradezco. Eso es suficiente. Thank you. That's enough.
¿Cómo le fue con su entrevista? How did it go with your interview?
Muy bien, gracias. Very well, thanks.
Todo está caro aquí. Everything is expensive here.
Yo sé. Especialmente la gasolina. I know. Especially the gasoline.
Sí. La gasolina es cara. Y todo lo demás. Yes. The gasoline is expensive. And everything else.
Tell me you have thirty dollars in the drawer. I have thirty dollars in the drawer.
Todo está caro aquí. Everything is expensive here.
Yo sé. Todo, especialmente la gasolina. I know. Everything, especially the gasoline.
Aquí están treinta dólares. ¿Es suficiente? Here are thirty dollars. Is it enough?
Sí. Es suficiente. Yes. It's enough.
Cómo se dice "Eso es más que suficiente?" That's more than enough.
How does one say "cincuenta" in English? Fifty.
And "sesenta"? Sixty.
Now say "Treinta y cinco" in English. Thirty five.
Veintiocho. Eso es más que suficiente. Twenty eight. That's more than enough.
¿Se acuerda cómo decir "Buenos días" en inglés? Good morning.
Do you remember how to say "Hello" in English? Hello.
¿Cómo le fue con su entrevista? How did it go with your interview?
Muy bien, gracias. Very well, thank you.
Eso es caro. That's expensive.
Eso no es caro. That's not expensive.

Protest in English, "Sí, es caro". Yes, it is expensive.
Ask me if I think so. Do you think so?
Sí. Creo que sí. Yes. I think so.
Tell me you don't agree. I don't agree.
Treinta y cinco dólares es demasiado dinero para un libro. Thirty five dollars is too much money for a book.
No es mucho. It's not much.
Tell me you don't agree. Thirty five dollars is too much money for a book. I don't agree. Thirty five dollars is too much money for a book.
¿Se acuerda cómo se dice "especialmente" en inglés? Especially.
Treinta y cinco dólares es demasiado para un libro. Thirty five dollars is too much for a book.
Cuarenta y cinco dólares es demasiado dinero para un libro. Forty five dollars is too much money for a book.
No estoy de acuerdo. I don't agree.
¿No está de acuerdo? You don't agree?
Bueno. No voy a comprar el libro entonces. Fine. I'm not going to buy the book, then.
En dólares es caro. In dollars it's expensive.
Usted habla demasiado rápido. You speak too fast.
Lo siento. Usted habla demasiado rápido. No le entiendo. I'm sorry. You speak too fast. I don't understand you.
Ask me if I have enough money. Do you have enough money?
Now ask me if I have enough money to buy the book. Do you have enough money to buy the book?
Tell me you have forty one dollars. I have forty one dollars.
¿Cuarenta y un? Usted tiene suficiente, entonces. Forty one? You have enough, then.
Eso es demasiado. That's too much.
No, pero es suficiente. No, but it's enough.
Cuesta demasiado. It costs too much.
No es caro. It's not expensive.
No estoy de acuerdo. I don't agree.
En dólares no es demasiado caro. In dollars it's not too expensive.
Aquí es más caro. Here it's more expensive.
¿Usted tiene suficiente dinero? Do you have enough money?
Usted habla muy rápido. You speak very fast.
Usted habla inglés demasiado rápido. You speak English too fast.

How does one say in English, "Usted habla inglés demasiado rápido para mí"? You speak English too fast for me.

Aquí es más caro. Here it's more expensive.

Buenos días. Good morning.

¿Quién es ese? Who is that?

Do you remember how to say "Mi esposo" in English? My husband.

¿Quién es esa? Who is that?

Mi esposa. My wife.

Ese es mi esposo. That's my husband.

Now say in English, "Esa es mi esposa". That's my wife.

Pregunte "¿Ese es su esposo?" That's your husband?

Ahora pregunte "¿Esa es su esposa? That's your wife?

Using the contraction, say "¿Quién es ese?" in English. Who's that?

How does one say "Su esposa está aquí" in English? Your wife is here.

Su esposo está aquí. Your husband is here.

Mi esposa está por allá. My wife is over there.

Tell me that your wife would like something to drink. My wife would like something to drink.

A mí me gustaría beber algo. I'd like something to drink.

A mi esposo le gustaría beber algo. My husband would like something to drink.

A mi esposo le gustaría tomar algo de vino. My husband would like to have some wine.

A mí me gustaría tomar algo de té helado. I'd like to have some iced tea.

A mi esposo le gustaría tomar algo de agua. My husband would like to have some water.

Algo de agua, por favor. Some water, please.

Tell me that your wife would like to have some water. My wife would like to have some water.

Café para mí, por favor. Coffee for me, please.

A mi esposo le gustaría algo de café. My husband would like some coffee.

¿Y qué le gustaría a usted? And what would you like?

Algo de té helado, por favor. Some iced tea, please.

Me gustaría algo de café. I'd like some coffee.

¿Y qué le gustaría a usted? And what would you like?

Agua para mí. Water for me.

Ask in English, "¿Dónde está mi esposo?" Where is my husband?

Now ask in English, "¿Dónde está mi esposa?" Where is my wife?

Ask this again but with a contraction. Where's my wife?
Answer in English, "Su esposa no está aquí". Your wife isn't here.
Su esposo no está aquí. Your husband isn't here.
¿Mi esposo? My husband?
A mi esposa le gustaría algo de café. My wife would like some coffee.
A mi esposo le gustaría algo de agua. My husband would like some water.
¿Tiene usted vino? Do you have any wine?
No, no tengo. No, I don't.
No, Señora. No tengo. No, ma'am. I don't.
Lo siento. No tengo. I'm sorry. I don't.
Aquí el vino es más caro. Here the wine is more expensive.
Todo está caro aquí, especialmente el vino. Everything is expensive here, especially the wine.
Lo siento. Usted habla demasiado rápido. I'm sorry. You speak too fast.
Ask in English, "¿Quién es ese?" Who is that?
Ask this again but with a contraction. Who's that?
Tell me you don't know. I don't know.
¿Me entiende? Do you understand me?
Lo siento. Usted habla demasiado rápido. I'm sorry. You speak too fast.
¿Entiende inglés? Do you understand English?
¿Me entiende? Do you understand me?
Conteste que no brevemente. No I don't.
Say "ahora" in English. Now.
Now say in English, "Lo siento. Usted habla demasiado rápido." I'm sorry. You speak too fast.
¿Quién está por allá? Who's over there?
Esa es mi esposa. That's my wife.
¿Qué quiere hacer su esposa? What does your wife want to do?
A mi esposa le gustaría comer algo. My wife would like to have something to eat.
¿Su esposa quiere beber algo? Does your wife want to have something to drink?
¿Quiere usted beber algo? Do you want to have something to drink?
¿Y usted? ¿Qué le gustaría beber? And you? What would you like to drink?
¿Café o agua? Coffee or water?
Agua, por favor. Water, please.
Tell me you would like some water, but without ice. I would like some water, but without ice.
Agua, por favor, pero sin hielo. Water please, but without ice.

Su esposa puede tomar algo de agua. Your wife can have some water.
Y usted puede tomar algo de café. And you can have some coffee.
Muchas gracias. Thank you very much.
¿Dónde está su esposa? Where is your wife?
¿Mi esposa? Yo no sé. My wife? I don't know.
Mi esposa no está aquí. My wife isn't here.
¿Le gustaría cenar conmigo? Would you like to have dinner with me?
Lo siento, pero no puedo. I'm sorry, but I can't.
Voy a cenar con mi esposo. I'm going to have dinner with my husband.
Voy a cenar con mi esposo esta noche. I'm going to have dinner with my husband tonight.
Entonces, ¿a usted le gustaría beber algo? Then would you like to have something to drink?
Answer that yes you would. Yes I would.
Ask me in English, "¿Qué le gustaría beber?" What would you like to drink?
Café. Coffee.
Agua, por favor. Pero sin hielo. Water, please. But without ice.
Usted puede tomar algo de vino. You can have some wine.
No, es demasiado caro. No, it's too expensive.
¿De verdad? Really?
Tell me that it's too expensive for you. It's too expensive for me.
Sí. Aquí es más caro. Yes. Here it's more expensive.
¿Una cerveza entonces? A beer then?
How does one say "De acuerdo" in English? Okay.
Por favor, deme algo de café. Please give me some coffee.
¿Su esposo también quiere café? Does your husband want coffee too?
No sé. Mi esposo no está aquí. I don't know. My husband isn't here.
Use the number one to say in English, "Un café, por favor." One coffee, please.
Aquí está su café, señora. Here's your coffee, ma'am.
Y allí está mi esposo. And there's my husband.
Y su esposa. And your wife.
¿Cómo le fue con su entrevista? How did it go with your interview?
Muy bien, gracias. Very well, thanks.

End of speaking/listening lesson. Continue with the reading for Lesson 21.

Reading for Lesson 21

As you listen to the student read and make corrections as necessary, continue watching for correct pronounciation of the "th" sound in words like "thanks" and "everything".

<u>Reading Practice</u>
Would you like something to drink?
Sure. What do you have?
I have beer, wine, coffee and water.
I'd like some wine please.
Here.
Thanks.
The wine is very expensive here.
I know. Everything is expensive here.
How did your job interview go?
It went well. I have another interview there tomorrow.
Who is that over there?
That is my wife Yolanda. I am having lunch with her.
Where are you having lunch?
We are having lunch at a Chinese restaurant.
Hello Yolanda. This is my friend Julio.
Hello Julio. It's nice to meet you.
It's nice to meet you too.
Where are you from, Julio?
I am from Los Angeles, California. And you?
I am from Acapulco.
Roberto, would you and Yolanda like to have dinner with me tomorrow night?
Sure, at what time?
How about nine o'clock?
That's too late. How about seven o'clock?
Okay. Seven o'clock is fine.

LEVEL 1: LESSON 22

Teaching Tip: Watch for the student's pronounciation of the "o" in the word "dollar". Most Spanish speakers pronounce it like a Spanish "o". Make sure the student pronounces it as the "a" in "father".

Remember that rápido means "fast" in English. Say "fast". Fast.
Say "Muy rápido" in English. Very fast.
Now say, "Usted habla inglés muy rápido". You speak English very fast.
Ask, "¿Su esposo también habla rápido?" Does your husband speak fast too?
Answer, "Sí, demasiado rápido". Yes, too fast.
Pero su esposo no está aquí. But your husband isn't here.
¿Mi esposo? My husband?
Tell me that your husband isn't here. My husband isn't here.
Pero mi esposo no está aquí. But my husband isn't here.
Es demasiado caro. It's too expensive.
Ask in English, "¿Qué es demasiado caro?" What is too expensive?
Conteste, "este libro". This book.
Este libro. Este libro es demasiado caro. This book. This book is too expensive.
¿Cuánto cuesta? How much does it cost?
Cincuenta dólares. Cuesta cincuenta dólares. Fifty dollars. It costs fifty dollars.
"Qué ridículo" se dice "How ridiculous. Say, "How ridiculous.". How ridiculous.
Say in English, "Qué ridículo." How ridiculous.
Now say, "Qué ridículo. Sesenta dólares por este libro". How ridiculous. Sixty dollars for this book.
Yo sé. I know.
Please say, "Cincuenta dólares, no sesenta." Fifty dollars, not sixty.
Say again, "fifty dollars, not sixty". Fifty dollars, not sixty.
Bueno, cincuenta dólares es caro también. Well, fifty dollars is expensive too.
"I agree" means "Estoy de acuerdo" in English. Say "I agree". I agree.

¿Cómo se dice "Estoy de acuerdo" en inglés? I agree.
Diga "sesenta dólares" en inglés. Sixty dollars.
Cuarenta y cinco dólares. Forty five dollars.
Sesenta y un dólares. Sixty one dollars.
Cincuenta y seis dólares. Fifty six dollars.
Veintiún. Twenty one.
¿Sesenta y ocho? Eso es demasiado caro. Sixty eight? That's too expensive.
En dólares es demasiado caro. In dollars it's too expensive.
Estoy de acuerdo. I agree.
Aquí está más caro. Here it's more expensive.
Para decir "Le voy a dar" se dice "I'm going to give you." Repita, "I'm going to give you." I'm going to give you.
How do you say "Le voy a dar"? I'm going to give you.
Say in English, "cincuenta y tres dólares." Fifty three dollars.
Tell me that's not enough. That's not enough.
Eso no es suficiente dinero. That's not enough money.
¿Quién es ese? Who's that?
Ese es mi esposo. That's my husband.
Use a contraction and ask me where my wife is. Where's your wife?
¿Mi esposa? No sé. My wife? I don't know.
Para decir "Ella anda por aquí en un lugar", diga "She's around here someplace". She's around here someplace.
Tell me that your wife's around here someplace. My wife's around here someplace.
Now ask "¿Dónde está su esposo?" Where's your husband?
Mi esposo no está aquí. My husband isn't here.
Él está por aquí en un lugar. He's around here someplace.
Mi esposo está por allá. My husband is over there.
Él está por allá. He is over there.
Tell me that he is over there with his friend Rodolfo. He is over there with his friend Rodolfo.
¿Mi esposo? Él está por allá. My husband? He's over there.
Él está por allá con su amigo. He's over there with his friend.
Usando la contracción, diga "Él está". He's.
Ahora diga, "He is". He is.
Using the contraction, say "Ella está" in English. She's.
Ahora diga, "She is". She is.

Usando la contracción, diga, "Ella está por ahí en un lugar". She's around here someplace.
Say in English, "¿Mi esposa? Ella está por allá." My wife? She's over there.
¿Ella está por allá? Is she over there?
Ella no está por allá. Ella está aquí. She's not over there. She's here.
¿Qué le gustaría beber a su esposo? What would your husband like to drink?
¿Qué le gustaría beber? What would he like to drink?
A mí me gustaría. I'd like.
Tell me he'd like some coffee. He'd like some coffee.
O agua. Or water.
A él le gustaría algo de café. He'd like some coffee.
A ella le gustaría algo de agua. She'd like some water.
Para decir "Pase" se dice "Come in". Say "Come in". Come in.
Pase, por favor. Come in, please.
"Mucho gusto en conocerlo" se dice "Pleased to meet you". Repita "Pleased to meet you". Pleased to meet you.
Diga, "Hola, soy Angela". Hello, I'm Angela.
Mucho gusto en conocerla. Pleased to meet you.
Mucho gusto en conocerlo. Pleased to meet you.
Por favor pase. Please come in.
Mucho gusto en conocerla. Pleased to meet you.
Gracias. Mucho gusto en conocerlo también. Thanks. Pleased to meet you too.
Ask me what I would like to drink. What would you like to drink?
Pase. Come in.
Mucho gusto en conocerla. Pleased to meet you.
¿Y su esposa? And your wife?
¿Qué le gustaría beber a ella? What would she like to drink?
Soy Rosa Montero. I'm Rosa Montero.
Mucho gusto en conocerla, Señora Montero. Pleased to meet you, Mrs. Montero.
Mucho gusto en conocerla, Señora Montero. Soy Robert Johnson. Pleased to meet you, Mrs. Montero. I'm Robert Johnson.
Mucho gusto en conocerlo, Señor Johnson. Pleased to meet you, Mr. Johnson.
Hola, Señora Johnson. Hello, Mrs. Johnson.
Para preguntar "¿Dónde viven ustedes?" se dice "Where do you live?" Repita "Where do you live? Where do you live?
Repeat, "Where do you live?" Where do you live?
Ask in English, "¿Dónde viven ustedes?" Where do you live?

Now ask, "¿Dónde viven ustedes dos?" Where do you two live?
Say in English "Viven". Live.
Ustedes viven. You live.
Usted vive. You live.
Yo vivo. I live.
Mucho gusto en conocerla, Señorita Johnson. Pleased to meet you, Miss Johnson.
Por favor, pase. Please, come in.
Pase por favor. Come in please.
¿Dónde vive usted? Where do you live?
Yo vivo en Guadalajara. I live in Guadalajara.
La palabra "mes" se dice "month". Repita, "month". Month.
Cómo se dice "mes" en inglés? Month.
Ahora diga, "Un mes". A month.
"Por un mes" se dice "For a month". Repita, "For a month". For a month.
Say in English, "Estoy en los Estados Unidos por un mes". I'm in the United States for a month.
Repeat in parts. "I'm in the United States". I'm in the United States.
For a month. For a month.
Diga en inglés "Estoy en los Estados Unidos por un mes". I'm in the United States for a month.
Ask me where I live. Where do you live?
Yo vivo en Guadalajara. ¿Y usted? ¿Usted vive aquí? I live in Guadalajara. And you? Do you live here?
Sí, en la Avenida Parque. Yes, on Park Avenue.
Nosotros vivimos aquí. We live here.
Nosotros vivimos. We live.
Nosotros vivimos aquí. We live here.
Nosotros vivimos aquí en la Avenida Parque. We live here, on Park Avenue.
Nosotros vivimos en Guadalajara. We live in Guadalajara.
Yo estoy en los Estados Unidos por un mes. I'm in the United States for a week.
Estamos en los Estados Unidos por un mes. We're in the United States for a week.
Nos gustaría beber algo. We'd like to have something to drink.
Para preguntar, "¿Cómo qué?" se dice "Like what?" "Repita, Like what?" Like what?
Say in English, "Nos gustaría beber algo". We'd like to have something to drink.
Ask in English, "¿Cómo qué?" Like what?
¿Qué le gustaría beber? What would you like to drink?

Nos gustaría algo de café. We'd like some coffee."
¿Su esposa también quiere café? Does your wife want coffee too?
Para contestar esto brevemente, diga "Yes, she does". Repeat "Yes, she does". Yes, she does.
Pregunte en inglés, "¿Su esposa también quiere café? Does your wife want coffee too?
Conteste brevemente que "Sí, ella quiere". Yes, she does.
A mi esposo y a mí. My husband and I.
A mi esposo y a mí nos gustaría algo de agua. My husband and I would like some water.
Nos gustaría algo de agua. We'd like some water.
A ella le gustaría algo de agua. She'd like some water.
Pero a él le gustaría algo de café. But he'd like some coffee.
No, nos gustaría algo de vino. No, we'd like some wine.
Tell me that you're in the United States for a month. I'm in the United States for a month.
Say in English, "Nosotros estamos in los Estados Unidos por un mes." We're in the United States for a month.
Tell me that here, the wine is more expensive. Here, the wine is more expensive.
How does one say "especialmente" in English? Especially.
Especialmente el vino California. Especially the California wine.
Pase. Come in.
Buenos diás, Señora. Good morning, ma'am.
Soy Charles Johnson. I'm Charles Johnson.
Gusto conocerlo, Señor Johnson. Soy Rosa Montero. Pleased to meet you, Mr. Johnson. I'm Rosa Montero.
Ask Mrs. Montero if her husband is here. Mrs. Montero, is your husband here?
No, él no está aquí. No, he isn't here.
Lo siento. No está aquí. I'm sorry. He isn't here.
¿Dónde viven ustedes en México? Where do you live in Mexico?
Tell me that you live in Guadalajara. We live in Guadalajara.
¿Y usted, Señor? ¿Dónde vive usted? And you, sir? Where do you live?
Yo vivo en México también. Estoy en los Estados Unidos por un mes. I live in Mexico too. I'm in the United States for a month.
How do you ask "Who is that?" with a contraction? Who's that?
"¿Quién puede ser?" se dice "Who can it be?" Repita, "Who can it be?" Who can it be?

Ask in English, "¿Quién puede ser?" Who can it be?
Yo no sé. I don't know.
"Esta hora" se dice "This hour". Repita, "This hour". This hour.
Say this in English: "A esta hora". At this hour.
¿Quién puede ser a esta hora? Who can it be at this hour?
No tengo ninguna idea. I have no idea.
Ask me who can it be at this hour. Who can it be at this hour?
Tell me you have no idea. I have no idea.
Pedro, el Señor Johnson está aquí. Pedro, Mr. Johnson is here.
How does one ask "¿A esta hora?" in English? At this hour?
Sí. No sé por qué. Yes. I don't know why.
Pase, por favor, Señor Johnson. Come in please, Mr. Johnson.
Señor Johnson, mi esposo Pedro. Mr. Johnson, my husband Pedro.
Mucho gusto conocerlo. Pleased to meet you.
Ask me if I would like some coffee. Would you like some coffee?
Señor Johnson, ¿le gustaría algo de café? Mr. Johnson, would you like some coffee?
Answer that yes you would. Yes, I would.
Oh, su esposa está aquí también. Oh, your wife is here too.
¿Su esposa también quiere café? Does your wife want coffee too?
Conteste brevemente que sí. Yes, she does.
Me gustaría beber algo. I would like to drink something.
¿Cómo qué? Like what?

End of speaking/listening lesson. Continue with the reading for Lesson 22.

Reading for Lesson 22

Have the student read the days of the week below. Then he/she is to read the sentences and phrases below to you out loud.

Days of the Week (Días de la Semana)
Sunday
Monday
Tuesday
Wednesday
Thursday
Friday
Saturday

Conversation 1

You speak English very fast. Does your husband speak fast too?
Not too fast. He speaks Spanish very fast, but not English.
This book is very expensive.
How much is it?
Forty five dollars. How ridiculous.
I agree. Forty-five dollars is too much money for a book. Especially one that is so *small (pequeño)*.

Conversation 2

Hello, Mrs. Montero. How are you? My name is Michael Smith.
Pleased to meet you, Mr. Smith.
Pleased to meet you too.
Helena, who can it be at this hour?
That's my husband. Bobby, this is Michael Smith.
Mr. Smith, this is my husband Robert.
Pleased to meet you, Robert.
Thanks. Please come in, Mr. Smith. Would you like some coffee?
No thanks. But I would like a glass of water if that's all right.
Sure.
So (Así que) where are you from, Mr. Smith?
I'm from Mexico. I live in Guadalajara. I am in the United States for a week.
My husband is from Guadalajara too. We are going to visit there in a month.

LEVEL 1: LESSON 23

Teaching tip: When you get to the expression "It costs an arm and a leg", make sure the student pronounces the second "s" in "costs". Also, watch the student's pronounciation of "girl" which is often said "gerol" (rhyming with Carol) by the Spanish speaker. "Girl" doesn't have much of any vowel sound in it, sounding like "grl".

Say in English, "Pase, por favor". Come in, please.
In English, "It's good to see you" means "es bueno verlo o es bueno verla". Repeat, "It's good to see you. It's good to see you.
Please say in English, "Es bueno verlo". It's good to see you.
¿Cómo se dice en inglés a una mujer, "Es bueno verla?" It's good to see you.
Para decir "Buenas tardes" se dice "Good afternoon". Repita, "Good afternoon". Good afternoon.
Buenas tardes, Mike. Es bueno verlo. Good afternoon, Mike. It's good to see you.
Es bueno verlo también. It's good to see you too.
Para preguntar, "¿Cómo ha estado?", diga, "How have you been?" Repita, "How have you been?" How have you been?"
Now say in English "Es bueno verlo. ¿Cómo ha estado?" It's good to see you. How have you been?
Bien, gracias. ¿Y usted? Fine, thanks. And you?
Ask me how I have been. How have you been?
Para responder, "No puedo quejarme" diga "I can't complain. Repita, "I can't complain. I can't complain.
Ask me if I would like to have something to drink. Would you like to have something to drink?
Claro. Sure.
¿Cómo qué? Like what?
Say "Buenas Tardes" in English. Good afternoon.
Now say, "Es bueno verla" in English. It's good to see you.

¿Cómo ha estado? How have you been?
No puedo quejarme. I can't complain.
Do you remember how to say, "Mucho gusto conocerlo"? Pleased to meet you.
Now say, "Mucho gusto conocerla". Pleased to meet you.
"Ms." Quiere decir "señora", "señorita" o mujer professional. Diga "Hello Ms. Johnson." Hello Ms. Johnson.
¿Cómo se dice "Señora o Señorita Johnson" en inglés? Ms. Johnson.
Ahora diga "Hola, Señora o Señorita Johnson." Hello, Ms. Johnson.
¿Le gustaría beber algo? Would you like to have something to drink?
¿Qué tiene usted? What do you have?
Tengo café o agua. I have coffee or water.
Café, por favor. Coffee, please.
¿Con o sin azúcar? With or without sugar?
Say "Sin azúcar, por favor" in English. Without sugar, please.
¿Qué quiere beber su esposo? What does your husband want to drink?
Solo un vaso de agua. Only a glass of water.
Es todo. That's all.
¿Solo un vaso de agua? ¿Es todo? Only a glass of water? That's all?
Si, es todo. Yes, that's all.
¿Cómo ha estado? How have you been?
No puedo quejarme. I can't complain.
Say that it's good to see me. It's good to see you.
Es bueno verlo también. It's good to see you too.
¿Quiere él algo de agua? Does he want some water?
¿O le gustaría algo de café? Or would he like some coffee?
A él le gustaría algo de café. He'd like some coffee.
Aquí el café es más caro. Here coffee is more expensive.
Una expresión Americana es decir "Cuesta un brazo y una pierna". Esto es una manera de decir que algo es carísimo. Se dice "It costs an arm and a leg." Repita en partes, "It costs". It costs.
Otra vez, y acuérdese pronunciar la ese. Diga, "It costs". It costs.
An arm. An arm.
And a leg. And a leg.
Say again, "It costs". It costs.
An arm. An arm.
And a leg. And a leg.
Ahora repita la primera mitad, "It costs an arm". It costs an arm.

Ahora diga, "And a leg". And a leg.
Repita, "It costs an arm and a leg." It costs an arm and a leg.
¿Cómo se dice "Cuesta un brazo y una pierna"? It costs an arm and a leg.
Ahora diga, "Aquí el café es más caro. Cuesta un brazo y una pierna." Here coffee is more expensive. It costs an arm and a leg.
¿Cómo se dice "Mucho más caro"? Much more expensive.
Aquí el café es mucho más caro. Here coffee is much more expensive.
Cuesta un brazo y una pierna. It costs an arm and a leg.
Para decir "taza" se dice "cup". Repita "cup". Cup.
Say "taza" in English. Cup.
Una taza. A cup.
Ask in English, "¿Cuánto por una taza? How much for a cup?
Tell me that a cup of coffee costs six dollars. A cup of coffee costs six dollars.
¿Seis dólares por una taza de café? ¡Qué ridículo! Six dollars for a cup of coffee? How ridiculous!
Yo sé. Cuesta un brazo y una pierna aquí. I know. It costs an arm and a leg here.
Seis dólares por una taza de café? ¡Qué ridículo! Six dollars for a cup of coffee? How ridiculous!
Estoy de acuerdo. I agree.
¿Dónde está su esposo? Where is your husband?
¿Dónde está él? Where is he?
¿Mi esposo? No sé. My husband? I don't know.
Él está por aquí en un lugar. He's around here someplace.
¿Dónde está su esposa? Where is your wife?
¿Mi esposa? No sé. My wife? I don't know.
No tengo ningúna idea. I have no idea.
No sé dónde está. I don't know where she is.
Say in English "Mi esposo no está aquí". My husband isn't here.
Ask in English "¿Dónde está su esposa? ¿Dónde está ella?" Where is your wife? Where is she?
Ella está con su esposa. She is with your wife.
Ask me where I live. Where do you live?
¿Dónde viven ustedes dos? Where do you two live?
Nosotros vivimos en México. We live in Mexico.
¿Dónde en México viven? Where in Mexico do you live?
"En el estado" se dice "In the state" en inglés. Repita, "In the state". In the state.
En el estado de Michoacán. In the state of Michoacan.

¿Dónde viven ustedes dos? Where do you two live?
Nosotros vivimos en México. We live in Mexico.
¿Dónde en México viven? Where in Mexico do you live?
Vivimos en el estado de Michoacán. We live in the state of Michoacan.
¿Tienen ustedes hijos? Do you have any children?
En inglés "han crecido" se dice "grown up". Repita "grown up". Grown up.
¿Cómo se dice "han crecido" en inglés? Grown up.
Ask "¿Tienen ustedes hijos?" Do you have any children?
Sí, pero ya han crecido. Yes but they're already grown up.
Ya han crecido. They're already grown up.
¿Tienen ustedes hijos? Do you have any children?
Sí, pero ya han crecido. Yes, but they're already grown up.
¿Tienen ustedes hijos? Do you have any children?
Sí, tenemos hijos. Yes, we have children.
No, no tenemos hijos. No, we don't have any children.
¿Dónde en México vive? Where in Mexico do you live?
Nosotros vivimos en el estado de Michoacán. We live in the state of Michoacan.
Ask me how many dollars do I have. How many dollars do you have?
Now ask me how many children do I have. How many children do you have?
Tenemos tres hijos. We have three children.
"Boy" es niño en inglés. Diga "boy". Boy.
Dos niños. Two boys.
Niños. Boys.
Dos niños. Two boys.
¿Cuántos hijos tiene? How many children do you have?
Tenemos dos niños. We have two boys.
"Girl" es "niña" en inglés. Diga "girl". Girl.
Una niña. A girl.
Tenemos dos niños. We have two boys.
Y una niña. And one girl.
Tenemos una niña. We have one girl.
Nos gustaría un niño. We'd like a boy.
Nos gustaría un niño algún día. We'd like a boy some day.
Nos gustaría un niño. We'd like a boy.
Pero tenemos tres niñas. But we have three girls.
Nos gustaría un niño algún día. We'd like a boy some day.
¿Cuántos hijos? How many children?

¿tres hijos? Three children?
Tenemos cinco hijos. We have five children.
tres niños. Three boys.
Y dos niñas. And two girls.
Eso es mucho. That's a lot.
Tenemos una niña. We have one girl.
Y un niño. And one boy.
En inglés la palabra "big" quiere decir "grande". Diga "big". Big.
El niño es grande. The boy is big.
La niña es grande. The girl is big.
¿Es grande el niño? Is the boy big?
Sí, él es grande. Yes, he's big.
Él es grande. He's big.
Él no es grande. He's not big.
¿Es grande la niña? Is the girl big?
Ella no es grande. She's not big.
El niño es muy grande. The boy is very big.
¿Cuántos hijos tiene usted? How many children do you have?
Say that you have four children. I have four children.
Usted tiene dos, ¿verdad? You have two, right?
¿Perdón? Excuse me?
Usted tiene dos, ¿verdad? You have two, right?
No, nosotros tenemos cuatro hijos. No, we have four children.
How does one say, "Los niños son grandes" in English? The boys are big.
Para decir "Ellos son grandes", se dice "They are big". Repita "They are big." They are big.
How does one say "Ellos son grandes" in English? They are big.
Say again in English "Ellos son grandes." They are big.
Diga en inglés con una contracción, "Ellos son grandes." They're big.
Say in English with a contraction, "Ellos están aquí". They're here.
¿Están ellos aquí? Are they here?
No están por allá. They're not over there.
¿Quién está por allá? Who's over there?
Solo mi esposa. Only my wife.
Say "Esa es mi esposa" in English. That's my wife.
¿Cuántos hijos tienen? How many children do you have?
Tenemos tres hijos. We have three children.

Tenemos dos niños. We have two boys.
Son grandes. They're big.
Y una niña. And one girl.
¿Ella es grande? Is she big?
Para contestar "No, no es" se puede decir "No, she's not" o "No, she isn't". Repita, "No, she's not. No, she's not.
Now say "No, she isn't". No, she isn't.
Pregunte "¿Ella es grande?" Is she big?
Conteste "No, no es". No she isn't. (Or "No, she's not".)
Para decir en inglés, "Ella no es grande" se puede decir "She's not big" o "She isn't big". Repeat "She's not big." She's not big.
No es grande. She isn't big.
Los niños son muy grandes. The boys are very big.
Ellos son muy grandes. They're very big.
¿Son muy grandes los niños? Are the boys very big?
¿Son muy grandes? Are they very big?
Sí, son grandes. Yes, they're big.
¿Son muy grandes los niños?" Are the boys very big?
Sí son muy grandes. Yes, they're very big.
¿Es usted mexicano, Señor Martinez? Are you Mexican, Mr. Martinez?
Sí, soy mexicano. Yes, I'm Mexican.
¿Y dónde vive usted en Mexico? And where do you live in Mexico?
Yo vivo en Guadalajara. I live in Guadalajara.
Mi esposa y yo vivimos en Guadalajara. My wife and I live in Guadalajara.
How does one say in English, "No soy mexicano. Soy colombiano." I'm not Mexican. I'm Colombian.
¿Tiene hijos? Do you have any children?
Sí, tenemos tres hijos. Yes, we have three children.
¿Tienen hijos? Do you have any children?
Sí, tenemos. Yes, we do.
Sí, tenemos tres. Yes, we have three.
¿Tienen ustedes niños? Do you have any boys?
Sí, tenemos dos niños. Yes, we have two boys.
¿Y una niña? And one girl?
Sí, tenemos una niña. Yes we have one girl.
¿Dónde están los hijos? ¿Estan aquí con usted? Where are the children? Are they here with you?

¿Y su esposa? ¿Está aquí también? And your wife? Is she here too?
Usted habla inglés muy bien, señor. You speak English very well, sir.
No, no muy bien. Pero se lo agradezco. No, not very well. But thank you.

End of speaking/listening lesson. Continue with the reading for Lesson 23.

Reading for Lesson 23

Read the following conversation with your student, taking care to read slowly so the student can follow along with you. The student can read the conversation alone after you read it together.

<u>Reading Practice</u>

Are you Mexican, Mr. Ortega?

Yes, I am. And you?

I'm from Perú.

Oh, so you're Peruvian?

Yes I am. Where in Mexico are you from, Mr. Ortega?

My wife and I live in the state of Jalisco, in the city of Guadalajara.

Do you have any children?

I have six. Three boys and three girls.

That's a lot.

Not over there. Many people in Guadalajara have more children than we do.

I only have two boys, but my wife and I would like a girl some day.

Would you like to have a cup of coffee?

Okay, but not here. The coffee is too expensive here.

Really?

Yes. It costs eight dollars for a cup.

How ridiculous!

I know. It costs an arm and a leg.

Excuse me?

Oh, when someone says that something costs an arm and a leg, it means that something is very expensive.

Oh, now I understand. That is very funny. So the coffee here costs an arm and a leg. Ha ha.

Yeah, really. It's very expensive.

I agree. So how is your wife? Is she here too?

No. She is in Guadalajara with the children. They are all small.

One of my sons is grown up, but the other one is small too.

LEVEL 1: LESSON 24

Teaching Tip: Spanish speakers often say "childrens" instead of "children". A simple exercise to correct this is to have them say the word "children" with the "n" stressed twice as long. It's as if you're saying "childrenn". The student can pronounce the word "children" in this way ten times before beginning the lesson and any other time as needed.

"Espere" se dice "wait" en inglés. Repita "wait". Wait.
Say in English, "Espere, por favor". Wait, please.
Para decir "solo un momento" se dice "just a moment". Diga "Just a moment". Just a moment.
Espere solo un momento. Wait just a moment.
Solo un momento, por favor. Just a moment, please.
Pase. Come in.
How does one say in English, "Espere"? Wait.
Now say in English, "Solo un momento, por favor". Just a moment, please.
Do you remember how to say in English, "Gusto en conocerla"? Pleased to meet you.
Gusto en conocerla, Señorita Johnson. Pleased to meet you, Miss Johnson.
Si no sabe si es casada o no, se usa "Ms." Repita "Ms.". Ms.
Say in English, "Pleased to meet you, Ms. Johnson." Pleased to meet you, Ms. Johnson.
¿Cómo ha estado? How have you been?
No puedo quejarme. I can't complain.
Ask in English, "¿Dónde viven ustedes? Where do you live?
Answer in English, "Nosotros vivimos en Guadalajara." We live in Guadalajara.
Now ask in English, "¿Cuántos hijos tiene usted?" How many children do you have?
Dos niños. Tenemos dos niños. Two boys. We have two boys.
Tell me that the boys are big. The boys are big.
Son grandes. They're big.

Son muy grandes. They're very big.
How does one say, "Ellos están por allá" in English? They're over there.
Los niños están por allá. The boys are over there.
Y su esposa, ¿dónde está? And your wife, where is she?
Ella está por allá también. She's over there too.
¿Dónde está su esposo? Where is your husband?
¿Mi esposo? Él está por allá. My husband? He is over there.
¿Tienen niñas ustedes? Do you have any girls?
Sí. Tenemos tres niñas. Yes, we have three girls.
Say, "Podemos" in English. We can.
How does one say in English, "Podemos esperar"? We can wait.
Ask in English, "¿Pueden ustedes esperar?" Can you wait?
Usted puede esperar. You can wait.
Nosotros queremos. We want.
Queremos muchos hijos. We want a lot of children.
Ustedes tienen muchos hijos. You have a lot of children.
Espere. Wait.
No queremos muchos hijos. We don't want a lot of children.
Tenemos suficiente con tres. We have enough with three.
Vivimos en Mexico. We live in Mexico.
Mi esposa y yo vivimos en Mexico. My wife and I live in Mexico.
Con los hijos. With the children.
Mi esposa y yo vivimos en Mexico con nuestros hijos. My wife and I live in Mexico with our children.
Tell me that the children are in Mexico. The children are in Mexico.
Ellos están en Mexico. They're in Mexico.
¿Dónde están? Where are they?
Las niñas están aquí. The girls are here.
Do you remember how to say, "Las niñas son grandes" in English? The girls are big.
Las niñas grandes. The big girls.
Las niñas son grandes. The girls are big.
Yo sé. Ellas son muy grandes. I know. They're very big.
Las niñas grandes. The big girls.
¿Dónde están? Where are they?
La niña está aquí. The girl is here.
La niña es grande. The girl is big.
La niña grande está aquí. The big girl is here.

Say "El niño grande está aquí" in English. The big boy is here.
¿Y la niña pequeña? And the little girl?
¿La niña pequeña es de ustedes? The little girl is yours?
El niño pequeño. The little boy.
El niño pequeño no es de nosotros. The little boy isn't ours.
Tell me that your boy is little. My boy is little.
How does one say in English, "Nuestro niño es pequeño" in English? Our boy is little.
Now say in English, "Nuestro niño". Our boy.
Please say in English, "Nuestro niño no es grande". Our boy isn't big.
Tiene solo cinco años. He's only five years old.
Tiene solo siete años. He's only seven years old.
Él es pequeño. He's little.
¿De verdad? Really?
Sí, de verdad. Yes, really.
"Nuestra" se dice "Our". Repita, "Our". Our.
How does one say, "Nuestra niña"? Our girl.
Ask me in English, ¿Dónde está su niña? Where's your girl?
Answer in English, "¿Nuestra niña grande o nuestra niña pequeña?" Our big girl or our little girl?
Say in English, "La niña grande". The big girl.
Su niña grande. Your big girl.
Nuestra niña pequeña está por allá. Our little girl is over there.
Ella no es pequeña. She isn't little.
Ella es muy grande. She's very big.
¿De verdad? Really?
Nuestra niña pequeña está aquí. Our little girl is here.
Ella está por aquí en un lugar. She's around here someplace.
Ask me if she would like to have something to drink. Would she like to have something to drink?
Sí. Le gustaría algo de agua. Yes, she'd like some water.
Sí, le gustaría. Yes, she would.
Pero ella puede esperar. But she can wait.
Do you remember how to say "Pase" in English? Come in.
Para decir "Tome un asiento" se dice "Have a seat." Say "have a seat". Have a seat.
Tome un asiento, por favor. Have a seat, please.
Gusto en conocerla Señora o Señorita Johnson. Pleased to meet you, Ms. Johnson.

Gusto en conocerlo, Señor Martinez. Pleased to meet you, Mr. Martinez.
Say "tome un asiento" in English. Have a seat.
Tome un asiento, por favor. Have a seat, please.
¿Le gustaría beber algo? Would you like to have something to drink?
Sí. Me gustaría algo de café, por favor. Yes. I'd like some coffee, please.
Sí. Nos gustaría algo de café, por favor. Yes, we'd like some coffee, please.
Pero podemos esperar. But we can wait.
¿Dónde está el baño? Where is the bathroom?
Perdón, ¿dónde está el baño? Excuse me, where is the bathroom?
Está por allá. It's over there.
En inglés "Siga derecho" se dice "Continue straight ahead". Diga "Continue straight ahead". Continue straight ahead.
Siga derecho. Está por allá. Continue straight ahead. It's over there.
¿El baño? Siga derecho. The bathroom? Continue straight ahead.
"Por el pasillo" se dice "through the hall" en inglés. Repita "through the hall". Through the hall.
How do you say "Por el pasillo" in English? Through the hall.
Siga derecho por el pasillo. Continue straight ahead through the hall.
El baño está por allá. The bathroom is over there.
¿De verdad? Really?
Sí, de verdad. Siga derecho por el pasillo. Yes, really. Continue straight ahead through the hall.
Say in English, "El niño pequeño". The little boy.
How does one say in English, "Nuestros cuatro niños"? Our four boys.
La niña grande. The big girl.
Las cuatro niñas grandes. The four big girls.
Sus cuatro niñas grandes. Your four big girls.
Sus cuatro niñas son grandes. Your four girls are big.
Sí, yo sé. Yes, I know.
Nuestra niña también es grande. Our girl is big too.
Ella está aquí con nosotros. She's here with us.
Con nosotros. With us.
Ella está aquí con nosotros. She's here with us.
Ask this in English, "Perdón, ¿dónde está el baño?" Excuse me, where is the bathroom?
Answer in English, "No tengo ninguna idea. Lo siento." I have no idea. I'm sorry.
Yo sé dónde está. I know where it is.

Siga derecho por el pasillo. Continue straight ahead through the hall.
¿Sabe usted dónde está el baño? Do you know where the bathroom is?
Sí, siga derecho. Yes, continue straight ahead.
"Family" means "familia" in English. Say "family". Family.
Try to say "Su familia" in English. Your family.
Now ask, "¿Cómo está su familia?" How is your family?
"Parents" means "padres" in English. Say "parents". Parents
How do you say "familia" in English? Family.
How do you say "padres" in English" Parents.
Ask in English, "¿Cómo están sus padres? How are your parents?
Bien, gracias. Fine, thanks.
¿Y su familia? ¿Cómo está su familia? And your family? How is your family?
Muy bien también. Very well too.
Try to say "Dos familias" in English. Two families.
Do you remember how to say "padres" in English? Parents.
Nuestra familia. Our family.
In English, ask me where my family is. Where is your family?
¿Mi familia? My family?
Mi esposa está aquí. My wife is here.
Los niños pequeños están en México. The little children are in Mexico.
La niña grande está aquí con nosotros. The big girl is here with us.
Tell me I have a big family. You have a big family.
Yo sé. I know.
Buenos días, Sra. Johnson. Good morning, Mrs. Johnson.
Now say good morning to Ms. Campbell. Good morning, Ms. Campbell.
¿Quién es este niño pequeño? Who is this little boy?
¿Es su niño pequeño? Is he your little boy?
Sí, es de nosotros. Yes, he is ours.
¿Entiende inglés él? Does he understand English?
Diga que no, brevemente. No, he doesn't.
No, no puede. No, he can't.
¿Cuántos niños tienen? How many boys do you have?
¿Y ustedes tienen niñas? And do you have any girls?
Tenemos una niña. We have one girl.
¿Una niña pequeña? A little girl?
How does one say, "Tiene siete años" in English? She is seven years old.
Y tenemos un niño pequeño. And we have a little boy.

Él tiene ocho años. He is eight years old.
Su niño pequeño quiere algo. ¿Qué quiere? Your little boy wants something. What does he want?
¿Dónde está el baño, por favor? Where is the bathroom, please?
Tell me that the bathroom is over there. The bathroom is over there.
Se lo agradezco. Thank you.

End of speaking/listening lesson. Continue with the reading for Lesson 24.

Reading for Lesson 24

Read the following conversation with your student, taking care to read slowly so the student can follow along with you. The student can read the conversation alone after you read it together.

Reading Practice

Your little boy wants something. What he does want?

He wants to *use the bathroom (usar el baño)*.

Oh, sure. Continue straight ahead through the hall.

Thanks.

Does your little boy understand English?

No, he doesn't. He only speaks Spanish.

He doesn't? But you speak English very well.

Yes. My son lives in Guadalajara with his mother. He is in the United States for a month.

My wife and son will come to live here in the United States in September.

Would he like to have something to drink?

Yes, he would. Do you have orange juice?

Yes. Would he like a small, medium or large?

A small, please. But with no ice.

Okay. And you? Would you like something to drink too?

Only a glass of water. With ice.

Is your wife here?

Yeah, she's around here someplace.

Then, would your wife like something too?

Yes. A *large glass (vaso grande)* of iced tea.

Okay.

Excuse me, but do you know what time it is?

Yes, it's four thirty.

Thanks.

Sure.

LEVEL 1: LESSON 25 (LESSONS 21 – 24 REVIEW)

This is one of two consecutive review lessons. I recommend you spend at least two days on each one. This review is needed because of the extensive material covered up to this point. Even so, there is some new learning intertwined with these lessons.

Teaching Tip: When you get to the prompts speaking about a car (coche), some English learners may have the habit of saying "caro", which is a Spanglish term. They should know you are speaking about a car when you say "coche" but every so often you may have to explain this to them if they haven't heard the term "coche" before. Note: At the end of day one of this lesson you may take the Lesson 25 reading or review any previous reading your student may have had difficulty with. But make sure to do the Lesson 25 reading by the end of this review.

Gusto en conocerla, Señora Martinez. ¿Está su esposo en San Diego también?
Pleased to meet you, Mrs. Martinez. Is your husband in San Diego too?
Conteste en inglés que sí, brevemente. Yes, he is.
¿Estan sus hijos aquí también? Are your children here too?
Sí, nuestros hijos están aquí con nosotros también. Yes, our children are here with us too.
Hola. Hello.
Hola, ¿cómo le va? Hello, how's it going?
Muy bien. ¿Y usted? ¿Cómo ha estado? Very well. And you? How have you been?
¿Está su esposo en San Diego también? Is your husband in San Diego too?
Conteste en inglés que sí, brevemente. Yes, he is.
Now ask, "¿Está su esposa en San Diego también?" Is your wife in San Diego too?
Conteste que sí, brevemente. Yes, she is.
Now ask, "¿Dónde está el baño?" in English. Where is the bathroom?
Siga derecho por el pasillo. Continue straight ahead through the hall.
El baño esta por allá. The bathroom is over there.
El baño esta por allá, por el pasillo. The bathroom is over there, through the hall.

How do you say "Un niño grande" in English? A big boy.
Now say in English, "Tenemos un niño grande." We have a big boy.
Nuestro niño es grande. Our boy is big.
Try to say, "Una niña pequeña" in English. A little girl.
Nosotros también tenemos una niña pequeña. We have a little girl too.
Nuestra niña no es grande. Our girl isn't big.
¿Cuántos hijos tiene? How many children do you have?
Tengo tres hijos. I have three children.
Tenemos tres hijos. We have three children.
¿Son grandes? Are they big?
"Ya" se dice "already" en inglés. Repita, "Already". Already.
Ahora diga, "Sí. Ya han crecido". Yes. They're already grown up.
Ask me where they are. Where are they?
Estan aquí con nosotros. They are here with us.
¿Dónde está el baño? Where is the bathroom?
El baño está por allá. The bathroom is over there.
Tell me you can wait. I can wait.
Now tell me your family is in the United States. My family is in the United States.
Mi familia está en México. My family is in Mexico.
Mi familia ya está en México. My family is already in Mexico.
Mi familia está conmigo. My family is with me.
Mi famililia ya está conmigo. My family is already with me.
Nuestra familia está con nosotros. Our family is with us.
¿Cuántas personas? How many people?
To ask, "¿Cuántas personas hay?" say "How many people are there?" Repeat, "How many people are there?" How many people are there?
¿En su familia? In your family?
¿Cuántas personas hay en su familia? How many people are there in your family?
Repeat in English, "Seven. My parents, four sisters and me". Seven, my parents, four sisters and me.
Ask me how many people are in my family. How many people are there in your family?
Siete. Mis padres, cuatro hermanas y yo. Seven. My parents, four sisters and me.
Seis. Mis padres, cuatro hermanas y yo. Six. My parents, three sisters and me.
Now ask where Lydia is. Where is Lydia?
Ella está por aquí en algún lugar. She's around here someplace.
¿Cuántas personas hay en su familia? How many people are there in your family?

Hay tres personas. There are three people.

Mis padres y yo. My parents and me.

¿Solo tres? Only three?

Say in English, "En mi familia". In my family.

Ask in English, "¿Cuántas personas hay?" How many people are there?

Hay tres personas. There are three people.

Hay tres personas en mi familia. There are three people in my family.

Do you remember how to say "hermanos" in English? Brothers.

tres hermanos. Three brothers.

¿Cuántas personas hay en su familia? How many people are there in your family?

Tell me that there are six people in your family. There are six people in my family.

Mis padres, tres hermanos y yo. My parents, three brothers and me.

¿Cuántas personas hay en su familia? How many people are there in your family?

Seis. Mis padres, tres hermanos y yo. Six. My parents, three brothers and me.

"Coche" is "car" in English. Repeat, "car". Car.

Coche mío. My car.

Say "En mi coche" in English. In my car.

How do you say "Coche" in English? Car.

Now say, "Tengo un coche". I have a car.

"New" quiere decir "nuevo". Repita, "New". New.

Try to say "coche nuevo" in English. New car.

Tengo un coche nuevo. I have a new car.

Ask me in English if I have a car. Do you have a car?

¿Tiene un coche nuevo? Do you have a new car?

¿Está aquí su coche? Is your car here?

¿Está en los Estados Unidos su familia? Is your family in the United States?

Los hijos están aquí con nosotros. The children are here with us.

¿Cuántas personas hay en su familia? How many people are there in your family?

Hay cinco personas en nuestra familia. There are five people in our family.

Tenemos un coche. We have a car.

Tenemos un coche nuevo. We have a new car.

Ya tenemos un coche nuevo. We already have a new car.

Tenemos un coche grande. We have a big car.

"Suficientemente" se puede decir "Enough" en inglés. Repita, "Enough". Enough.

¿Cómo cree que se dice "Suficientemente grande"? Big enough.

Ahora diga, "Mi coche es suficientemente grande". My car is big enough.

Can you say this in English, "Mi coche es suficientemente grande para nuestra familia"? My car is big enough for our family.
Say this again, "My car is big enough for our family." My car is big enough for my family.
"Para mis necesidades" se dice "for my needs" en inglés. Diga "for my needs". For my needs.
Say "Mi coche es suficientemente grande para mis necesidades". My car is big enough for my needs.
tres personas. Three people.
Hay tres personas en nuestra familia. There are three people in my family.
Su coche es muy pequeño. Your car is very small.
Es suficientemente grande para mis necesidades. It's big enough for my needs.
¿Tiene un coche? Do you have a car?
Sí, tenemos un coche. Yes, we have a car.
Ask me if I have a car. Do you have a car?
Sí, tengo un coche. Yes, I have a car.
Sí, tenemos un coche. Yes, we have a car.
Nos gustaría algo de gasolina. We'd like some gas.
Algo de gasolina. Some gas.
Say in English, "Deme algo de gasolina". Give me some gas.
Now say in English, "Por favor, deme algo de gasolina". Give me some gas please.
En inglés, "Diez galones" se dice "Ten gallons" Repita, "Ten gallons". Ten gallons.
How do you say, "Diez galones de gasolina" in English? Ten gallons of gas.
Now say, "Diez galones de gasolina, por favor". Ten gallons of gas, please.
Quince galones de gasolina, por favor. Fifteen gallons of gas, please.
"En la bomba número doce" se dice "On pump twelve" Repita, "On pump twelve". On pump twelve.
Me gustaría veinte dólares de gasolina en la bomba número catorce, por favor. I'd like twenty dollars of gas on pump fourteen, please.
Me gustaría treinta dólares de gasolina en la bomba número diez, por favor. I'd like thirty dollars of gas on pump ten, please.
Me gustaría veinticinco dólares de gasolina en la dieciséis, por favor. I'd like twenty five dollars of gas on sixteen please.
Me gustaría veintiocho en la diez, por favor. I'd like twenty eight on ten, please.
Espere. Wait.
Eso es mucha gasolina. That's a lot of gas.
Eso es mucha gasolina ¿no cree? That's a lot of gas, don't you think?

Eso es demasiado. That's too much.
Repeat after me, "That's too much, don't you think?" That's too much, don't you think?
Me gustaría veintiocho en la once, por favor. I'd like twenty eight on eleven, please.
Eso es demasiado. That's too much.
Eso es demasiado, ¿no cree? That's too much, don't you think?
Es suficiente. That's enough.
Ask in English, "¿Es suficiente?" Is it enough?
¿Treinta galones? Eso es demasiado. Thirty gallons? That's too much.
La palabra "Worth" significa "Valor". Repita, "I´d like ten dollars worth of gas, please. I'd like ten dollars' worth of gas, please.
Esto es literalmente, "Me gustaría el valor de diez dólares en gasolina, por favor". Pero la palabra "valor" se sobrentiende en español, y por eso no se usa. No es necesario usarla en inglés tampoco, pero el uso es común. Usando la palabra "Worth", diga otra vez "Me gustaría diez dólares en gasolina, por favor." I'd like ten dollars' worth of gas, please.
Por favor, deme diez dólares en gasolina. Please give me ten dollars' worth of gas.
Ask me if I have enough gas. Do you have enough gas?
Answer that no, you don't. No, I don't.
Say in English, "No tengo suficiente gasolina". I don't have enough gas.
Now say in English, "Voy a comprar algo de gasolina". I'm going to buy some gas.
¿Cuánta gasolina? How much gas?
Voy a comprar. I'm going to buy.
Quince dólares en gasolina. Fifteen dollars' worth of gas.
Voy a comprar quince dólares de gasolina. I'm going to buy fifteen dollars of gas.
Tell me in English that you are going to buy fifteen dollars of gas. I'm going to buy fifteen dollars of gas.
"Milla" se dice "Mile" en inglés. Repita, "Mile". Mile.
¿Cómo se dice "Milla" en inglés? Mile.
Ahora pregunte, "Cuántas millas?" How many miles?
Cincuenta millas. Fifty miles.
Entonces, voy a comprar algo de gasolina. Then I'm going to buy some gas.
Por favor, deme dieciséis dólares en gasolina. Please give me sixteen dollars worth of gas.
Espere. Wait.
Eso es suficiente gasolina. That's enough gas.
Usted tiene un coche pequeño. You have a small car.

Pero es suficiente para mis necesidades. But it's enough for my needs.
Eso es suficiente gasolina. That's enough gas.
Es suficiente para cincuenta millas. That's enough for fifty miles.
"Treasure Island" literalmente quiere decir "Isla de Tesoros". Repita, "Treasure Island". Treasure Island
Me voy a Treasure Island. I'm going to Treasure Island.
A Treasure Island. To Treasure Island.
Me voy a Treasure Island con unos amigos. I'm going to Treasure Island with some friends.
Me voy a Treasure Island con unos amigos más tarde. I'm going to Treasure Island with some friends later.
Me voy a Treasure Island. I'm going to Treasure Island.
¿Por qué Treasure Island? Why Treasure Island?
¿Por qué no? Why not?
¿Cuántas millas son de aquí a Treasure Island? How many miles is it from here to Treasure Island?
Sesenta millas. Son sesenta millas a Treasure Island. Sixty miles. It's sixty miles to Treasure Island.
¿Cuántas millas son de aquí a Treasure Island? How many miles is it from here to Treasure Island?
¿Cuántas millas son de aquí? How many miles is it from here?
Cuarenta. Forty.
¿De verdad? Really?
Tengo un coche grande. I have a big car.
Y tengo mucha gasolina en el coche. And I have a lot of gas in the car.
Y vamos a Treasure Island. And we're going to Treasure Island.
Try to say, "Si usted quiere" in English. If you want.
Si usted quiere. If you want.
Vamos a Treasure Island si usted quiere. We're going to Treasure Island if you want.
How do you say "Rápido" in English? Fast.
Say "Muy rápido" in English. Very fast.
Now say in English, "Usted habla inglés muy rápido". You speak English very fast.
Ask in English, "¿Su esposo también habla rápido?" Does your husband speak fast too?
Answer in English, "Sí, demasiado rápido". Yes, too fast.
Pero su esposo no está aquí. But your husband isn't here.
Ask me where he is. Where is he?

¿Mi esposo? My husband?
Mi esposo no está aquí. My husband isn't here.
Do you remember how to say, "Es demasiado caro" in English? It's too expensive.
¿Qué es demasiado caro? What is too expensive?
How do you say "Este libro" in English? This book.
Ask in English, "¿Qué es demasiado caro? What is too expensive?
Answer in English, "Este libro. Este libro es demasiado caro". This book. This book is too expensive.
¿Cuánto cuesta? How much does it cost?
Cincuenta dólares. Cuesta cincuenta dólares. Fifty dollars. It costs fifty dollars.
Say in English, "Qué ridículo." How ridiculous.
Now say, "Qué ridículo. Sesenta dólares por este libro". How ridiculous. Sixty dollars for this book.
Please say, "Cincuenta dólares, no sesenta" in English. Fifty dollars, not sixty.
Bueno, cincuenta dólares es caro también. Well, fifty dollars is expensive too.
¿Cómo se dice "Estoy de acuerdo" en inglés? I agree.
Diga "Sesenta dólares" en inglés. Sixty dollars.
How does one say, "Cuarenta y cinco dólares" in English? Forty five dollars.
Sesenta y un dólares. Sixty one dollars.
Cincuenta y seis dólares. Fifty six dollars.
Veintiún. Twenty one.
¿Sesenta y ocho? Eso es demasiado caro. Sixty eight? That's too expensive.
En dólares es demasiado caro. In dollars it's too expensive.
Estoy de acuerdo. I agree.
Aquí está más caro. Here it's more expensive.
How do you say in English, "Le voy a dar"? I'm going to give you.
Say in English, "Cincuenta y tres dólares." Fifty three dollars.
Now say, "Le voy a dar cincuenta y tres dólares" in English. I'm going to give you fifty three dollars.
Eso no es suficiente. That's not enough.
Eso no es suficiente dinero. That's not enough money.
¿Quién es ese? Who's that?
Ese es mi esposo. That's my husband.
¿Dónde está su esposa? Where's your wife?
¿Mi esposa? No sé. My wife? I don't know.
¿Dónde está su esposo? Where's your husband?
Mi esposo no está aquí. My husband isn't here.

Él está por aquí en algún lugar. He's around here someplace.

Mi esposo está por allá. My husband is over there.

Él está por allá. He is over there.

Él está por allá con su amigo Rodolfo. He is over there with his friend Rodolfo.

¿Mi esposo? Él está por allá. My husband? He's over there.

Tell me that he's over there with his friend. He's over there with his friend.

Usando la contracción, diga en inglés, "Él está". He's.

Usando la contracción, diga en inglés, "Ella está por ahí en algún lugar". She's around here someplace.

¿Mi esposa? Ella está por allá. My wife? She's over there.

Ask me if she is over there. Is she over there?

Ella no está por allá. Ella está aquí. She's not over there. She's here.

¿Qué le gustaría beber a su esposo? What would your husband like to drink?

¿Qué le gustaría beber? What would he like to drink?

A mí me gustaría. I'd like.

Tell me that he'd like some coffee or water. He'd like some coffee or water.

Now tell me he'd like some coffee. He'd like some coffee.

A ella le gustaría algo de agua. She'd like some water.

Do you remember how to say, "Pase, por favor" in English? Come in, please.

Diga, "Hola, soy Angela". Hello, I'm Angela.

Mucho gusto en conocerla. Pleased to meet you.

Mucho gusto en conocerlo. Pleased to meet you.

Por favor, pase. Please, come in.

Tell me that you're pleased to meet me. Pleased to meet you.

Gracias. Mucho gusto en conocerlo también. Thanks. Pleased to meet you too.

¿Qué le gustaría beber? What would you like to drink?

Me gustaría algo de té helado por favor. I'd like some iced tea, please.

¿Y su esposa? And your wife?

¿Qué le gustaría beber a ella? What would she like to drink?

Soy Rosa Montero. I'm Rosa Montero.

Mucho gusto en conocerla, Señora Montero. Pleased to meet you, Mrs. Montero.

Mucho gusto en conocerla, Señora Montero. Soy Robert Johnson. Pleased to meet you, Mrs. Montero. I'm Robert Johnson.

Mucho gusto en conocerlo, Señor Johnson. Pleased to meet you, Mr. Johnson.

Hola, Señora Johnson. Hello, Mrs. Johnson.

Ask in English, "¿Dónde viven ustedes?" Where do you live?

Now ask in English "¿Dónde viven ustedes dos?" Where do you two live?

Say "Viven" in English. Live.
"We live" means "Nosotros vivimos" in English. Repeat, "We live". We live.
Answer in English, "Nosotros vivimos". We live.
Now say in English, "Ustedes viven". You live.
Usted vive. You live.
Yo vivo. I live.
Nosotros vivimos. We live.
Mucho gusto en conocerla, Señorita Johnson. Pleased to meet you, Miss Johnson.
Por favor, pase. Please, come in.
Pase por favor. Come in please.
Ask me where I live. Where do you live?
Tell me that you live in Guadalajara. I live in Guadalajara.
Nosotros vivimos en Guadalajara. We live in Guadalajara.
¿Cómo se dice "mes" en inglés? Month.
Ahora diga, "Un mes". A month.
Say in English, "Estoy en los Estados Unidos por un mes". I'm in the United States for a month.
¿Dónde vive usted? Where do you live?
Yo vivo en Guadalajara. ¿Y usted? ¿Usted vive aquí? I live in Guadalajara. And you? Do you live here?
Sí, en la Avenida Parque. Yes, on Park Avenue.
Nosotros vivimos aquí. We live here.
Nosotros vivimos aquí en la Avenida Parque. We live here, on Park Avenue.
Nosotros vivimos en Guadalajara. We live in Guadalajara.
¿Y usted? ¿Usted vive aquí? And you? Do you live here?
Sí, en la Avenida Parque. Yes, on Park Avenue.
Yo estoy en los Estados Unidos por un mes. I'm in the United States for a month.
Nos gustaría beber algo. We'd like to have something to drink.
¿Cómo qué? Like what?
¿Qué le gustaría beber? What would you like to drink?
Nos gustaría algo de café. We'd like some coffee.
¿Su esposa también quiere café? Does your wife want coffee too?
Answer in English, "Sí, ella quiere". Yes, she does.
A mi esposo y a mí. My husband and I.
A mi esposo y a mí nos gustaría algo de agua. My husband and I would like some water.
Nos gustaría algo de agua. We'd like some water.

A ella le gustaría algo de agua. She'd like some water.
Pero a él le gustaría algo de café. But he'd like some coffee.
Ask if we would like some coffee. Would you like some coffee?
No, nos gustaría algo de vino. No, we'd like some wine.
Aquí, el vino es más caro. Here, wine is more expensive.
Especialmente el vino California. Especially the California wine.
Pase. Come in.
Buenos diás, Señora. Good morning, ma'am.
Soy Charles Johnson. I'm Charles Johnson.
Gusto en conocerlo, Señor Johnson. Soy Rosa Montero. Pleased to meet you, Mr. Johnson. I'm Rosa Montero.
Señora Montero, ¿está su esposo aquí? Mrs. Montero, is your husband here?
No, él no está aquí. No, he isn't here.
Lo siento. No está aquí. I'm sorry. He isn't here.
¿Dónde viven ustedes en México? Where do you live in Mexico?
Vivimos en Guadalajara. We live in Guadalajara.
¿Y usted, Señor? ¿Dónde vive usted? And you, sir? Where do you live?
Yo vivo en México también. Estoy en los Estados Unidos por un mes. I live in Mexico too. I'm in the United States for a month.
¿Quién es ese? Who's that?
In English, "¿Quién puede ser?" means "Who can it be?" Repeat, "Who can it be? Who can it be?
Ask in English, "¿Quién puede ser?" Who can it be?
Say that you don't know. I don't know.
Say this in English: "A esta hora". At this hour.
¿Quién puede ser a esta hora? Who can it be at this hour?
No tengo ninguna idea. I have no idea.
Pedro, el Señor Johnson está aquí. Pedro, Mr. Johnson is here.
¿A esta hora? At this hour?
Sí. No sé por qué. Yes. I don't know why.
Pase por favor, Señor Johnson. Come in please, Mr. Johnson.
Señor Johnson, mi esposo Pedro. Mr. Johnson, my husband Pedro.
Mucho gusto en conocerlo. Pleased to meet you.
Señor Johson, ¿le gustaría algo de café? Mr. Johnson, would you like some coffee?
Sí, me gustaría. Yes, I would.
Oh, su esposa está aquí también. Oh, your wife is here too.
¿Su esposa también quiere café? Does your wife want coffee too?

En inglés, conteste brevemente que sí. Yes, she does.
Please say, "Es bueno verlo" in English. It's good to see you.
Hola, Mike. Es bueno verlo. Hello, Mike. It's good to see you.
Es bueno verlo también. It's good to see you too.
Now say in English "Es bueno verlo. ¿Cómo ha estado?" It's good to see you. How have you been?
Bien, gracias. ¿Y usted? Fine, thanks. And you?
¿Cómo ha estado? How have you been?
No puedo quejarme. I can't complain.
Try to say in English, "Nosotros no podemos quejarnos". We can't complain.
Repeat, "We can't complain". We can't complain.
¿Le gustaría beber algo? Would you like to have something to drink?
Claro. Sure.
Ahora diga "Hola, Señora o Señorita Johnson. Es bueno verla" Hello, Ms. Johnson. It's good to see you.
Es bueno verlo también. It's good to see you too.
¿Le gustaría beber algo? Would you like to have something to drink?
¿Qué tiene usted? What do you have?
Tengo café o agua. I have coffee or water.
Café, por favor. Coffee, please.
Para decir "con o sin azúcar", diga "With or without sugar". Repita, "With or without sugar". With or without sugar.
Me gustaría un café, por favor. I would like a coffee, please.
Ask, "¿Con o sin azúcar?" With or without sugar?
Sin azúcar, por favor. Without sugar, please.
¿Qué quiere beber su esposo? What does your husband want to drink?
Solo un vaso de agua. Only a glass of water.
Es todo. That's all.
¿Solo un vaso de agua? ¿Es todo? Only a glass of water? That's all?
Sí, es todo. Yes, that's all.
¿Cómo ha estado? How have you been?
No puedo quejarme. I can't complain.
Es bueno verla. It's good to see you.
Es bueno verlo también. It's good to see you too.
¿Quiere él algo de agua? Does he want some water?
¿O le gustaría algo de café? Or would he like some coffee?
A él le gustaría algo de café. He'd like some coffee.

¿Con o sin azúcar? With or without sugar?
Aquí el café es más caro. Here coffee is more expensive.
Do you remember how to say in English, "Cuesta un brazo y una pierna." It costs an arm and a leg.
Now say in English, "Aquí el café es más caro. Cuesta un brazo y una pierna." Here coffee is more expensive. It costs an arm and a leg.
¿Cómo se dice "Mucho más caro"? Much more expensive.
Aquí el café es mucho más caro. Here coffee is much more expensive.
Cuesta un brazo y una pierna. It costs an arm and a leg.
"Cup" means "taza" in English. Repeat, "cup". Cup.
Say "taza" in English. Cup.
Una taza. A cup.
¿Cuánto por una taza? How much for a cup?
Una taza de café cuesta quince dólares. A cup of coffee costs fifteen dollars.
¿Cinco dólares por una taza de café? ¡Qué ridículo! Fifteen dollars for a cup of coffee? How ridiculous!
Yo sé. Cuesta un brazo y una pierna aquí. I know. It costs an arm and a leg here.
¿Quince dólares por una taza de café? ¡Qué ridículo! Fifteen dollars for a cup of coffee? How ridiculous!
Estoy de acuerdo. I agree.
Ask in English, "¿Dónde está su esposo? Where is your husband?
¿Dónde está él? Where is he?
¿Mi esposo? No sé. My husband? I don´t know.
Él está por aquí en algún lugar. He's around here someplace.
¿Dónde está su esposa? Where is your wife?
¿Mi esposa? No sé. My wife? I don't know.
No tengo ninguna idea. I have no idea.
No sé dónde está. I don't know where she is.
Say in English "Mi esposo no está aquí". My husband isn't here.
Ask in English "¿Dónde está su esposa? ¿Dónde está ella?" Where is your wife? Where is she?
Ella está con su esposa. She is with your wife.
¿Dónde vive usted? Where do you live?
¿Dónde viven ustedes dos? Where do you two live?
Nosotros vivimos en México. We live in Mexico.
¿Dónde en México viven? Where in Mexico do you live?
En el estado de Michoacan. In the state of Michoacan.

¿Dónde viven ustedes dos? Where do you two live?
Nosotros vivimos en México. We live in Mexico.
¿Dónde en México viven? Where in Mexico do you live?
Vivimos en el estado de Michoacán. We live in the state of Michoacan.
¿Tienen ustedes hijos? Do you have any children?
Sí, pero ya han crecido. Yes but they're already grown up.
¿Tienen ustedes hijos? Do you have any children?
Sí, tenemos hijos. Yes, we have children.
No, no tenemos hijos. No, we don't have any children.
¿Dónde en México viven? Where in Mexico do you live?
Nosotros vivimos en el estado de Michoacan. We live in the state of Michoacan.
¿Cuántos dólares tiene usted? How many dollars do you have?
¿Cuántos hijos tienen ustedes? How many children do you have?
Tenemos tres hijos. We have three children.
Dos niños. Two boys.
¿Cuántos niños tienen? How many children do you have?
Tenemos dos niños. We have two boys.
Una niña. A girl.
Tenemos dos niños y una niña. We have two boys and one girl.
Tenemos una niña. We have one girl.
Nos gustaría un niño. We'd like a boy.
Nos gustaría un niño algún día. We'd like a boy some day.
Nos gustaría un niño. We'd like a boy.
Pero tenemos tres niñas. But we have three girls.
Nos gustaría un niño algún día. We'd like a boy some day.
Tenemos cinco hijos. We have five children.
tres niños y dos niñas. Three boys and two girls.
Eso es mucho. That's a lot.
Tenemos una niña y un niño. We have one girl and one boy.
El niño es grande. The boy is big.
La niña es grande. The girl is big.
¿Es grande el niño? Is the boy big?
Sí, él es grande. Yes, he's big.
El no es grande. He's not big.
¿Es grande la niña? Is the girl big?
Ella no es grande. She's not big.
El niño es muy grande. The boy is very big.

¿Cuántos hijos tiene usted? How many children do you have?
Tengo cuatro hijos. I have four children.
Usted tiene dos, ¿ verdad? You have two, right?
¿Perdón? Excuse me?
Usted tiene dos, ¿verdad? You have two, right?
No, nostotros tenemos cuatro hijos. No, we have four children.
Los niños son grandes. The boys are big.
How do you say "Ellos son grandes" in English? They are big.
Now say this with a contractión,"They're big." They're big.
Ellos están aquí. They're here.
¿Están ellos aquí? Are they here?
No están por allá. They're not over there.
¿Quién está por allá? Who's over there?
Solo mi esposa. Only my wife.
Esa es mi esposa. That's my wife.
¿Cuántos hijos tienen? How many children do you have?

End of speaking/listening lesson. Continue with the reading for Lesson 25.

Reading for Lesson 25

As in the other lessons, read the following conversation with your student, taking care to read slowly so the student can follow along with you. The student can read the conversation alone after you read it together.

Reading Practice

I'd like twenty five dollars worth of gas on pump seventeen, please.

Twenty five on seventeen? Okay.

Excuse me, how many miles is it to Treasure Island?

It's not far. *Maybe (Quizás)* thirty or forty miles.

Good. I'm going there with some friends, and they're very hungry.

There are some good restaurants on the island. It is not very far away.

You have a very small car.

I know. But it's enough for my needs and big cars are too expensive.

Yes, but is your car big enough for your friends? There are a lot of people in your car.

Yes, some friends and some family.

How many people are in your car? Six or seven?

Seven.

With you, that's eight.

You're right. But Treasure Island isn't far. Oh, where is the bathroom?

Over there, *next to the telephone (al lado del teléfono).*

Okay thanks.

No problem. Oh, do your friends want to use the bathroom too? Sometimes there is a lot of *traffic on the bridge* (*tráfico en el puente*) to the island.

There is? (¿Hay?)

Yes, there is.

LEVEL 1: LESSON 26 (REVIEW CONTINUATION)

Remember to take at least two days on this review lesson. Note: At the end of day one of this lesson you may take the Lesson 26 reading or review any previous reading your student may have had difficulty with. But make sure to do the Lesson 26 reading by the end of this review.

Teaching Tip: When you get to the question, "Do you live around here?", it is common for Spanish speakers to say, "You live around here?". Watch for that and don't let them get away with it! Make sure they don't omit the "do".

Tenemos tres hijos. We have three children.

Tenemos dos niños. We have two boys.

Y una niña. And one girl.

¿Ella es grande? Is she big?

Para contestar "No, no es" se puede decir "No, she's not" o "No, she isn't". Repita, "No, she's not. No, she's not.

Now say "No, she isn't". No, she isn't.

Ask in English "¿Ella es grande?" Is she big?

Answer in English, "No, no es". No she isn't. (Or) No, she's not.

Los niños son muy grandes. The boys are very big.

Ellos son muy grandes. They're very big.

¿Son muy grandes los niños? Are the boys very big?

¿Son muy grandes? Are they very big?

Sí, son grandes. Yes, they're big.

¿Es usted mexicano, Señor Martinez? Are you Mexican, Mr. Martinez?

Sí, soy mexicano. Yes, I'm Mexican.

¿Y dónde vive usted en Mexico? And where do you live in Mexico?

Yo vivo en Guadalajara. I live in Guadalajara.

Mi esposa y yo vivimos en Guadalajara. My wife and I live in Guadalajara.

¿Tiene hijos? Do you have any children?

Sí, tenemos tres hijos. Yes, we have three children.

¿Tienen hijos? Do you have any children?

Conteste brevemente que si tienen. Yes, we do.

Sí, tenemos tres. Yes, we have three.

¿Tiene usted niños? Do you have any boys?

Sí, tenemos dos niños. Yes, we have two boys.

¿Y una niña? And one girl?

Sí, tenemos una niña. Yes we have one girl.

¿Dónde están los hijos? ¿Estan aquí con usted? Where are the children? Are they here with you?

Answer that "Yes, they are here with me". Yes, they are here with me.

¿Y su esposa? ¿Está aquí también? And your wife? Is she here too?

Tell me that "Yes, she is here too". Yes, she is here too.

Usted habla inglés muy bien, señor. You speak English very well, sir.

No, no muy bien. Pero se lo agradezco. No, not very well. But thank you.

Espere, por favor. Wait, please.

Para decir "solo un momento" se dice "just a moment". Diga "Just a moment". Just a moment.

Espere solo un momento. Wait just a moment.

Solo un momento, por favor. Just a moment, please.

Gusto en conocerla, Señorita Johnson. Pleased to meet you, Miss Johnson.

Si no sabe si es casada o no, se usa "Ms." Repita "Ms.". Ms.

Say, "Pleased to meet you, Ms. Johnson." Pleased to meet you, Ms. Johnson.

Ask in English, "¿Dónde viven ustedes?" Where do you live?

Nosotros vivimos en Colombia. We live in Columbia.

Nosotros vivimos en Perú. We live in Peru.

Nosotros vivimos en El Salvador. We live in El Salvador.

¿Cuántos hijos tiene usted? How many children do you have?

Dos niños. Tenemos dos niños. Two boys. We have two boys.

Los niños son grandes. The boys are big.

Son grandes. They're big.

Ellos están por allá. They're over there.

Los niños están por allá. The boys are over there.

Y su esposa, ¿dónde está? And your wife, where is she?

Ella está por allá también. She's over there too.

¿Mi esposo? El está por allá. My husband? He is over there.

¿Tienen niñas ustedes? Do you have any girls?

Sí. Tenemos tres niñas. Yes, we have three girls.
Say in English, "Podemos". We can.
Now say in English, "Podemos esperar". We can wait.
Ask me in English if I can wait. Can you wait?
Usted puede esperar. You can wait.
Nosotros queremos. We want.
Queremos muchos hijos. We want a lot of children.
Ustedes tienen muchos hijos. You have a lot of children.
Ya tienen muchos hijos. You already have a lot of children.
Espere. No queremos muchos hijos. Wait. We don't want a lot of children.
Tenemos suficiente con tres. We have enough with three.
Y nosotros tenemos suficiente con once. And we have enough with eleven.
Vivimos en El Salvador. We live in El Salvador.
Mi esposa y yo vivimos en El Salvador. My wife and I live in El Salvador.
Con los hijos. With the children.
Mi esposa y yo vivimos en El Salvador con nuestros hijos. My wife and I live in El Salvador with our children.
Los hijos están en Perú. The children are in Peru.
Utilizando la contracción, diga en inglés, "Ellos están en Perú". They're in Peru.
¿Dónde están? Where are they?
Las niñas están aquí. The girls are here.
Las niñas son grandes. The girls are big.
Las niñas grandes. The big girls.
La niña está aquí. The girl is here.
La niña es grande. The girl is big.
La niña grande está aquí. The big girl is here.
El niño grande está aquí. The big boy is here.
¿Y la niña pequeña? And the little girl?
¿La niña pequeña es de ustedes? The little girl is yours?
El niño pequeño. The little boy.
El niño pequeño no es de nosotros. The little boy isn't ours.
Say in English, "Mi niño es pequeño". My boy is little.
Nuestro niño es pequeño. Our boy is little.
Nuestro niño. Our boy.
Nuestro niño no es grande. Our boy isn't big.
Tiene solo cinco años. He's only five years old.
Tiene solo siete años. He's only seven years old.

Él es pequeño. He's little.
¿De verdad? Really?
Sí, de verdad. Yes, really.
¿Dónde está su niña? Where's your girl?
¿Nuestra niña grande o nuestra niña pequeña? Our big girl or our little girl?
La niña grande. The big girl.
Su niña grande. Your big girl.
Nuestra niña grande está por allá. Our big girl is over there.
Ella es muy grande. She's very big.
¿De verdad? ¿Cree que sí? Really? Do you think so?
Nuestra niña pequeña está aquí. Our little girl is here.
Ella está por aquí en algún lugar. She's around here someplace.
¿Le gustaría beber algo? Would she like to have something to drink?
Sí. Le gustaría algo de agua. Yes, she'd like some water.
Sí, le gustaría. Yes, she would.
Pero ella puede esperar. But she can wait.
Pase. Tome un asiento, por favor. Come in. Have a seat, please.
Gusto conocerla Señora o Señorita Johnson. Pleased to meet you, Ms. Johnson.
Gusto conocerlo, Sr. Martinez. Pleased to meet you, Mr. Martinez.
Tome un asiento, por favor. Have a seat, please.
¿Le gustaría beber algo? Would you like to have something to drink?
Sí. Me gustaría algo de café, por favor. Yes, I'd like some coffee, please.
Sí. Nos gustaría algo de café, por favor. Yes, we'd like some coffee, please.
Pero podemos esperar. But we can wait.
¿Dónde está el baño? Where is the bathroom?
Perdón, ¿dónde está el baño? Excuse me, where is the bathroom?
Está por allá. It's over there.
Siga derecho. Está por allá. Continue straight ahead. It's over there.
¿El baño? Siga derecho. The bathroom? Continue straight ahead.
How do you say "por el pasillo" in English? Through the hall.
Siga derecho por el pasillo. Continue straight ahead through the hall.
El baño está por allá. The bathroom is over there.
¿De verdad? Really?
Sí, de verdad. Siga derecho por el pasillo. Yes, really. Continue straight ahead through the hall.
El niño pequeño. The little boy.
Nuestros cuatro niños. Our four boys.

La niña grande. The big girl.
Las cuatro niñas grandes. The four big girls.
Sus cuatro niñas son grandes. Your four girls are big.
Sí, yo sé. Yes, I know.
Nuestra niña también es grande. Our girl is big too.
Ella está aquí con nosotros. She's here with us.
Perdón, ¿dónde está el baño? Excuse me, where is the bathroom?
No tengo ninguna idea. Lo siento. I have no idea. I'm sorry.
Yo sé dónde está. I know where it is.
Siga derecho por el pasillo. Continue straight ahead through the hall.
¿Sabe usted dónde está el baño? Do you know where the bathroom is?
Sí, siga derecho. Yes, continue straight ahead.
¿Cómo está su familia? How is your family?
How do you say "familia" in English? Family.
How do you say "padres" in English?" Parents.
Now ask in English, "¿Cómo están sus padres?" How are your parents?
Bien, gracias. Fine, thanks.
¿Y su familia? ¿Cómo está su familia? And your family? How is your family?
Dos familias. Two families.
Padres. Parents.
Nuestra familia. Our family.
¿Dónde está su familia? Where is your family?
¿Mi familia? My family?
Los hijos pequeños están en Mexico. The little children are in Mexico.
La niña grande está aquí con nosotros. The big girl is here with us.
Tiene una familia grande. You have a big family.
Yo sé. I know.
Buenos días, Señora Johnson. Good morning, Mrs. Johnson.
Now say good morning to Ms. Campbell. Good morning, Ms. Campbell.
¿Quién es este niño pequeño? Who is this little boy?
¿Es su niño pequeño? Is he your little boy?
Sí, es de nosotros. Yes, he is ours.
¿Entiende inglés él? Does he understand English?
Diga brevemente que no en inglés. No, he doesn´t.
No, no puede. No, he can't.
¿Cuántos niños tienen? How many boys do you have?
¿Y ustedes tienen niñas? And do you have any girls?

Tenemos una niña. We have one girl.
¿Una niña pequeña? A little girl?
Tiene siete años. She is seven years old.
Y tenemos un niño pequeño. And we have a little boy.
Él tiene ocho años. He is eight years old.
Su niño pequeño quiere algo. ¿Qué quiere? Your little boy wants something. What does he want?
¿Dónde está el baño, por favor? Where is the bathroom, please?
El baño está por allá. The bathroom is over there.
Gracias. Thank you.
Gusto en conocerla, Señora Martinez. ¿Está su esposo en Nueva York también? Pleased to meet you, Mrs. Martinez. Is your husband in New York too?
¿Están sus hijos aquí también? Are your children here too?
Sí, nuestros hijos están aquí con nosotros también. Yes, our children are here with us too.
Hola. Hello.
Hola, ¿cómo le va? Hello, how's it going?
Muy bien. ¿Y usted? ¿Cómo ha estado? Very well. And you? How have you been?
Ask in English where the bathroom is. Where is the bathroom?
Say in English, "Un niño grande". A big boy.
Now say in English, "Tenemos un niño grande". We have a big boy.
Nuestro niño es grande. Our boy is big.
Una niña pequeña. A little girl.
Nosotros también tenemos una niña pequeña. We have a little girl too.
Nuestra niña no es grande. Our girl isn't big.
¿Cuántos hijos tiene? How many children do you have?
Tengo tres hijos. I have three children.
Tenemos tres hijos. We have three children.
¿Son grandes? Are they big?
¿Dónde están? Where are they?
Estan aquí con nosotros. They are here with us.
¿Dónde está el baño? Where is the bathroom?
El baño está por allá. The bathroom is over there.
Puedo esperar. I can wait.
Mi familia está en los Estados Unidos. My family is in the United States.
Mi familia está en Mexico. My family is in Mexico.
Mi familia está conmigo. My family is with me.

Nuestra familia está con nosotros. Our family is with us.
¿Cuántas personas? How many people?
¿Cuántas personas hay? How many people are there?
En su familia. In your family.
¿Dónde está Lydia? Where is Lydia?
Ella está por aquí en un lugar. She's around here someplace.
¿Cuántas personas hay en su familia? How many people are there in your family?
Hay tres personas. There are three people.
¿Solo tres? Only three?
Say in English, "En mi familia". In my family.
Now ask in English, "¿Cuántas personas hay? How many people are there?
Hay tres personas. There are three people.
Hay tres personas en mi familia. There are three people in my family.
Ask me how many people there are in my family. How many people are there in your family?
Answer in English, "Hay seis personas en mi familia". There are six people in my family.
Do you remember how to say, "En mi coche" in English? In my car.
Say "coche" in English. Car.
Tengo un coche. I have a car.
Tengo un coche nuevo. I have a new car.
¿Tiene un coche? Do you have a car?
¿Tiene un coche nuevo? Do you have a new car?
¿Está aquí su coche? Is your car here?
¿Está en los Estados Unidos su familia? Is your family in the United States?
Los hijos están aquí con nosotros. The children are here with us.
¿Cuántas personas hay en su familia? How many people are there in your family?
Hay cinco personas en nuestra familia. There are five people in our family.
Tenemos un coche. We have a car.
Tenemos un coche nuevo. We have a new car.
Tenemos un coche grande. We have a big car.
Suficientemente grande. Big enough.
Mi coche es suficientemente grande. My car is big enough.
Mi coche es suficientemente grande para nuestra familia. My car is big enough for our family.
Say in English, "Mi coche es suficientemente grande para mis necesidades". My car is big enough for my needs.

Si usted quiere. If you want.
tres personas. Three people.
Si usted quiere. If you want.
Hay tres personas en nuestra familia. There are three people in my family.
Su coche es muy pequeño. Your car is very small.
Es suficientemente grande para mis necesidades. It's big enough for my needs.
¿Tiene un coche? Do you have a car?
Sí, tenemos un coche. Yes, we have a car.
Ask me if I have a car. Do you have a car?
Sí, tengo un coche. Yes, I have a car.
Sí, tenemos un coche. Yes, we have a car.
Nos gustaría algo de gasolina. We'd like some gas.
Now say in English, "Por favor, deme algo de gasolina". Give me some gas please.
Diez galones de gasolina, por favor. Ten gallons of gas, please.
Quince galones de gasolina, por favor. Fifteen gallons of gas, please.
En la bomba número doce. On pump twelve.
Me gustaría veinte dólares de gasolina en la bomba catorce, por favor. I'd like twenty dollars of gas on pump fourteen, please.
Me gustaría treinta dólares de gasolina en la bomba diez, por favor. I'd like thirty dollars of gas on pump ten, please.
Me gustaría veinticinco dólares de gasolina en la dieciséis, por favor. I'd like twenty five dollars of gas on sixteen, please.
Me gustaría veintiocho en la diez, por favor. I'd like twenty eight on ten, please.
Espere. Wait.
Eso es mucha gasolina. That's a lot of gas.
Eso es mucha gasolina, ¿no cree? That's a lot of gas, don't you think?
Eso es demasiado. That's too much.
Eso es demasiado, no cree? That's too much, don't you think?
Me gustaría veintiocho en la once, por favor. I'd like twenty eight on eleven, please.
Eso es demasiado. That's too much.
Es suficiente. That's enough.
¿Es suficiente? Is it enough?
¿Treinta galones? Eso es demasiado. Thirty gallons? That's too much.
Me gustarían diez dólares en gasolina, por favor. I'd like ten dollars' worth of gas, please.
Por favor, deme diez dólares en gasolina. Please give me ten dollars' worth of gas.
¿Tiene usted suficiente gasolina? Do you have enough gas?

Conteste que no, brevemente. No, I don't.
No tengo suficiente gasolina. I don't have enough gas.
Voy a comprar algo de gasolina. I'm going to buy some gas.
¿Cuánta gasolina? How much gas?
Voy a comprar quince dólares de gasolina. I'm going to buy fifteen dollars of gas.
¿Cuántas millas? How many miles?
Cincuenta millas. Fifty miles.
Entonces, voy a comprar algo de gasolina. Then I'm going to buy some gas.
Por favor, deme dieciséis dólares de gasolina. Please give me sixteen dollars' worth of gas.
Espere. Eso es suficiente gasolina. Wait. That's enough gas.
Usted tiene un coche pequeño. You have a small car.
Pero es suficiente para mis necesidades. But it's enough for my needs.
Eso es suficiente gasoline. That's enough gas.
Es suficiente para cincuenta millas. That's enough for fifty miles.
Tell me you're going to Treasure Island. I'm going to Treasure Island.
Me voy a Treasure Island con unos amigos. I'm going to Treasure Island with some friends.
Tell me in English that you are going to Treasure Island with some friends later. I'm going to Treasure Island with some friends later.
¿Por qué Treasure Island? Why Treasure Island?
¿Por qué no? Why not?
¿Cuántas millas son de aquí a Treasure Island? How many miles is it from here to Treasure Island?
Sesenta millas. Son sesenta millas a Treasure Island. Sixty miles. It's sixty miles to Treasure Island.
¿Cuántas millas son de aquí a Treasure Island? How many miles is it from here to Treasure Island?
¿Cuántas millas son de aquí? How many miles is it from here?
¿De verdad? Really?
How does one say, "Tengo un coche grande" in English? I have a big car.
Y tengo mucha gasolina en el coche. And I have a lot of gas in the car.
Y vamos a Treasure Island. And we're going to Treasure Island.

End of speaking/listening lesson. Continue with the reading for Lesson 26.

Reading for Lesson 26

Read the following with your student. Make sure he uses proper intonation in all the questions and make sure he doesn´t drop any sounds in words having contractions, such as "we're" and "how's". See that your student doesn't pronounce the word "kid" as "keed".

Reading Practice

Hello Robert. How are you doing?

I´m fine, Luis. And you? How's your family?

We´re well. My wife is fine and so are my *kids (hijos)*.

I'm glad to hear it (Me alegra oírlo).

How many people are there in your family?

There are five. My wife, my two sons, my daughter and *myself (yo)*.

There are six *in mine (en la mía)*. My wife, my three daughters and my two sons.

You have five kids?

Yes, I do.

So what are you doing today?

We are going to Treasure Island later.

You are? That's *great (maravilloso, fantástico, etc)*.

Thanks.

I was there last year (Estuve allí el año pasado). I *went (fui)* with some friends.

How many miles is it from here?

It´s about ninety miles from here. But *you have to remember (tienes que acordarte)* that there is a lot of traffic when you enter San Francisco.

So it's a trip (Así que es un viaje) of about two hours from here?

Yeah. Well I hope you have fun.

Thanks. It was good seeing you.

It was good seeing you too.

LEVEL 1: LESSON 27

Teaching Tip: Watch the student's pronounciation of "grandmother", that it's not "grandmudder" or "grandmatter". Have the student relax the jawline on the "o" so it is like a short "ut" and stress the "th" sound so it doesn't sound like a "d".

¿Cuántos hijos tiene usted, Sr. Martinez? How many children do you have, Mr. Martinez?

Dos. Mi esposa y yo tenemos dos hijos, un niño pequeño y una niña pequeña. Two. My wife and I have two children, a little boy and a little girl.

Say "coche" in English. Car.

Now say in English, "nuestro coche". Our car.

En nuestra familia. In our family.

¿Cuántas personas hay? How many people are there?

¿En su familia? In your family?

Ask me how many people there are in my family. How many people are there in your family?

Cinco personas. Five people.

Hay cinco personas en nuestra familia. There are five people in our family.

Tenemos tres hijos. We have three children.

Un niño y dos niñas. One boy and two girls.

Tenemos tres hijos, un niño y dos niñas. We have three children, one boy and two girls.

Tell me that the girls are here in the United States. The girls are here in the United States.

Con nosotros. With us.

Las niñas están aquí en los Estados Unidos con nosotros. The girls are here in the United States with us.

Nuestro niño pequeño está en Mexico. Our little boy is in Mexico.

¿De verdad? Really?

Sí, de verdad. Yes, really.
"Grandmother" means "abuela" in English. Repeat, "Grandmother". Grandmother.
Say in English, "Con su abuela". With his grandmother.
Now say in English, "Está en México con su abuela". He's in Mexico with his grandmother.
Nuestro niño pequeño está con su abuela en México. Our little boy is with his grandmother in Mexico.
¿Está en México? He's in Mexico?
¿Con quién? With whom?
Answer in English, "Con su abuela". With his grandmother.
Nuestra familia es grande. Our family is big.
Tenemos una familia grande. We have a big family.
No tenemos una familia grande. We don't have a big family.
Hay tres personas en nuestra familia. There are three people in our family.
Tenemos una familia pequeña. We have a small family.
Una familia pequeña. A small family.
Tenemos una familia pequeña. We have a small family.
Tenemos un coche pequeño. We have a small car.
Tenemos una familia pequeña y un coche pequeño. We have a small family and a small car.
¿Dónde está el baño? Where is the bathroom?
Está por allá. It's over there.
In English, "Word" means "palabra". Repeat, "word". Word.
Para preguntar "¿Cómo se dice esta palabra en inglés?" se dice, "How do you say this word in English?" Repeat, "How do you say this word in English?" How do you say this word in English?
Say again, "How do you say this word in English?" How do you say this word in English?
Diga esta pregunta en inglés: "¿Cómo se dice 'gasolina' en inglés?" How do you say "gasolina" in English?
Ask me how to say 'gasolina' in English. How do you say gasolina en English?
Now say in English, "Diez galones, por favor". Ten gallons please.
Es suficiente. It's enough.
Para cuarenta millas. For forty miles.
¿Es suficiente? Is that enough?
Espere. Wait.
Me gustaría treinta galones. I'd like thirty gallons.

Veinte dólares en gasolina, por favor. Twenty dollars worth of gas, please.
Tell me that your car is too big. My car is too big.
¿Tiene un coche grande? Do you have a big car?
Conteste que sí, brevemente. Yes, I do.
Pregúnteme cómo se dice coche en inglés. How do you say "coche" in English?
Say in English, "Quiero un coche pequeño". I want a small car.
La palabra "smaller" quiere decir "más chiquito" o "más pequeño". Repeat, "smaller". Smaller.
Tell me that you want a smaller car. I want a smaller car.
El que tengo yo usa demasiada gasolina. The one I have uses too much gas.
El que tengo yo. The one I have.
El que tengo yo usa demasiada gasolina. The one I have uses too much gas.
Quiero un coche más pequeño. I want a smaller car.
¿Un coche más chiquito? ¿Por qué? A smaller car? Why?
El que tengo yo usa demasiado gasolina. The one I have uses too much gas.
Me gustaría tener un coche más chiquito. I'd like to have a smaller car.
¿Un coche más chiquito? ¿Por qué? A smaller car? Why?
El que tengo yo usa demasiada gasolina. The one I have uses too much gas.
Quiero un coche más pequeño. I want a smaller car.
How does one say, "Más caro" in English? More expensive.
Quiero un coche más chiquito. I want a smaller car.
¿Tiene usted suficiente gasolina? Do you have enough gas?
Por favor, deme dieciséis dólares en gasolina. Please, give me sixteen dollars worth of gas.
Espere. Wait.
Deme quince dólares en gasolina. Give me fifteen dollars worth of gas.
¿A dónde va usted, señorita? Where are you going, miss?
Voy a Treasure Island. I'm going to Treasure Island.
Voy a Treasure Island mañana. I'm going to Treasure Island tomorrow.
¿Cuántas millas? How many miles?
¿Cuántas millas son de aquí a Treasure Island? How many miles is it from here to Treasure Island?
¿Cuántas millas son? How many miles is it?
Está lejos. It's far.
Cómo se dice. How do you say.
¿Cómo se dice esta palabra? How do you say this word?
Está lejos. It's far.

¿Quéda lejos Treasure Island? Is Treasure Island far?
Yo no sé. I don't know.
Setenta millas. Seventy miles.
Diecisiete millas. Seventeen miles.
Setenta y tres. Seventy three.
Setenta y cinco. Seventy five
No, setenta y un. No, seventy one.
Está setenta y un millas. It's seventy one miles.
Espere. Wait.
Usted habla demasiado rápido. You speak too fast.
Usted habla demasiado rápido para mí. You speak too fast for me.
Setenta y cuatro. Seventy four.
Sesenta y dos. Sixty two.
Está lejos. It's far.
Está lejos Treasure Island. Treasure Island is far.
Tell me that it's far. It's far.
Now ask me if I have enough gas. Do you have enough gas?
Diga que sí, brevemente. Yes, I do.
Yo tengo un coche pequeño. I have a small car.
Quiero un coche más grande. I want a bigger car.
Quiero un coche más caro. I want a more expensive car.
La palabra "camino" quiere decir "road". Repita, "Road". Road.
Say "El camino" in English. The road.
¿Cuál es el camino a Treasure island? Which is the road to Treasure Island?
El camino. The road.
El camino a Treasure Island. The road to Treasure Island.
¿Cuál es el camino a Treasure Island? Which is the road to Treasure Island?
Perdón, ¿cuál es el camino a Treasure Island? Excuse me, which is the road to Treasure Island?
¿Treasure Island? Está lejos. Treasure Island? It's far.
¿Cuántas millas? How many miles?
¿Cuántas millas son de aquí a Treasure Island? How many miles is it from here to Treasure Island?
Setenta y cinco. Seventy five.
Son setenta y cinco millas. It's seventy five miles.
¿Cuál es el camino a Treasure Island? Which is the road to Treasure Island?

"Tome el Camino Figueroa" se dice, "Take Figueroa Road". Repita, "Take Figueroa Road". Take Figueroa Road.

Está todo derecho. It's straight ahead.

Tome el camino Figueroa por setenta y cinco millas. Take Figueroa Road for seventy five miles.

Tome el camino Figueroa. Take Figueroa Road.

Está todo derecho. It's straight ahead.

Espere. Wait.

Ese no es el camino a Treasure Island. That's not the road to Treasure Island.

El camino a Treasure Island. The road to Treasure Island.

Está por allá. Is over there.

El camino a Treasure Island está por allá. The road to Treasure Island is over there.

¿Todo derecho? Straight ahead?

Sí, todo derecho. Yes, straight ahead.

¿Cuánta gasolina quiere? How much gas do you want?

Ask him in English how much gas he wants. How much gas do you want?

Por favor deme dieciseis dólares en gasolina. Please give me sixteen dollars worth of gasoline.

Gracias. Thank you.

De nada. You're welcome.

Espere. Wait.

¿Quéda lejos Treasure Island? Is Treasure Island far?

No, no está lejos. No, it's not far.

No está lejos Treasure Island. Treasure Island isn't far.

Setenta y ocho millas. Seventy eight miles.

Son setenta y ocho millas a Treasure Island. It's seventy eight miles to Treasure Island.

¿Es este el camino a Treasure Island? Is the road to Treasure Island?

¿Es este el camino? Is this the road?

¿Es este el camino a Treasure Island? Is this the road to Treasure Island?

¿Perdón, es este el camino a Treasure Island? Excuse me, is this the road to Treasure Island?

¿Cuál es el camino a Treasure Island? Which is the road to Treasure Island?

El camino a Treasure Island. The road to Treasure Island.

Está todo derecho. It is straight ahead.

Ask me if I have enough gas. Do you have enough gas?

Tell me that you have a lot of gas. I have a lot of gas.

Tengo un coche pequeño. I have a small car.
"Bigger" quiere decir "Más grande". Repita, "Bigger". Bigger.
Tell me you'd like a bigger car. I'd like a bigger car.
Pero no está lejos Treasure Island. But Treasure Island isn't far.
Buenos días, señora. Good morning, ma'am.
¿Cuánta gasolina quiere? How much gas do you want?
Quince dólares en gasolina, por favor. Fifteen dollars worth of gas, please.
Ask me which is the road to Treasure Island. Which is the road to Treasure Island?
¿Es este el camino a Treasure Island? Is this the road to Treasure Island?
Sí, sí es. Yes it is.
Treasure Island está todo derecho. Treasure Island is straight ahead.
¿Cuántas millas son de aquí a Treasure Island? How many miles is it from here to Treasure Island?
"No está tan lejos" se dice "It's not that far". Repita, It's not that far". It's not that far.
Sesenta o setenta millas. Sixty or seventy miles.
Solo sesenta o setenta millas. Only sixty or seventy miles.
No está tan lejos. It's not that far.
Usted tiene una familia grande. You have a big family.
Sí, hay siete personas en nuestra familia. Yes, there are seven people in our family.
Adiós, señor. Goodbye, sir.

End of speaking/listening lesson. Continue with the reading for Lesson 27.

Reading for Lesson 27

See if your student can read the following conversation out loud by himself. If any word is mispronounced, have the student stop right away and see if he can figure out how to pronounce it correctly on his own. If he can´t, go ahead and pronounce the word for him.

Reading Practice

You have a very big family.
I know. There are fourteen people in my family.
Your parents, you, and eleven brothers and sisters?
Yes. And you? How big is your family?
Not that big (No tan grande). I have a brother and sister in Los Angeles. My mom and dad live here in San Jose.
Do you know if this is the road to Treasure Island?
Yes, it is. Continue north on the highway and it will take you to Figueroa Avenue. Then take Figueroa Avenue west to Treasure Island.
Treasure Island, how far is it from here?
Oh, about sixty or seventy miles. Do you have enough gas?
I think so.
You need to be sure (Tienes que estar seguro), because sometimes there is a lot of traffic on the highway at this time.
You're right.
There is a cheap gas station on North Eighty Street. It's not far from here.
Oh, how do you say this word?
Which word?
This one.
Oh, that word is "expensive". It means that something costs a lot.
Like the gasoline.
Yes, like the gasoline.
Well, *have a nice day (qué tengas un buen día).*
You too, *friend (amigo).*

LEVEL 1: LESSON 28

Teaching Tip: When you get to the part in the lesson where the student will say "an old Chevy" make sure that they pronounce the "ch" sound as a "sh" sound. This may seem impractical and you may be thinking "My student may never have to say the word 'Chevy' in real life" but Spanish speakers struggle with the "sh" sound, often putting a "ch" sound in words like "ship", "shepherd", "shall" and others.

Para decir "La gasolina es cara" se dice "The gasoline is expensive". Repita "The gasolina is expensive". The gasolina is expensive.

Es cara. It's expensive.

¿Qué es cara? What is expensive?

La gasolina. The gasoline.

La gasolina es cara. The gasoline is expensive.

¿Es cara? Is it expensive?

¿Es cara la gasolina? Is the gasoline expensive?

¿Es muy cara la gasolina en los Estados Unidos? Is gas very expensive in the United States?

No, no es muy caro. No, it's not very expensive.

"Es carísima" se dice "It's extremely expensive". Repita, "It's extremely expensive." It's extremely expensive.

Repeat after me, "Extremely". Extremely.

Ex. Ex.

Treme. Treme.

Ly. Ly.

Extremely. Extremely.

Now repeat, "Extremely expensive". Extremely expensive.

Say in English, "La gasolina es carísima aquí". The gasoline is extremely expensive here.

La gasolina es muy cara en los Estados Unidos. The gasoline is very expensive in the United States.
Para decir "Es mejor caminar" diga "It's better to walk". Repita "It's better to walk." It's better to walk.
¿Es mejor caminar? Is it better to walk?
Sí. Es mejor caminar si es posible. Yes. It's better to walk if it's possible.
Es mejor caminar si es posible. It's better to walk if it's possible.
"To use a bicicycle" means "usar una bicicleta" in English. Repeat, "to use a bicycle". To use a bicycle.
How do you say "usar una bicicleta" in English? To use a bicycle.
Now say "Es mejor caminar o usar una bicicleta. It's better to walk or use a bicycle.
Me gusta caminar. I like to walk.
Yo uso una bicicleta. I use a bicycle.
Es mejor caminar si es possible. It's better to walk if possible.
O usar una bicicleta. Or use a bicycle.
La gasolina es cara en los Estados Unidos. The gas is expensive in the Estados Unidos.
La gasolina es carísima en los Estados Unidos. The gas is extremely expensive in the United States.
En inglés la palabra "prefiero" se dice "I prefer". Repita "I prefer". I prefer.
Prefiero caminar. I prefer to walk.
Prefiero caminar si es possible. I prefer to walk if it's possible.
Me gustaría comprar una bicicleta. I would like to buy a bicycle.
¿Una bicicleta? ¿Por qué? A bicycle? Why?
Quiero comprar una bicicleta porque la gasolina es cara aquí. I want to buy a bicycle because the gasoline is expensive here.
La gasolina es carísima. The gas is extremely expensive.
Ask in English, "¿Son caras las bicicletas en los Estados Unidos?" Are bicycles expensive in the United States?
Answer in English, "No son muy caras". They're not very expensive.
Ask again in English, "¿Son caras?" Are they expensive?
No, no son muy caras. No, they're not very expensive.
Me gustaría comprar una bicicleta. I would like to buy a bicycle.
¿Es cara la gasolina en Mexico? Is gas expensive in Mexico?
No, no es muy caro. No, it's not very expensive.
Soy mexicano. Vivo en Guadalajara. I'm Mexican. I live in Guadalajara.
Voy a los Estados Unidos. I'm going to the United States.
"Un Chevy Viejo" se dice "an old Chevy." Repita "An old Chevy". An old chevy.

Tengo un Chevy viejo. I have an old Chevy.
Tengo un coche, un Chevy viejo. I have a car, an old Chevy.
Tengo un coche pequeño. I have a small car.
Me gustaría un coche más grande. I would like a bigger car.
Me gustaría un coche más grande, como su Chevy. I would like a bigger car, like your Chevy.
Para decir "Prefiero tener" se dice "I prefer to have". Repita "I prefer to have". I prefer to have.
Prefiero tener un coche pequeño. I prefer to have a small car.
Prefiero tener un coche pequeño si es posible. I prefer to have a small car if it's possible.
Voy a los Estados Unidos con mi familia. I'm going to the United States with my family.
¿Cuántas personas hay en su familia? How many people are there in your family?
Hay tres personas en nuestra familia. There are three people in our family.
Tenemos una familia pequeña. We have a small family.
Nuestra familia es más grande. Our family is bigger.
Hay cinco personas en nuestra familia. There are five people in our family.
¿Es cara la gasolina en los Estados Unidos? Is gasoline expensive in the United States?
Un dólar por galón. One dollar per gallon.
Ask me in English how many gallons I want. How many gallons do you want?
Say in English, "Quiero veinte galones". I want twenty gallons.
Espere. Wait.
Eso es demasiado. That's too much.
Aquí es más caro. Here it's more expensive.
Dos dólares por galón. Two dollars per gallon.
"That's nothing" means "Eso no es nada" in English. Repeat "That's nothing". That's nothing.
¿Dos dólares por galón? Eso no es nada. Two dollars per gallon? That's nothing.
Son cinco dólares por galón donde vivo yo. It's five dollars per gallon where I live.
Eso no es nada. That's nothing.
Son cinco dólares por galón donde vivo yo. It's five dollars per gallon where I live.
¿Son cinco dólares por galón donde vive usted? It's five dollars per gallon where you live?
"Are you serious?" means "¿En serio?" in English. Repeat, "Are you serious?" Are you serious?

Sí. Yes.

Es mejor caminar, entonces. It's better to walk, then.

Puede decir eso otra vez. You can say that again.

Es mejor caminar, entonces. It's better to walk, then.

Ask me if Treasure Island is far. Is Treasure Island far?

Para preguntar "¿Qué tan lejos está?" se dice "How far is it?" Repita "How far is it?" How far is it?

¿Queda lejos Treasure Island? Is Treasure Island far?

Ask in English, "¿Qué tan lejos está?" How far is it?

Answer in English, "No muy lejos". Not very far.

No está lejos. It's not far.

¿Cuál es el camino a Treasure Island? Which is the road to Treasure Island?

El camino a Treasure Island. The road to Treasure Island.

Todo derecho. Straight ahead.

Está todo derecho. It's straight ahead.

Do you remember how to say "lejos" in English? Far.

Todo derecho. Straight ahead.

¿Qué tan lejos está? How far is it?

Setenta millas. Seventy miles.

No, setenta y cinco millas. No, seventy five miles.

You can say "gas" instead of "gasoline" if you want. Repeat, "gas". Gas.

Tell me you want some gas. I want some gas.

Now tell me you need some gas. I need some gas.

Usted necesita algo de gasolina. You need some gas.

Necesito algo de gasolina. I need some gas.

Usted necesita gasolina. You need gas.

Ask me if I need any gas. Do you need any gas?

Conteste que sí, brevemente. Yes, I do.

Necesito algo de gasolina. I need some gas.

Por favor, deme quince dólares en gasolina. Please give me fifteen dollars worth of gasoline.

Para decir "Quince dólares en gasolina" se dice "fifteen dollars worth of gasoline".

Repita "fifteen dollars worth of gas". Fifteen dollars worth of gas.

Tenemos un coche pequeño. We have a small car.

Pero nuestro coche es un Chevy grande. But our car is a big Chevy.

Tell me that you have a big car. I have a big car.

Now tell me you would like a small car because your Chevy uses too much gasoline.
I would like a small car because my Chevy uses too much gasoline.
Prefiero tener un coche pequeño. I prefer to have a small car.
Prefiero tener un coche más pequeño. I prefer to have a smaller car.
Ask me if I have a big family. Do you have a big family?
Conteste que sí, brevemente. Yes, I do.
Now ask me how many people there are in my family. How many people are there in your family?
Hay seis personas en nuestra familia. There are six people in our family.
Perdón. Excuse me.
¿Cuál es el camino a Treasure Island? Which is the road to Treasure Island?
¿Es este el camino a Treasure Island? Is this the road to Treasure Island?
Say the word "Este" in English. This.
¿Es este el camino? Is this the road?
¿Es este el camino a Treasure Island? Is this the road to Treasure Island?
Sí. Está todo derecho. Yes, it's straight ahead.
To say, "Está a la derecha" say "It's to the right". Repeat, "It's to the right". It's to the right.
Now just say, "to the right". To the right.
Está a la derecha. It's to the right.
A la derecha. To the right.
Está a la derecha. It's to the right.
Vaya a la derecha. Go to the right.
No está todo derecho. It's not straight ahead.
Vaya a la derecha. Go to the right.
How does one say "Usted quiere" in English? You want.
El camino que usted quiere. The road you want.
Está a la derecha. Is to the right.
El camino que usted quiere está a la derecha. The road you want is to the right.
¿A la derecha? To the right?
¿O todo derecho? Or straight ahead?
¿A la derecha o todo derecho? To the right or straight ahead?
Vaya todo derecho. Go straight ahead.
¿De verdad? Really?
Sí, de verdad. Yes, really.
Espere. Wait.
"A la izquierda" se dice, "To the left". Repeat, "To the left". To the left.

Say "A la izquierda" in English. To the left.
Vaya a la izquierda. Go to the left.
Espere. El camino que usted quiere está a la izquierda. Wait. The road you want is to the left.
¿A la izquierda? To the left?
Sí. El camino que usted quiere está a la izquierda. Yes. The road you want is to the left.
El camino que yo quiero. The road I want.
¿El camino que yo quiero está a la izquierda? Is the road I want to the left?
No, está todo derecho. No, its straight ahead.
No a la derecha. Not to the right.
Vaya a la izquierda. Go to the left.
Ese es el camino que usted quiere. That's the road you want.
Ask me if I'm sure. Are you sure?
Sí. Vaya a la derecha. Yes. Go to the right.
"Y luego" se dice "and then". Repita "and then". And then.
Vaya a la izquierda y luego. Go to the left and then.
Vaya a la izquierda y luego todo derecho. Go to the left and then straight ahead.
A la izquierda y luego todo derecho. To the right and then straight ahead.
Ese es el camino a Treasure Island. That's the road to Treasure Island.
¿Qué tan lejos está? How far is it?
Son setenta millas. It's seventy miles.
Son setenta millas a Treasure Island. It's seventy miles to Treasure Island.
Necesito algo de gasolina. I need some gas.
Por favor, deme veinte galones. Please give me twenty gallons.
¿Cuánto le debo? How much do I owe you?
Un dólar por galón. One dollar per gallon.
Eso es veinte dólares. That's twenty dollars.
Un dólar por galón. Eso es veinte dólares. One dollar per gallon. That's twenty dollars.
Aquí están veinte dólares. Here's twenty dollars.
¿Este es el camino a Treasure Island? Is this the road to Treasure Island?
El camino que usted quiere. The road you want.
Está a la derecha. Is to the right.
El camino que usted quiere está a la derecha. The road you want is to the right.
Luego, vaya a la izquierda. Then, go to the left.
Espere. No entiendo. Wait. I don't understand.
Say that you are sorry. I'm sorry.

Now tell me I speak too fast. You speak too fast.
Usted habla demasiado rápido para mí. You speak too fast for me.
Por favor repita. Please repeat.
Lo siento. Usted habla demasiado rápido para mí. I'm sorry. You speak too fast for me.
Por favor repita. Please repeat.
Por favor, no hable demasiado rápido. Please don't speak too fast.
Por favor, no hable tan rápido. Please don't speak so fast.
¿Cuál es el camino a Treasure Island? Which is the road to Treasure Island?
¿Es este el camino a Treasure Island? Is this the road to Treasure Island?
No, el camino que usted quiere. No, the road you want.
Está por allá. Is over there.
No, el camino que usted quiere está por allá. No, the road you want is over there.
Por favor, no hable tan rápido. Please don't speak so fast.
Lo siento. I'm sorry.
Vaya a la derecha. Go the right.
Luego, vaya a la izquierda. Then go to the left.
Y luego setenta millas todo derecho. And then seventy miles straight ahead.
No está lejos Treasure Island. Treasure Island isn't far.
¿Cuántas millas? How many miles?
¿Cuántas millas son? How many miles is it?
Son setenta y cinco millas. It's seventy five miles.
Necesito algo de gasolina. I need some gas.
¿La gasolina es cara? Is gas expensive?
No, cuesta un dólar por galón. No, it costs one dollar per gallon.
No, cuesta sólo un dólar por galón. No, costs only one dollar per gallon.
Y usted tiene un coche pequeño. And you have a small car.
Sí, yo prefiero tener un coche pequeño. Yes, I prefer to have a small car.
¿Y usted? And you?
Say that you prefer to have a small car too. I prefer to have a small car too.
Tell me that the gasoline is not expensive here. The gasoline is not expensive here.
Entonces me gustarían doce dólares de gasolina. Then I'd like twelve dollars worth of gas.
¿Pero cuál es el camino a Treasure Island? But which is the road to Treasure Island?
¿A la izquierda o a la derecha? To the left or to the right?
¿O todo derecho? Or straight ahead?
Tell me that you don't know. I don't know.

Y ahora. And now.
Adiós. Goodbye.

End of speaking/listening lesson. Continue with the reading for Lesson 28.

Reading for Lesson 28

See if your student can read the following conversation out loud by himself. If any word is mispronounced, have the student stop right away and see if he can figure out how to pronounce it correctly on his own. If he can´t, go ahead and pronounce the word for him.

Reading Practice.

Is gas expensive around here?

No. It's two dollars per gallon.

That´s not too bad.

No, it's not. And you have a small car.

Yeah, I prefer to have a smaller car. Big cars are too expensive.

I know. I have one, and it costs an arm and a leg to fill it.

You're right. It does.

So where are you from?

I'm from Ecuador. I'm in the United States for the month.

Oh really? *Are you working or just visiting (Estás trabajando o solo visitando)?*

I'm visiting my family.

Do you have a big family?

Eleven brothers and six sisters.

Wow. *That's enormous (Es enorme)!*

I know. And they are all grown up and they have children too.

Are they all in the United States?

Yes, they are all here in Calfornia. Some live in San Jose and the others live in Los Angeles. *How about you (Y de usted)?* Do you have a big family?

My family is small. I have a brother and sister. They don't have any children.

Well, I need to put gas in my car. I need fifteen dollars worth of gas, I think.

Okay. You can use pump fourteen.

Thanks.

You're welcome.

Have a nice day.

You too.

LEVEL 1: LESSON TWENTY 29

Teaching tips: Towards the end of this lesson, your student will learn to say the word "Women". It's very important that you teach him to pronounce it as if it were "wemen". (Both "e" sounds are short as in the word "men"). Otherwise he will pronounce the words "women" and "woman" exactly the same. So make sure he says it as if to say "wemen" when he says "women". Also, be sure that the student doesn't pronounce the "l" in "should".

Say "millas" in English. Miles.
Now ask, "¿Cuántas millas?" How many miles?
Ask me in English which is the road to Treasure Island. Which is the road to Treasure Island?
Now ask me how many miles to Los Angeles. How many miles to Los Angeles?
¿Es este el camino a Treasure Island? Is this the road to Treasure Island?
How does one ask, "¿Cuántas millas a San Francisco?" How many miles to San Francisco?
¿Es este el camino a San Francisco? Is this the road to San Francisco?
¿Cuál es el camino a San Francisco? Which is the road to San Francisco?
A la derecha. To the right.
Vaya a la derecha. Go to the right.
El camino que usted quiere. The road you want.
Está a la derecha. Is to the right.
Para decir "No puede perderlo" se dice "You can't miss it". Repita "You can't miss it". You can't miss it.
El camino que usted quiere está a la derecha. The road you want is to the right.
No puede perderlo. You can't miss it.
¿El camino que yo quiero está a la derecha? Is the road I want to the right?
¿O a la izquierda? Or to the left?
Vaya a la izquierda. Go to the left.

Luego a la derecha. Then to the right.
Y luego. And then.
Todo derecho. Straight ahead.
El camino está a la derecha. The road is to the right.
No puede perderlo. You can't miss it.
¿Qué tan lejos está? How far is it?
¿Qué tan lejos está San Francisco? How far is San Francisco?
Disculpe, ¿qué tan lejos a San Francisco? Excuse me, how far to San Francisco?
No está lejos. It's not far.
Son setenta millas. It's seventy miles.
Son ochenta millas. It's eighty miles.
Ese es el camino que usted quiere. That's the road you want.
Necesito algo de gasolina. I need some gas.
¿Cuánto cuesta? How much is it?
Un dólar por galón. One dollar per gallon.
Pero en Nueva York. But in New York.
La gasolina es más cara. Gas is more expensive.
Cuesta dos dólares por galón. It costs two dollars per gallon.
¿Dos dólares por galón? ¿En serio? Two dollars per gallon? Are you serious?
Sí, en serio. Yes, I'm serious.
"Con razón" se dice "No wonder". Repita, "No wonder". No wonder.
Say this in English, "Con razón usted". No wonder you.
Now say, "Con razón usted usa una bicicleta". No wonder you use a bicycle.
Sí, con razón uso una bicicleta. Yes, no wonder I use a bicycle.
"Debería" se dice "You should". Repita, "You should". You should.
Usted debería también. You should too.
Sí, yo debería también. Yes, I should too.
No puedo creer. I can't believe.
Tell me in English that you can't believe the price of gas here. I can't believe the price of gas here.
Now tell me that it costs an arm and a leg. It costs an arm an a leg.
"No puedo creerlo tampoco" se dice, "I can't believe it either". Repeat, "I can't believe it either". I can't believe it either.
Say in English, "Yo sé. No puedo creerlo tampoco." I know. I can't believe it either.
Con razón usted usa una bicicleta. No wonder you use a bicycle.
Sí, y usted debería usar una bicicleta también. Yes, and you should use a bicycle too.
Debería usar una bicicleta también. I should use a bicycle too.

To say "precio" use the word "price". Repeat, "price". Price.
Tell me you can't believe the price of gas here. I can't believe the price of gas here.
Con razón usted usa bicicleta. No wonder you use a bicycle.
Son dos dólares por galón. It's two dollars per gallon.
No puedo creer el precio. I can't believe the price.
Say "Yo puedo" in English. I can.
Now, in English say "¿Puedo?" like a question. Can I?
Ask in English, "¿Puedo comprar algo?" Can I buy something?
¿Puedo comprar algo en San Francisco? Can I buy something in San Francisco?
No, usted no puede. No, you can't.
¿Por qué no? Why not?
¿Por qué? Why?
¿Por qué no? Why not?
Repeat after me, "You can't because". You can't because.
Usted no puede porque. You can't because.
¿Por qué? Why?
¿Por qué no? Why not?
No puede porque no tiene suficiente dinero. You can't because you don't have enough money.
Y yo necesito algo de dinero también. And I need some money too.
Usted ya tiene dinero. You already have money.
Pero necesito más. But I need more.
¿Cuánto necesita? How much do you need?
¿Cuánto necesito? How much do I need?
Necesito ochenta dólares. I need eighty dollars.
¿Qué soy yo, un banco? What am I, a bank?
Usted ya tiene ochenta dólares. You already have eighty dollars.
"Store" quiere decir "tienda" en inglés. Repita "store". Store.
Now say "Las tiendas" in English. The stores.
La tienda. The store.
Para decir "tienda departamental" se dice "Department store". Diga "department store". Department store.
Say "Las tiendas" in English. The stores.
How does one say in English, "tienda departamental?" Department store.
Para decir "Las tiendas están cerradas" en inglés, diga "The stores are closed". Diga "The stores are closed". The stores are closed.
Las tiendas departamentales están cerradas. The department stores are closed.

¿Por qué? Why?
Repeat after me, "It's the Fourth of July". It's the Fourth of July.
Tell me the stores are closed because it's the Fourth of July. The stores are closed because it's the Fourth of July.
Remember that "cerrada" or "cerrado" means "closed" in English. Repeat, "closed". Closed.
Say in English, "Las tiendas están cerradas". The stores are closed.
Las tiendas están cerradas porque es el Cuatro de Julio. The stores are closed because it's the Fourth of July.
¿Están cerradas las tiendas? Are the stores closed?
Say, "No, they're open". No, they're open.
No, están abiertas. No, they're open.
Say "Estan abiertas" in English. They're open.
Abiertas. Open.
Cerradas. Closed.
Están cerradas ahora. They're closed now.
¿Están abiertas las tiendas departamentales? Are the department stores open?
Tell me the department stores are open now. The department stores are open now.
Las tiendas más pequeñas están cerradas. The smaller stores are closed.
¿Qué hora es? What time is it?
No tengo ninguna idea. I have no idea.
Yo sé. I know.
Yo sé que hora es. I know what time it is.
Son las nueve. It's nine o'clock.
¿Están abiertas las tiendas? Are the stores open?
No, están cerradas. No, they're closed.
"Early" quiere decir "temprano". Repita, "early". Early.
¿Tan temprano? So early?
¿Por qué? Why?
Porque. Because.
Porque es tarde. Because it's late.
No es tarde. It's not late.
Es muy tarde. Son las once. It's very late. It's eleven o'clock.
No es tarde. It's not late.
Las once es tarde. Eleven o'clock is late.
No es tarde. It's not late.
Pero las tiendas están cerradas. But the stores are closed.

Estan cerradas por el cuatro de Julio. They're closed for the Fourth of July.
Tell me that San Francisco is far. San Francisco is far.
Ochenta y cinco millas. Eighty five miles.
Ochenta y cinco millas, pero las tiendas están cerradas. Eighty five miles, but the stores are closed.
Tell me you want to buy something. I want to buy something.
Mi esposo quiere comprar algo. My husband wants to buy something.
Mi esposo quiere comprar algo mañana. My husband wants to buy something tomorrow.
Él necesita algo de dinero. He needs some money.
Ask me what time it is. What time is it?
Now ask me if it is late. Is it late?
Son las diez. It's ten o'clock.
¿Por qué? Why?
¿Por qué pregunta? Why do you ask?
Porque mi esposa quiere comprar algo. Because my wife wants to buy something.
Ella quiere comprar algo. She wants to buy something.
Mi esposa quiere. My wife wants.
Mi esposa quiere comprar algo. My wife wants to buy something.
Ella quiere comprar algo. She wants to buy something.
¿Dónde? Where?
En una tienda departamental. In a department store.
¿Estan abiertas las tiendas? Are the stores open?
Las tiendas pequeñas están cerradas. The small stores are closed.
Las tiendas más grandes están abiertas. The bigger stores are open.
Las tiendas departamentales están abiertas ahora. The department stores are open now.
Están abiertas ahora. They're open now.
Están abiertas esta noche. They're open tonight.
Están abiertas tarde esta noche. They're open late tonight.
¿Y mañana? And tomorrow?
Mañana están cerradas. Tomorrow they're closed.
Mañana están cerradas por el cuatro de Julio. Tomorrow they're closed for the Fourth of July.
¿Dónde están las tiendas departamentales? Where are the department stores?
Están en la Avenida Parque. They're on Park Avenue.
Vaya a la izquiera. Go to the left.

Y luego, todo derecho. And then straight ahead.
Mi esposa quiere comprar algo. My wife wants to buy something.
En una tienda departamental. In a department store.
¿Qué quiere comprar ella? What does she want to buy?
Algo para nuestro niño pequeño. Something for our little boy.
Ask me if I have enough money. Do you have enough money?
Tell me in English that you have eighty dollars. I have eighty dollars.
Pero eso no es suficiente. But that's not enough.
Sí es. Yes it is.
San Francisco es caro. San Francisco is expensive.
Y mi esposa. And my wife.
Mi esposa necesita mucho dinero. My wife needs a lot of money.
Nueva York es caro. New York is expensive.
Y mi esposa necesita mucho dinero. And my wife needs a lot of money.
Para decir "Mujeres son", se dice "Women are". Repita, "Women are". Women are.
Say "Usted sabe" in English. You know.
Now say "Usted sabe como". You know how.
How do you say "Mujeres son" in English? Women are.
Para decir, "Usted sabe como son las mujeres", diga "You know how women are". You know how women are.
"Men" quiere decir "hombres" en inglés. Cómo cree que se dice "Hombres son" en inglés? Men are.
How does one say, "Usted sabe como son las mujeres"? You know how women are.
Ahora diga, "Usted sabe como son los hombres". You know how men are.
Diga, "Mi esposa necesita mucho dinero". My wife needs a lot of money.
Usted sabe como son las mujeres. You know how women are.
Ahora diga, "Mi esposo necesita mucho dinero". My husband needs a lot of money.
Usted sabe como son los hombres. You know how men are.
Usted sabe como son las mujeres. You know how women are.
"People" quiere decir "gente". Repita, "People". People.
Now say, "Usted sabe cómo es la gente". You know how people are.

End of speaking/listening lesson. Continue with the reading for Lesson 29.

Reading for Lesson 29

Have the student attempt reading the conversation below, taking care to pause slightly at the commas and to use proper intonation on the questions. Correct any mistakes as before.

Reading Practice

I can't believe (No puedo creer) the price of gas around here. It costs an arm and a leg just *to fill up the tank (llenar el tanque)* of my car.
Yeah, California is expensive.
Everything costs too much around here.
It's not just in California (No es solo en California). Everything is expensive *everywhere (en todos lugares).*
I am from Oregon and everything is expensive there too.
You're right (Tiene razón). The price of everything is expensive, especially the gas.
I know. The price per gallon is ridiculous. No wonder you use a bicycle.
Yes. It is cheaper.
I should buy one too.
I use a bicycle when I go *somewhere in town (algún lugar en el pueblo),* but I still need to use my car sometimes.
Do you know if the departments stores are still open?
Yeah. They close in two hours.
Are they open tomorrow?
No, because it's the Fourth of July.
Oh, that's right. *I forgot (se me olvidó).*
I can take you to the store if you'd like. My wife wants to buy something for tomorrow.
Okay. At what time?
Well we need to go soon if we want to get there *before the stores close (antes de que cierren las tiendas).*
How about in ten minutes? I need to get some money.
All right. I'll see you in ten minutes.
Okay.

LEVEL 1: LESSON 30

Teaching tip: Watch to see if your student drops the final "s" sound in words like "stores" or "needs" If they do, have them stop and resay the word.

How does one say "Ellas quieren" in English. They want.
Now say in English, "Ellas quieren comprar todo". They want to buy everything.
Do you remember how to say in English, "Usted sabe como es la gente". You know how people are.
Usted sabe como es la gente. Ellos quieren comprar todo. You know how people are. They want to buy everything.
Sí, yo sé. Yes, I know.
Son sólo las ocho. It´s only eight o'clock.
Tell me "good morning" in English. Good morning.
Ask me in English how I am. How are you?
Now tell me "good morning" in English and ask me how I am. Good morning, how are you?
Answer in English, "Bien gracias, ¿y usted?" Fine thanks, and you?
¿Cómo está su esposa? How is your wife?
Ella está bien también. She's fine too.
Ella está bien también, gracias. She's fine too, thanks.
¿Y usted, señorita? ¿Cómo está? And you, miss? How are you?
¿Y cómo está usted, señorita? And how are you miss?
No muy bien. Not very well.
¿No muy bien? ¿ Por qué no? Not very well? Why not?
Porque me gustaría comprar algo. Because I'd like to buy something.
Y no puedo. And I can't.
¿Usted no puede? ¿Por qué no? You can't? Why not?
Porque las tiendas están cerradas. Because the stores are closed.
¿De verdad? Really?

Sí, están cerradas. Yes, they're closed.
Es tarde. It's late.
Es porque. It's because.
Es porque es tarde. It's because it's late.
Es demasiado tarde. It's too late.
Pero están abiertas mañana. But they're open tomorrow.
Usted puede comprar algo mañana. You can buy something tomorrow.
En una tienda departamental. In a department store.
¿Qué quiere comprar? What do you want to buy?
Mi esposo quiere comprar algo. My husband wants to buy something.
Para nuestra niña pequeña. For our little girl.
Entonces, vaya a la tienda departamental. Then go to the department store.
En la Avenida Parque. On Park Avenue.
Mañana las tiendas están abiertas. Tomorrow the stores are open.
Ask me where Park Avenue is. Where is Park Avenue?
Do you remember how to say, "Está por allá"? It's over there.
Vaya a la derecha. Go to the right.
Siga derecho. Continue straight ahead.
Por una milla. For a mile.
Entonces a la izquierda. Then to the left.
No se lo puede perder. You can't miss it.
Mi esposo necesita algo de dinero. My husband needs some money.
Tell me that you need some money too. I need some money too.
Porque voy a Washington D. C. Because I'm going to Washington, D.C.
¿Usted va a Washington? You're going to Washington.
"Fin de semana" se dice "weekend" en inglés. Repita, "weekend". Weekend.
Sí, voy allí este fin de semana. Yes, I'm going there this weekend.
Tell me you're going to Washington D.C. this weekend. I'm going to Washington D.C. this weekend.
Tell me you're going over there this weekend. I'm going over there this weekend.
¿Qué va a hacer allí? What are you going to do there?
¿Perdón? Excuse me?
¿Qué va a hacer allí? What are you going to do there?
¿Qué voy a hacer allí? What am I going to do there?
Voy a ver algunos amigos. I'm going to see some friends.
Voy a ver algunos amigos en Washington D.C. I'm going to see some friends in Washington D.C.

En inglés, "Unos amigos" se dice "A few friends". Repita, "A few friends". A few friends.
¿Cómo se dice "Unos amigos" en inglés? A few friends.
Voy a ver a unos amigos. I'm going to see a few friends.
Tengo unos amigos allí. I have a few friends there.
In English, "to work" means "trabajar". Repeat, "to work". To work.
Y voy a trabajar. And I'm going to work.
Tengo unos amigos allí y voy a trabajar. I have a few friends there and I'm going to work.
¿Va a trabajar? Are you going to work?
Un poco. A little.
Voy a ver unos amigos. I'm going to see a few friends.
In English, "Do I know them?" means "¿Los conozco?" Repeat, "Do I know them?" Do I know them?
Say in English, "¿Unos amigos? Los conozco yo?" A few friends? Do I know them?
Answer in English, "No, usted no los conoce". No, you don't know them.
How does one say, "fin de semana" in English"? Weekend.
Voy a ver a unos amigos en Washington D.C. este fin de semana. I'm going to see a few friends in Washington D.C. this weekend.
¿En Washington? ¿Los conozco yo? In Washington? Do I know them?
No, usted no los conoce. No, you don't know them.
Mis amigos. My friends.
Algunos amigos. Some friends.
Yo voy a ver a mis amigos. I'm going to see my friends.
Y voy a trabajar. And I'm going to work.
Voy a trabajar un poco. I'm going to work a little.
Y voy a ver a unos amigos. And I'm going to see a few friends.
"Tal vez" se dice "Maybe" en inglés. Repita, "Maybe". Maybe.
Ask me in English if I am going to work. Are you going to work?
Say "Tal vez" in English. Maybe.
Sí, creo que sí. Yes, I think so.
Creo que sí. I think so.
Creo que no. I don't think so.
¿Va a ver a Leo? Are you going to see Leo?
Creo que no. I don't think so.
Tal vez. Maybe.
¿Leo trabaja en Washington? Does Leo work in Washington?

¿Leo trabaja en Washington, D. C.? Does Leo work in Washington, D.C.?
Creo que sí. I think so.
No sé. I don't know.
¿Va a ver a Leo? Are you going to see Leo?
Creo que no. I don't think so.
Tal vez. Maybe.
¿Trabaja Leo en Washington? Does Leo work in Washington?
No. Él trabaja en Nueva York. No. He works in New York.
Creo que trabaja en Nueva York. I think he works in New York.
Él vive en Nueva York. He lives in New York.
Creo que vive en Nueva York. I think he lives in New York.
Entonces, ¿va usted a ver a Charles? Then are you going to see Charles?
Él está allí también. He is there too.
Yo creo que sí. I think so.
Voy a ver a Charles. I'm going to see Charles.
Si él trabaja en Washington, D. C. If he works in Washington, D. C.
Pero voy a trabajar también. But I'm going to work too.
Y ver a unos amigos. And to see a few friends.
Voy a ver a unos amigos. I'm going to see a few friends.
Por favor, deme. Please give me.
Unos dólares. A few dollars.
¿Qué soy yo, un banco?" What am I, a bank?
Por favor deme unos dólares. Please give me a few dollars.
Porque necesito tomar un taxi. Because I need to take a taxi.
¿Qué soy yo, un banco? What am I, a bank?
Claro. Sure.
To say "Aeropuerto" in English, say "Airport". Repeat, "Airport". Airport.
How does one say "aeropuerto" in English? Airport.
Now say, "Al aeropuerto". To the airport.
Voy al aeropuerto. I'm going to the airport.
Necesito tomar un taxi al aeropuerto. I need to take a taxi to the airport.
Tell me you're going to Washington, D.C. I'm going to Washington, D. C.
Cortésmente pídame unos dólares para un taxi. Please give me a few dollars for a taxi.
Say that you need to take a taxi to the airport. I need to take a taxi to the airport.
Voy a Washington, D.C. Mi amiga María vive allí. I'm going to Washington, D.C. My friend Mary lives there.

Ella trabaja allí. She works there.
¿Qué tan lejos está Washington, D.C.? How far is Washington D.C.?
Ochenta millas. Eighty miles.
¿Va usted hoy? Are you going today?
No sé. Tal vez. I don't know. Maybe.
Creo que no. I don't think so.
Pero me gustaría ver Washington. But I'd like to see Washington.
Y tengo amigos allí. And I have friends there.
Para decir "Necesito pedir indicaciones" diga en inglés, "I need to ask for directions" Repeat, I need to ask for directions." I need to ask for directions.
¿Por qué? Why?
Tell me you need to ask for directions. I need to ask for directions.
"I´m lost" quiere decir "Me he perdido" en inglés. Literalmente dice "Estoy perdido", pero así es como se dice "Me he perdido". Repita, "I'm lost". I'm lost.
Tell me in English that you're lost. I'm lost.
Now say in English, "Creo que me he perdido". I think I'm lost.
How does one ask, "¿Se ha perdido?" Are you lost?
Tal vez. Maybe.
Sí, me he perdido. Yes, I'm lost.
Diga en inglés, "Necesito pedir indicaciones." I need to ask for directions.
Repita en partes: I need to. I need to.
Ask for directions. Ask for directions.
Repita, "I need to ask for directions". I need to ask for directions.
¿Se ha perdido? Are you lost?
Creo que sí. Necesito pedir indicaciones. I think so. I need to ask for directions.
¿Por qué? Why?
Creo que me he perdido. Necesito pedir indicaciones. I think I'm lost. I need to ask for directions.

End of speaking/listening lesson. Continue with the reading for Lesson 30.

Reading for Lesson 30

Read the following sentences out loud with your student. Next, have your student read them out loud to you by his or herself.

Reading Practice

Excuse me.

How are you doing?

Fine, thanks.

How may I help you (Cómo puedo ayudarle)?

I am not from around here (No soy de por aquí). I think I'm lost.

Where do you want to go (A dónde quiere ir)?

I want to find (Quiero encontrar) Highway 20 North.

Oh, *that's easy (es fácil)*. Go straight for about four miles and turn right on Garden Avenue. Then turn left on First Street. You will see the Highway 20 exit on the right.

Okay so I go straight for about four miles and then I turn left on Garden Avenue.

No, no no. You need to turn left on Garden Avenue.

Oh, right. Sorry. I go straight for about four miles then I turn left on Garden Avenue.

That's it.

After this I turn left on First Street and I will see Highway 20 on the right?

You got it.

Great! I have been driving around for nearly an hour *(Llevo casi una hora conduciendo)* and getting nowhere *(y sin llegar a ninguna parte)*.

It can be confusing (Puede ser confuso).

So I noticed (Así lo noté). Well, thank you.

No problem. *Drive safely (Maneje con seguridad)*.

I will.

LEVEL 1: LESSON 31

Watch for the student's tendency to pronounce "New York" as "New Jork". Make sure the student pronounces "bookstore" with the jawline dropping slightly, so the "oo" sounds like the "oo" in "crook" not the "oo" in "boo".

"Voy a parar" se dice "I'm going to stop". Repita, "I'm going to stop". I'm going to stop.
Say in English, "Voy a parar aquí". I'm going to stop here.
Voy a parar el coche. I'm going to stop the car.
¿Usted se va a parar? You're going to stop?
Sí. Voy a parar aquí. Yes. I'm going to stop here.
¿Por qué? Why?
Necesito pedir indicaciones. I need to ask for directions.
Tell me you're lost. You need to ask for directions. I'm lost. I need to ask for directions.
Say, "Buenas noches, señor" in English. Good evening, sir.
Buenas noches. Good evening.
Voy a parar aquí. I'm going to stop here.
¿Es este el camino a Washington, D.C.? Is this the road to Washington, D.C.?
"A la derecha" se dice "To the right" en inglés. Repita, "To the right". To the right.
Voy a parar aquí. I'm going to stop here.
¿Cómo se dice "A la derecha" en inglés? To the right.
Ahora diga, "No, el camino que usted quiere está a la derecha". No, the road you want is to the right.
¿Es este el camino a Washington, D.C.? Is this the road to Washington, D.C.?
No, el camino que usted quiere está a la derecha. No, the road you want is to the right.
¿A la derecha? To the right?
Sí, a la derecha. Yes, to the right.

Para decir "A la izquierda", diga, "To the left". Repita, "To the left". To the left.
"Vaya a la izquierda" se dice "Go to the left". Repita, "Go to the left". Go to the left.
Ask in English, "¿A la izquierda?" To the left?
Now answer in English, "Sí. Vaya a la izquierda". Yes. Go to the left.
No puede perderlo. You can't miss it.
El camino que usted quiere está a la derecha. The road you want is to the right.
¿A la izquierda? To the left?
No, vaya a la derecha y entonces a la izquierda. No, go to the right and then to the left.
Vaya a la derecha allí. Go to the right there.
Y entonces vaya a la izquierda en la Avenida Lincoln. And then go the left on Lincoln Avenue.
Say in English, "Vaya a la derecha allí en la Calle Primera". Go to the right there on First Street.
Now say in English, "Vaya a la derecha allí en la Calle Primera y entonces vaya a la izquierda en la Avenida Lincoln". Go to the right there on First Street and then go to the left on Lincoln Avenue.
How does one say, "Vaya a la izquierda y entonces todo derecho"? Go to the left and then straight ahead.
Siga derecho. Go straight ahead.
"Traffic light" es como se dice "Semáforo" en inglés. Repita, "Traffic light". Traffic light.
Say "Semáforo" in English. Traffic light.
Now say in English, "Siga derecho por tres semáforos". Continue straight ahead for three traffic lights.
Siga derecho por dos semáforos. Continue straight ahead for two traffic lights.
Ask me if the department stores are open now. Are the department stores open now?
No, es tarde. Creo que las tiendas departamentales están cerradas. No, it's late. I think the department stores are closed.
No es tarde. It's not late.
Son las once. Sí es tarde. It's eleven o'clock. It is late.
Yo no creo. I don't think so.
¿Usted no cree? You don't think so?
Es muy tarde. It's very late.
Yo no creo. I don't think so.
¿Usted no cree? ¿De dónde es usted? You don't think so? Where are you from?
Soy de Nueva York. I'm from New York.
Con razón. No wonder.

Usted cree que no es tarde. You think it isn't late.
Con razón usted cree que no es tarde. No wonder you think it isn't late.
En Nueva York nunca es tarde. In New York it is never late.
Nunca es tarde allí. It's never late there.
Tell me that I'm right. You're right.
Tell me that you agree. I agree.
Nunca es tarde en Nueva York. It's never late in New York.
Nunca es tarde allí. It's never late there.
Pero es tarde aquí. But it's late here.
Y creo que las tiendas están cerradas. And I think the stores are closed.
Las tiendas aquí están cerradas. The stores here are closed.
Perdón, señorita. Excuse me, miss.
¿Es este el camino a Los Ángeles? Is this the road to Los Angeles?
Para decir "Al lado", diga "Next to". Repita, "Next to". Next to.
Usa las palabras "Over there" para decir "Allá". Repita, "Over there". Over there.
Say "Mi esposa está por allá" in English. My wife is over there.
¿Dónde? Where?
Allá. Over there.
Allá, al lado de la niña. Over there, next to the girl.
Mi esposo está por allá. My husband is over there.
¿Dónde? Where?
Allá, al lado del niño. Over there, next to the boy.
¿Es este el camino a Los Angeles? Is this the road to Los Angeles?
El camino que usted quiere está todo derecho. The road you want is straight ahead.
Al lado de la tienda de libros. Next to the book store.
El camino que usted quiere está todo derecho, al lado de la tienda de libros. The road you want is straight ahead, next to the book store.
¿Al lado de la tienda de libros? Next to the book store?
Sí, no puede perderlo. Yes, you can't miss it.
Siga derecho, y entonces a la izquierda. Continue straight ahead, then to the left.
Say "Millas" in English. Miles.
Ask in English, "¿Cuántas millas?" How many miles?
¿Cuál es el camino a Los Ángeles? Which is the road to Los Angeles?
¿Es este el camino a Los Ángeles? Is this the road to Los Angeles?
¿Qué tan lejos está Los Ángeles? How far is Los Angeles?
Tell me you need some. I need some gas.
"Por aquí" se dice "Around here". Repita, "Around here". Around here.

¿Cuánto cuesta por aquí? How much is it around here?

Un dólar por galón. One dollar per gallon.

"Es una broma?" se dice "Is this a joke?" en inglés. Repita "Is this a joke? Is this a joke?

¿Un dólar por galón? Es una broma? One dollar per gallon? Is this a joke?

No es broma. It's no joke.

¿Cuánto cuesta? How much is it?

Un dólar por galón. One dollar per gallon.

Pero en Nueva York. But in New York.

La gasolina es más cara. Gas is more expensive.

Pero en Nueva York la gasolina es más cara. But in New York gas is more expensive.

Tell me that the gas is more expensive around here. The gas is more expensive around here.

Cuesta dos dólares por galón. It's two dollars per gallon.

¿Dos dólares por galón? Two dollars per gallon?

Eso es nada. That's nothing.

En California cuesta cinco dólares por galón. In California it's five dollars per gallon.

¿Cinco dólares por gallon? ¡Qué ridículo! Five dollars per gallon? How ridiculous!

Eso todavía no es nada. That's still nothing.

¿Eso todavía no es nada? That's still nothing?

Sí. En Miami son seis dólares por galón. Yes. In Miami it's six dollars per gallon.

¿Cuánto por tres galones? How much for three gallons?

tres dólares. Three dollars.

¿tres dólares? ¿Es una broma? Three dollars? Is this a joke?

No es broma. Son tres dólares. It's no joke. It's three dollars.

Mañana voy a comprarme una bicicleta. Tomorrow I'm going to buy myself a bicycle.

Yo también. Me too.

Hoy voy a comprarme una bicicleta. Today I'm going to buy myself a bicycle.

Yo puedo. I can.

¿Puedo? Can I?

¿Puedo comprar algo? Can I buy something?

¿Puedo comprar algo en Nueva York? Can I buy something in New York?

No, no puede. No, you can't.

¿Por qué no? Why not?

Porque. Because.

Porque usted necesita el dinero. Because you need the money.

Para esta noche. For tonight.
Porque usted necesita el dinero para esta noche. Because you need the money for tonight.
Porque yo necesito. Because I need.
Porque necesito el dinero para esta noche. Because I need the money for tonight.
Tell me that you need eighty dollars. I need eighty dollars.
Y las tiendas están cerradas. And the stores are closed.
¿Usted necesita ochenta dólares? ¿Por qué? You need eighty dollars? Why?
"Tío" se dice "Uncle" en inglés. Repita, "Uncle". Uncle.
Ese es mi tío. That's my uncle.
¿Dónde? Where?
Allí, al lado de mi esposa. There, next to my wife.
Necesito comprar algo para mi tío. I need to buy something for my uncle.
¿Dónde está su tío? Where is your uncle?
Allí, al lado de las dos mujeres. There, next to the two women.
¿Dónde? Where?
Allí, al lado de las dos mujeres. There, next to the two women.

End of speaking/listening lesson. Continue with the reading for Lesson 31.

Reading for Lesson 31

Read the following sentences out loud with your student. Next, have your student read them out loud to you by his or herself.

<u>Reading Practice</u>

I tell you (Yo te digo), my girls are *having a great time (se están divirtiendo).*
They are? I'm glad.
Yes, they are having fun going to all the stores here in Sacramento.
You should tell them (Debes decirles) to go the Capitol Mall on the west side. There are a lot of great department stores there.
No thanks. *They've spent enough money already (Han gastado suficiente dinero ya).*
Relax *(Tranquilo).* Take it easy. They don't come to Washington all the time.
I know but *shopping (ir de compras)* is what they do all the time .
Fine. Maybe you could take them out to dinner. There are a lot of good restaurants at the Riverwalk.
The Riverwalk? Where is that?
Do you know where the book store is?
Is that the store close to the park?
Yes. *That's the one (Esa es).*
I know where that is.
Well, pass the store and turn right on Washington Street.
Okay.
Then turn left on Riverwalk Parkway.
That's it. You'll see a lot of good restaurants on Riverwalk Parkway.
Thanks. I think I'll take my daughters out to dinner there tonight.
Good. So now *you can be the one who will spend a lot of money (puedes ser tú el que va a gastar mucho dinero).*

LEVEL 1: LESSON 32 (LESSONS 27 – 31 REVIEW)

Note: This is an extra long review lesson. It is recommended you break this up in the sections as seen in this lesson. In this way, this long lesson is completed over a period of 3 – 4 days. Of course you can take more than one section per day, depending on how well the student has mastered the material. With each section, review a Reading Practice from the past that was more challenging for the student. When you get to the final section, do the Reading Practice at the end.

<u>Section One</u>

Ask this in English, "¿Cuántos hijos tiene usted, Sr. Martinez?" How many children do you have, Mr. Martinez?

Dos. Mi esposa y yo tenemos dos hijos, un niño pequeño y una niña pequeña. Two. My wife and I have two children, a little boy and a little girl.

How does one say "coche" in English? Car.

Nuestro coche. Our car.

En nuestra familia. In our family.

¿Cuántas personas hay? How many people are there?

¿En su familia? In your family?

¿Cuántas personas hay en su familia? How many people are there in your family?

Cinco personas. Five people.

Hay cinco personas en nuestra familia. There are five people in our family.

Tenemos tres hijos. We have three children.

Un niño y dos niñas. One boy and two girls.

Tenemos tres hijos, un niño y dos niñas. We have three children, one boy and two girls.

Las niñas están aquí en los Estados Unidos. The girls are here in the United States.

Con nosotros. With us.

Las niñas están aquí en los Estados Unidos con nosotros. The girls are here in the United States with us.

Nuestro niño pequeño está en Mexico. Our little boy is in Mexico.
¿De verdad? Really?
Sí, de verdad. Yes, really.
Remember that "Abuela" means "grandmother" in English. Repeat, "Grandmother". Grandmother.
Now say in English, "Él está con su abuela". He's with his grandmother.
Please say in English, "Él está con su tío." He's with his uncle.
Nuestro niño pequeño está con su abuela en México. Our little boy is with his grandmother in Mexico.
Nuestro niño pequeño está con su tío en México. Our little boy is with his uncle in Mexico.
¿Está en México? He's in Mexico?
¿Con quién? With whom?
Con su abuela. With his grandmother.
Con su tío. With his uncle.
Con su abuela y su tío. With his grandmother and his uncle.
Nuestra familia es grande. Our family is big.
Tenemos una familia grande. We have a big family.
No tenemos una familia grande. We don´t have a big family.
Hay tres personas en nuestra familia. There are three people in our family.
Tenemos una familia pequeña. We have a small family.
Una familia pequeña. A small family.
Tenemos una familia pequeña. We have a small family.
Tenemos un coche pequeño. We have a small car.
Tenemos una familia pequeña y un coche pequeño. We have a small family and a small car.
Ask me where the bathroom is. Where is the bathroom?
Está por allá. It's over there.
"That makes sense" significa "Eso tiene sentido" en inglés. Repita, "That makes sense". That makes sense.
Try to say, "Eso no tiene sentido" in English. That doesn't make sense.
Ask in English, "¿Cómo se dice esta palabra en inglés?" How do you say this word in English?
Ask me in English, "¿Cómo se dice gasolina en inglés?" How do you say gasolina in English?
Say in English, "Diez galones, por favor". Ten gallons please.
Es suficiente. It's enough.

Para cuarenta millas. For forty miles.
¿Es suficiente? Is that enough?
Espere. Wait.
Tell me you'd like thirty gallons. I'd like thirty gallons.
Veinte dólares en gasolina, por favor. Twenty dollars worth of gas, please.
Mi coche es demasiado grande. My car is too big.
Ask me if I have a big car. Do you have a big car?
Conteste que sí, brevemente. Yes, I do.
Quiero un coche pequeño. I want a small car.
Now tell me you want a smaller car. I want a smaller car.
El que tengo yo usa demasiado gasolina. The one I have uses too much gas.
Eso tiene sentido. That makes sense.
El que tengo yo. The one I have.
El que tengo yo usa demasiado gasolina. The one I have uses too much gas.
Quiero un coche más pequeño. I want a smaller car.
¿Un coche más pequeño? ¿Por qué? A smaller car? Why?
El que tengo yo usa demasiado gasolina. The one I have uses too much gas.
Me gustaría tener un coche más pequeño. I'd like to have a smaller car.
¿Un coche más pequeño? ¿Por qué? A smaller car? Why?
El que tengo yo usa demasiado gasolina. The one I have uses too much gas.
Quiero un coche más chico. I want a smaller car.
Más caro. More expensive.
Quiero un coche más pequeño. I want a smaller car.
¿Tiene usted suficiente gasolina? Do you have enough gas?
Por favor, deme dieciséis dólares de gasolina. Please, give me sixteen dollars worth of gas.
Espere. Wait.
Deme quince dólares de gasolina. Give me fifteen dollars worth of gas.
¿A dónde va usted, señorita? Where are you going, miss?
Voy a Treasure Island. I'm going to Treasure Island.
Voy a Treasure Island mañana. I'm going to Treasure Island tomorrow.
¿Cuántas millas? How many miles?
¿Cuántas millas son de aquí a Treasure Island? How many miles is it from here to Treasure Island?
¿Cuántas millas son? How many miles is it?
Está lejos. It's far.
Cómo se dice. How do you say.

¿Cómo se dice esta palabra? How do you say this word?
Está lejos. It's far.
¿Quéda lejos Treasure Island? Is Treasure Island far?
Yo no sé. I don't know.
Setenta millas. Seventy miles.
Diez y siete millas. Seventeen miles.
How does one say, "Setenta y tres" in English? Seventy three.
Now how does one say, "Setenta y cinco". Seventy five
Está a setenta y un millas. It's seventy one miles.
No, setenta y dos. No, seventy two.
Espere. Wait.
Usted habla demasiado rápido. You speak too fast.
Say "Setenta y cuatro" in English. Seventy four.
Sesenta y cuatro. Sixty four.
Está lejos. It's far.
Está lejos Treasure Island. Treasure Island is far.
Está lejos. It's far.
¿Tiene usted suficiente gasolina? Do you have enough gas?
Diga que sí, brevemente. Yes, I do.
Yo tengo un coche pequeño. I have a small car.
Quiero un coche más grande. I want a bigger car.
Quiero un coche más caro. I want a more expensive car.
How does one say "camino" in English? Road.
El camino. The road.
El camino a Treasure Island. The road to Treasure Island.
¿Cuál es el camino a Treasure Island? Which is the road to Treasure Island?
Perdón, ¿cuál es el camino a Treasure Island? Excuse me, which is the road to Treasure Island?
¿Treasure Island? Está lejos. Treasure Island? It's far.
¿Cuántas millas? How many miles?
¿Cuántas millas son de aquí a Treasure Island? How many miles is it from here to Treasure Island?
Setenta y cinco. Seventy five.
Son setenta y cinco millas. It's seventy five miles.
¿Cuál es el camino a Treasure Island? Which is the road to Treasure Island?
Tome el camino Figueroa. Take Figueroa Road.
Está todo derecho. It's straight ahead.

Tome el camino Figueroa por setenta y cinco millas. Take Figueroa Road for seventy miles.
Tome el camino Figueroa. Take Figueroa Road.
Está todo derecho. It's straight ahead.
Espere. Wait.
Ese no es el camino a Treasure Island. That's not the road to Treasure Island.
El camino a Treasure Island. The road to Treasure Island.
Está por allá. Is over there.
El camino a Treasure Island está por allá. The road to Treasure Island is over there.
¿Todo derecho? Straight ahead?
Sí, todo derecho. Yes, straight ahead.
¿Cuánta gasolina quiere? How much gas do you want?
Por favor deme dieciséis dólares de gasolina. Please give me sixteen dollars worth of gasoline.
Gracias. Thank you.
De nada. You're welcome.
Espere. Wait.
¿Quéda lejos Treasure Island? Is Treasure Island far?
No, no está lejos. No, it's not far.
No está lejos Treasure Island. Treasure Island isn't far.
Setenta y ocho millas. Seventy eight miles.
Son setenta y ocho millas a Treasure Island. It's seventy eight miles to Treasure Island.
¿Es este el camino a Treasure Island? Is the road to Treasure Island?
¿Es este el camino? Is this the road?
¿Es este el camino a Treasure Island? Is this the road to Treasure Island?
Perdón, ¿es este el camino a Treasure Island? Excuse me, is this the road to Treasure Island?
¿Cuál es el camino a Treasure Island? Which is the road to Treasure Island?
El camino a Treasure Island. The road to Treasure Island.
Está todo derecho. Is straight ahead.
Ask me if I have enough gas. Do you have enough gas?
Tengo mucha gasolina. I have a lot of gas.
Tengo un coche pequeño. I have a small car.
Me gustaría un coche más grande. I'd like a bigger car.
Pero no está lejos Treasure Island. But Treasure Island isn't far.
Buenos días, señora. Good morning, ma'am.

¿Cuánta gasolina quiere? How much gas do you want?
Quince dólares de gasolina, por favor. Fifteen dollars worth of gas, please.
Ask in English, "¿Cuál es el camino a Treasure Island?" Which is the road to Treasure Island?
¿Es este el camino a Treasure Island? Is this the road to Treasure Island?
Sí, sí es. Yes it is.
Treasure Island está todo derecho. Treasure Island is straight ahead.
¿Cuántas millas son de aquí a Treasure Island? How many miles is it from here to Treasure Island?
No está tan lejos. It's not that far.
Sesenta o setenta millas. Sixty or seventy miles.
Solo sesenta o setenta millas. Only sixty or seventy miles.
Do you remember how to say in English, "Usted tiene una familia grande". You have a big family.
Say in English, "Si, hay siete personas en nuestra familia". Yes, there are seven people in our family.
Adiós, señor. Goodbye, sir.
Remember that "La gasolina es cara" in English is "The gasoline is expensive".
Repeat "The gasoline is expensive". The gasoline is expensive.
Es cara. It's expensive.
¿Qué es cara? What is expensive?
La gasolina. The gasolina.
La gasolina es cara. The gasoline is expensive.
¿Es cara? Is it expensive?
Ask if the gasoline is expensive. Is the gasoline expensive?
¿Es muy cara la gasolina en los Estados Unidos? Is gas very expensive in the United States?
No, no es muy cara. No, it's not very expensive.
"Es carísima" se dice "it's extremely expensive". Repita, "It's extremely expensive." It's extremely expensive.
La gasolina es carísima aquí. The gasoline is extremely expensive here.
La gasolina es muy cara en los Estados Unidos. The gasolina is very expensive in the United States.
Para decir "Es mejor caminar" en inglés, diga "It's better to walk". Repita "It's better to walk." It's better to walk.
La gasolina es cara. Es mejor caminar. Gas is expensive. It's better to walk.
Ask in English, "¿Es mejor caminar?" Is it better to walk?

Answer in English, "Sí. Es mejor caminar si es posible." Yes. It's better to walk if it's possible.

Es mejor caminar si es posible. It's better to walk if it's possible.

"To use a bicicycle" means "usar una bicicleta" in English. Repeat, "to use a bicycle". To use a bicycle.

Repita, "To use". To use.

Ahora repita, "A bicycle". A bicycle.

Diga, "To use a bicycle." To use a bicycle.

How do you say "Usar una bicicleta" in English? To use a bicycle.

Now say in English, "Es mejor caminar o usar una bicicleta". It's better to walk or use a bicycle.

Tell me in English that you like to walk. I like to walk.

Now tell me that you use a bicycle. I use a bicycle.

Es mejor caminar si es posible. It's better to walk if possible.

o usar una bicicleta. Or use a bicycle.

How does one say in English, "La gasolina es cara en los Estados Unidos". The gas is expensive in the United States.

Now say in English, "La gasolina es carísima en los Estados Unidos". The gas is extremely expensive in the United States.

En inglés la palabra "prefiero" se dice "I prefer". Repita "I prefer". I prefer.

Prefiero caminar. I prefer to walk.

Prefiero caminar si es posible. I prefer to walk if it's possible.

Me gustaría comprar una bicicleta. I would like to buy a bicycle.

¿Una bicicleta? ¿Por qué? A bicycle? Why?

Quiero comprar una bicicleta porque la gasolina es cara aquí. I want to buy a bicycle because the gasoline is expensive here.

¿Son caras las bicicletas en los Estados Unidos? Are bicycles expensive in the United States?

No son muy caras. They're not very expensive.

¿Son caras? Are they expensive?

No, no son muy caras. No, they're not very expensive.

Tell me you would like to buy a bicycle. I would like to buy a bicycle.

Now ask me if the gas is expensive in Mexico. Is gas expensive in Mexico?

No, no es muy cara. No, it's not very expensive.

Soy mexicano. Vivo en Guadalajara. I'm Mexican. I live in Guadalajara.

Section Two

Tell me in English that you have an old Chevy. I have an old Chevy.
Tengo un coche, un Chevy viejo. I have a car, an old Chevy.
Tengo un coche pequeño. I have a small car.
Me gustaría un coche más grande. I would like a bigger car.
Me gustaría un coche más grande, como su Chevy. I would like a bigger car, like your Chevy.
Para decir "Prefiero tener" se dice "I prefer to have". Repita "I prefer to have". I prefer to have.
Prefiero tener un coche pequeño. I prefer to have a small car.
Prefiero tener un coche pequeño si es posible. I prefer to have a small car if it's possible.
Voy a los Estados Unidos con mi familia. I'm going to the United States with my family.
¿Cuántas personas hay en su familia? How many people are there in your family?
Hay tres personas en nuestra familia. There are three people in our family.
Tenemos una familia pequeña. We have a small family.
Nuestra familia es más grande. Our family is bigger.
Hay cinco personas en nuestra familia. There are five people in our family.
Ask me if gasoline is expensive in the United States. Is gasoline expensive in the United States?
Un dólar por galón. One dollar per gallon.
Ask me how many gallons do I want. How many gallons do you want?
Quiero veinte galones. I want twenty gallons.
Espere. Wait.
Eso es demasiado. That's too much.
Aquí es más caro. Here it's more expensive.
Dos dólares por galón. Two dollars per gallon.
"That's nothing" means "No es nada" in English. Repeat "That's nothing". That's nothing.
¿Dos dólares por galón? No es nada. Two dollars per gallon? That's nothing.
Son cinco dólares por galón donde vivo yo. It's five dollars per gallon where I live.
No es nada. That's nothing.
Tell me it's five dollars per gallon where you live. It's five dollars per gallon where I live.
Ask in English, "¿Son cinco dólares por galón donde vive usted? It's five dollars per gallon where you live?
¿En serio? Are you serious?

Sí. Yes.

Es mejor caminar, entonces. It's better to walk, then.

Puede decir eso otra vez. You can say that again.

¿Queda lejos Treasure Island? Is Treasure Island far?

Para preguntar "¿Qué tan lejos está?" se dice en inglés, "How far is it?" Repita "How far is it?" How far is it?

¿Queda lejos Treasure Island? Is Treasure Island far?

¿Qué tan lejos está? How far is it?

No muy lejos. Not very far.

No está lejos. It's not far.

¿Cuál es el camino a Treasure Island? Which is the road to Treasure Island?

El camino a Treasure Island. The road to Treasure Island.

Todo derecho. Straight ahead.

Está todo derecho. It's straight ahead.

Lejos. Far.

Todo derecho. Straight ahead.

¿Qué tan lejos está? How far is it?

Setenta millas. Seventy miles.

No, setenta y cinco millas. No, seventy five miles.

Tell me you want some gas. I want some gas.

Now tell me I need some gas. I need some gas.

Usted necesita algo de gasolina. You need some gas.

Necesito algo de gasolina. I need some gas.

Usted necesita gasolina. You need gas.

Ask me if I need gas. Do you need gas?

Conteste que sí, brevemente. Yes, I do.

Necesito algo de gasolina. I need some gas.

Por favor, deme quince dólares de gasolina. Please give me fifteen dollars worth of gas.

Para decir "Quince dólares de gasolina" se dice "fifteen dollars worth of gas".

Repita "fifteen dollars worth of gas". Fifteen dollars worth of gas.

Tenemos un coche pequeño. We have a small car.

Pero nuestro coche es un Chevy grande. But our car is a big Chevy.

Tengo un coche grande. I have a big car.

Me gustaría un coche pequeño porque mi Chevy usa demasiado gasolina. I would like a small car because my Chevy uses too much gasoline.

Prefiero tener un coche pequeño. I prefer to have a small car.

Prefiero tener un coche más pequeño. I prefer to have a smaller car.
Eso tiene sentido. That makes sense.
Ask me if I have a big family. Do you have a big family?
Conteste que sí, brevemente. Yes, I do.
¿Cuántas personas hay en su familia? How many people are there in your family?
Hay seis personas en nuestra familia. There are six people in our family.
Perdón. Excuse me.
¿Cuál es el camino a Treasure Island? Which is the road to Treasure Island?
¿Es este el camino a Treasure Island? Is this the road to Treasure Island?
Este. This.
¿Es este el camino? Is this the road?
¿Es este el camino a Treasure Island? Is this the road to Treasure Island?
Sí. Está todo derecho. Yes, it's straight ahead.
Está a la derecha. It's to the right.
A la derecha. To the right.
Está a la derecha. It's to the right.
Vaya a la derecha. Go to the right.
No está todo derecho. It's not straight ahead.
Vaya a la derecha. Go to the right.
Usted quiere. You want.
El camino que usted quiere. The road you want.
Está a la derecha. Is to the right.
El camino que usted quiere está a la derecha. The road you want is to the right.
¿A la derecha? To the right?
¿O todo derecho? Or straight ahead?
¿A la derecha o todo derecho? To the right or straight ahead?
Tell me to go straight ahead. Go straight ahead.
¿De verdad? Really?
Sí, de verdad. Yes, really.
Espere. Wait.
A la izquierda. To the left.
Now tell me to go to the left. Go to the left.
Espere. El camino que usted quiere está a la izquierda. Wait. The road you want is to the left.
¿A la izquierda? To the left?
Sí. El camino que usted quiere está a la izquierda. Yes. The road you want is to the left.

El camino que yo quiero. The road I want.
¿El camino que yo quiero está a la izquierda? Is the road I want to the left?
No, está todo derecho. No, it's straight ahead.
No a la izquiereda. Not to the left.
Vaya a la izquierda. Go to the left.
Ese es el camino que usted quiere. That's the road you want.
Vaya a la derecha. Go to the right.
Vaya a la izquierda. Go to the left.
To say "y luego" say "and then". Repeat, "and then". And then.
Vaya a la izquierda y luego. Go to the left and then.
Tell me to go to the left and then straight ahead. Go to the left and then straight ahead.
¿A la izquierda y luego todo derecho? To the right and then straight ahead.
Ese es el camino a Treasure Island. That's the road to Treasure Island.
Ask me how far it is. How far is it?
Son setenta millas. It's seventy miles.
Son setenta millas a Treasure Island. It's seventy miles to Treasure Island.
How do you say that you need some gas? I need some gas.
Por favor, deme veinte galones. Please give me twenty gallons.
¿Cuánto le debo? How much do I owe you?
Un dólar por galón. One dollar per gallon.
Eso es veinte dólares. That's twenty dollars.
Un dólar por galón. Eso es veinte dólares. One dollar per gallon. That's twenty dollars.
Aquí están veinte dólares. Here's twenty dollars.
Ask me if this is the road to Treasure Island. Is this the road to Treasure Island?
El camino que usted quiere. The road you want.
Está a la derecha. Is to the right.
Tell me that the road I want is to the right. The road you want is to the right.
Luego, vaya a la izquierda. Then, go to the left.
Espere. No entiendo. Wait. I don't understand.
Tell me that you are sorry. I'm sorry.
Usted habla demasiado rápido. You speak too fast.
Usted habla demasiado rápido para mí. You speak too fast for me.
Por favor repita. Please repeat.
Usted habla demasiado rápido para mí. You speak too fast for me.
Por favor repita. Please repeat.
Si usted quiere. If you want.

Por favor, no hable demasiado rápido. Please don't speak too fast.
Por favor, no hable tan rápido. Please don't speak so fast.
¿Cuál es el camino a Treasure Island? Which is the road to Treasure Island?
¿Es este el camino a Treasure Island? Is this the road to Treasure Island?
No, el camino que usted quiere. No, the road you want.
Está por allá. Is over there.
No, el camino que usted quiere está por allá. No, the road you want is over there.
Por favor, no hable tan rápido. Please don't speak so fast.
Lo siento. I'm sorry.
Vaya a la derecha. Go the right.
Luego, vaya a la izquierda. Then go to the left.
Y luego setenta millas todo derecho. And then seventy miles straight ahead.
No está lejos Treasure Island. Treasure Island isn't far.
¿Cuántas millas? How many miles?
¿Cuántas millas son? How many miles is it?
Son setenta y cinco millas. It's seventy five miles.
Necesito algo de gasolina. I need some gas.
Ask me if gas is expensive. Is gas expensive?
No, cuesta un dólar por galón. No, it's one dollar per gallon.
No, cuesta solo un dólar por galón. No, it's only one dollar per gallon.
Y usted tiene un coche pequeño. And you have a small car.
Sí, yo prefiero tener un coche pequeño. Yes, I prefer to have a small car.
¿Y usted? And you?
Tell me that you prefer to have a small car too. I prefer to have a small car too.
La gasolina no es cara aquí. The gasolina is not expensive here.
Entonces me gustarían doce dólares en gasolina. Then I'd like twelve dollars worth of gas.
¿Pero cuál es el camino a Treasure Island? But which is the road to Treasure Island?
¿A la izquierda o a la derecha? To the left or to the right?
¿O todo derecho? Or straight ahead?
No sé. I don't know.
Y ahora. And now.
Adiós Señor. Goodbye, sir.
Say "millas" in English. Miles.
Now ask, "¿Cuántas millas?" How many miles?
¿Cuál es el camino a Treasure Island? Which is the road to Treasure Island?
¿Cuántas millas a Los Ángeles? How many miles to Los Angeles?

¿Es este el camino a Treasure Island? Is this the road to Treasure Island?
En inglés "Nueva York" se dice "New York". Diga "New York". New York.
¿Cuántas millas a Nueva York? How many miles to New York?
Ask me if this is the road to New York. Is this the road to New York?
Now ask me which is the road to New York. Which is the road to New York?
A la derecha. To the right.
Say, "Vaya a la derecha" in English. Go to the right.
El camino que usted quiere. The road you want.
Está a la derecha. Is to the right.
Say "No puede perderlo" in English. You can't miss it.
¿El camino que yo quiero está a la derecha? Is the road I want to the right?
¿O a la izquierda? Or to the left?
Vaya a la izquierda. Go to the left.
Luego a la derecha. Then to the right.
Y luego. And then.
Todo derecho. Straight ahead.
El camino está a la derecha. The road is to the right.
No puede perderlo. You can't miss it.
¿Qué tan lejos está? How far is it?
¿Qué tan lejos está Nueva York? How far to New York?
Disculpe, ¿Qué tan lejos a Nueva York? Excuse me, how far to New York?
No está lejos. It's not far.
Son setenta millas. It's seventy miles.
Son ochenta millas. It's eighty miles.
Say in English, "Ese es el camino que usted quiere". That's the road you want.
Tell me you need some gas. I need some gas.
¿Cuánto cuesta? How much is it?
Un dólar por galón. One dollar per gallon.
Pero en Nueva York. But in New York.
La gasolina es más cara. Gas is more expensive.
Cuesta dos dólares por galón. It costs two dollars per gallon.
¿Dos dólares por galón? ¿En serio? Two dollars per gallon? Are you serious?
Sí, en serio. Yes, I'm serious.
Con razón. No wonder.
Con razón usted. No wonder you.
Con razón usted usa una bicicleta. No wonder you use a bicycle.
Sí, con razón uso una bicicleta. Yes, no wonder I use a bicycle.

¿How does one say, "Usted debería" in English? You should.
Usted debería también. You should too.
Sí, yo debería también. Yes, I should too.
No puedo creer. I can't believe.
Tell me in English that you can't believe the price of gas here. I can't believe the price of gas here.
How does one say in English, "Yo sé. No puedo creerlo tampoco". I know. I can't believe it either.
Con razón usted usa una bicicleta. No wonder you use a bicycle.
Sí, y usted debería usar una bicicleta también. Yes, and you should use a bicycle too.
Yo debería usar una bicicleta también. I should use a bicycle too.
No puedo creer el precio de gasolina aquí. I can't believe the price of gas here.
Con razón usted usa bicicleta. No wonder you use a bicycle.
Son dos dólares por galón. It's two dollars per gallon.
Say "Puedo" in English. I can.
¿Puedo? Can I?
¿Puedo comprar algo? Can I buy something?
¿Puedo comprar algo en Nueva York? Can I buy something in New York?
No, usted no puede. No, you can't.
¿Por qué no? Why not?
¿Por qué? Why?
¿Por qué no? Why not?
Porque. Because.
Usted no puede porque. You can't because.
¿Por que? Why?
¿Por qué no? Why not?
Porque no tiene suficiente dinero. Because you don´t have enough money.
Y yo necesito algo de dinero también. And I need some money too.
Usted ya tiene dinero. You already have money.
Pero necesito más. But I need more.
¿Cuánto necesita? How much do you need?
¿Cuánto necesito? How much do I need?
Tell me in English that you need eighty dollars. I need eighty dollars.
Usted ya tiene ochenta dólares. You already have eighty dollars.
"Store" quiere decir "tienda" en inglés. Repita "store". Store.
Now say "Las tiendas" in English. The stores.

Section Three

How does one say in English, "La tienda"? The store.
Para decir "tienda departamental" se dice "department store". Diga "department store". Department store.
Las tiendas. The stores.
Para decir "Las tiendas están cerradas" se dice "The stores are closed". Diga "The stores are closed". The stores are closed.
Now tell me that the department stores are closed. The department stores are closed.
¿Por qué? Why?
Porque es el cuatro de Julio. Because it's the Fourth of July.
Las tiendas están cerradas. The stores are closed.
Las tiendas están cerradas porque es el cuatro de Julio. The stores are closed because it's the Fourth of July.
Ask if the stores are closed. Are the stores closed?
No, están abiertas. No, they're open.
Están abiertas. They're open.
Abiertas. Open.
Cerradas. Closed.
Están cerradas ahora. They're closed now.
¿Están abiertas las tiendas departamentales? Are the department stores open?
Tell me that the department stores are open now. The department stores are open now.
Las tiendas más pequeñas están cerradas. The smaller stores are closed.
¿Qué hora es? What time is it?
No tengo ninguna idea. I have no idea.
Yo sé. I know.
Yo sé que hora es. I know what time it is.
Son las nueve. It's nine o´clock.
¿Están abiertas las tiendas? Are the stores open?
No, están cerradas. No, they're closed.
¿Tan temprano? So early?
¿Por qué? Why?
Porque. Because.
Porque es tarde. Because it's late.
No es tarde. It's not late.
"¿De qué esta hablando?" se dice, "What are you talking about?" Repeat, "What are you talking about?" What are you talking about?

Es muy tarde. Son las once. It's very late. It's eleven o'clock.
No es tarde. It's not late.
Las once es tarde. Eleven o'clock is late.
¿De qué está hablando? No es tarde. What are you talking about? It's not late.
Pero las tiendas están cerradas. But the stores are closed.
Estan cerradas por el cuatro de Julio. They're closed for the Fourth of July.
Está lejos Nueva York. New York is far.
Ochenta y cinco millas. Eighty five miles.
Ochenta y cinco millas, pero las tiendas están cerradas. Eighty five miles, but the stores are closed.
Tell me that you want to buy something. I want to buy something.
Mi esposo quiere comprar algo. My husband wants to buy something.
Mi esposo quiere comprar algo mañana. My husband wants to buy something tomorrow.
Él necesita algo de dinero. He needs some money.
Ask me what time it is. What time is it?
¿Es tarde? Is it late?
Son las diez. It's ten o'clock.
Ask in English, "¿Por qué?" Why?
Now ask in English, "¿Por qué pregunta?" Why do you ask?
Answer in English, "Porque mi esposa quiere comprar algo". Because my wife wants to buy something.
Ella quiere comprar algo. She wants to buy something.
Mi esposa quiere. My wife wants.
Mi esposa quiere comprar algo. My wife wants to buy something.
Ella quiere comprar algo. She wants to buy something.
¿Dónde? Where?
En una tienda departamental. In a department store.
Ask me if the stores are open. Are the stores open?
Las tiendas pequeñas están cerradas. The small stores are closed.
Las tiendas más grandes están abiertas. The bigger stores are open.
Las tiendas departamentales están abiertas ahora. The department stores are open now.
Están abiertas ahora. They're open now.
Están abiertas esta noche. They're open tonight.
Están abiertas tarde esta noche. They're open late tonight.
¿Y mañana? And tomorrow?

Mañana están cerradas. Tomorrow they're closed.
Mañana están cerradas por el cuatro de Julio. Tomorrow they're closed for the Fourth of July.
Ask me where the department stores are. Where are the department stores?
Están en la Avenida Parque. They're on Park Avenue.
Vaya a la izquiera. Go to the left.
Y luego, todo derecho. And then straight ahead.
Mi esposa quiere comprar algo. My wife wants to buy something.
En una tienda departamental. In a department store.
¿Qué quiere comprar ella? What does she want to buy?
Algo para nuestro niño pequeño. Something for our little boy.
Ask me if I have enough money. Do you have enough money?
Tengo ochenta dólares. I have eighty dollars.
Pero eso no es suficiente. But that's not enough.
Nueva York es caro. New York is expensive.
Y mi esposa. And my wife.
Mi esposa necesita mucho dinero. My wife needs a lot of money.
Nueva York es caro. New York is expensive.
Y mi esposa necesita mucho dinero. And my wife needs a lot of money.
Mujeres son. Women are.
Usted sabe. You know.
Usted sabe como. You know how.
Usted sabe como son las mujeres. You know how women are.
Mi esposa necesita mucho dinero. My wife needs a lot of money.
Usted sabe como son las mujeres. You know how women are.
Usted sabe como son los hombres. You know how men are.
Ellas quieren. They want.
Ellas quieren comprar todo. They want to buy everything.
Usted sabe como son las niñas. You know how girls are.
Usted sabe como son las niñas. Ellas quieren comprar todo. You know how girls are. They want to buy everything.
Sí, yo sé. Yes, I know.
Do you remember how to say, "Son solo las ocho" in English? It's only eight o´clock.
Buenos días, ¿cómo está? Good morning, how are you?
Bien gracias, ¿y usted? Fine thanks, and you?
¿Cómo está su esposa? How is your wife?
Ella está bien también. She's fine too.

Ella está bien también, gracias. She's fine too, thanks.
¿Y usted, señorita? ¿Cómo está? And you, miss? How are you?
¿Y cómo está usted, señorita? And how are you miss?
No muy bien. Not very well.
¿No muy bien? ¿Por qué? Not very well? Why?
Porque me gustaría comprar algo. Because I'd like to buy something.
Y no puedo. And I can't.
¿Por qué no? Why not?
How does one ask, "¿Por qué no puede?" in English? Why can't you?
Porque las tiendas están cerradas. Because the stores are closed.
¿De verdad? Really?
Sí, están cerradas. Yes, they're closed.
Es tarde. It's late.
Es porque. It's because.
Es porque es tarde. It's because it's late.
Es demasiado tarde. It's too late.
Pero están abiertas mañana. But they're open tomorrow.
Usted puede comprar algo mañana. You can buy something tomorrow.
En una tienda departamental. In a department store.
Ask me what I want to buy. What do you want to buy?
Mi esposo quiere comprar algo. My husband wants to buy something.
Para nuestra niña pequeña. For our little girl.
Entonces, vaya a la tienda departamental. Then go to the department store.
En la Avenida Parque. On Park Avenue.
Mañana las tiendas están abiertas. Tomorrow the stores are open.
Ask me where Park Avenue is. Where is Park Avenue?
Está por allá. It's over there.
Vaya a la derecha. Go to the right.
Siga derecho. Continue straight ahead.
Por una milla. For a mile.
Entonces a la izquierda. Then to the left.
Tell me that I can't miss it. You can't miss it.
Mi esposo necesita algo de dinero. My husband needs some money.
Tell me that you need some money too. I need some money too.
Porque voy a Washington D. C. Because I'm going to Washington, D.C.
Usted va a Washington. You're going to Washington.
Say that yes, you are going there this weekend. Yes, I'm going there this weekend.

Voy a Washington D.C. este fin de semana. I'm going to Washington D.C. this weekend.

Voy por allá este fin de semana. I'm going over there this weekend.

¿Qué va a hacer allí? What are you going to do there?

¿Perdón? Excuse me?

¿Qué va a hacer allí? What are you going to do there?

¿Qué voy a hacer allí? What am I going to do there?

Tell that you're going to see some friends. I'm going to see some friends.

Voy a ver a algunos amigos. I'm going to see some friends.

¿Cómo se dice "algunos amigos" en inglés? Some friends.

Voy a ver a algunos amigos en Washington D.C. I'm going to see some friends in Washington D.C.

"Unos amigos" se dice "A few friends". Repita, "A few friends". A few friends.

¿Cómo se dice "Unos amigos" en inglés? A few friends.

Ahora diga, "Voy a ver a unos amigos." I'm going to see a few friends.

Tengo unos amigos allí. I have a few friends there.

Y voy a trabajar. And I'm going to work.

Tengo unos amigos allí y voy a trabajar. I have a few friends there and I'm going to work.

Ask me if I'm going to work. Are you going to work?

Un poco. A little.

Voy a ver a unos amigos. I'm going to see a few friends.

¿Unos amigos? ¿Los conozco? A few friends? Do I know them?

No, usted no los conoce. No, you don't know them.

Voy a ver a unos amigos en Washington D.C. este fin de semana. I'm going to see a few friends in Washington D.C. this weekend.

¿En Washington? ¿Los conozco? In Washington? Do I know them?

No, usted no los conoce. No, you don't know them.

Say "Mis amigos" in English. My friends.

How does one say "Algunos amigos" in English? Some friends.

Tell me that you're going to see your friends. I'm going to see my friends.

Y voy a trabajar. And I'm going to work.

Voy a trabajar un poco. I'm going to work a little.

Y voy a ver a unos amigos. And I'm going to see a few friends.

Tal vez. Maybe.

¿Va usted a trabajar? Are you going to work?

Tal vez. Maybe.

Sí, creo que sí. Yes, I think so.
Creo que sí. I think so.
Creo que no. I don't think so.
¿Va a ver a Leo? Are you going to see Leo?
Creo que no. I don't think so.
Tal vez. Maybe.
Ask if Leo works in Washington. Does Leo work in Washington?
¿Leo trabaja en Washington, D. C.? Does Leo work in Washington, D.C.?
Creo que sí. I think so.
No sé. I don't know.
Ask me if I'm going to see Leo. Are you going to see Leo?
Creo que no. I don't think so.
Tal vez. Maybe.
¿Trabaja Leo en Washington? Does Leo work in Washington?
No. Él trabaja en Nueva York. No. He works in New York.
Creo que trabaja en Nueva York. I think he works in New York.
Tell me that he lives in New York. He lives in New York.
Creo que vive en Nueva York. I think he lives in New York.
¿Entonces, va usted a ver a Charles? Then are you going to see Charles?
Él está allí también. He is there too.
Yo creo que sí. I think so.
Voy a ver a Charles. I'm going to see Charles.
Si el trabaja en Washington, D. C. If he works in Washington, D. C.
Pero voy a trabajar también. But I'm going to work too.
Y ver a unos amigos. And to see a few friends.
Voy a ver a unos amigos. I'm going to see a few friends.
Por favor, deme. Please give me.
Unos dólares. A few dollars.
Por favor deme unos dólares. Please give me a few dollars.
Porque necesito tomar un taxi. Because I need to take a taxi.
Necesito tomar un taxi al aeropuerto. I need to take a taxi to the airport.
Voy a Washington, D.C. I'm going to Washington, D. C.
Por favor deme unos dólares para un taxi. Please give me a few dollars for a taxi.
Necesito tomar un taxi al aeropuerto. I need to take a taxi to the airport.
Diga en inglés, "Voy a Washington, D.C. Mi amiga María vive allí". I'm going to Washington, D.C. My friend Mary lives there.
Ella trabaja allí. She works there.

¿Qué tan lejos está Washington, D.C.? How far is Washington D.C.?
Ochenta millas. Eighty miles.
¿Va usted hoy? Are you going today?
No sé. Tal vez. I don't know. Maybe.
Creo que no. I don't think so.
Pero me gustaría ver Washington. But I'd like to see Washington.
Y tengo amigos allí. And I have friends there.
Necesito pedir indicaciones. I need to ask for directions.
¿Por qué? Why?
Creo que me perdí. I think I'm lost.
¿Usted está perdido? You're lost?
Creo que sí. Necesito pedir indicaciones. I think so. I need to ask for directions.
Voy a parar aquí. I'm going to stop here.
¿Por qué? Why?
Necesito pedir indicaciones. I need to ask for directions.
Me perdí. Necesito pedir indicaciones. I'm lost. I need to ask for directions.
Buenas noches, señor. Good evening, sir.
Buenas noches. Good evening.
¿Es este el camino a Washington, D.C.? Is this the road to Washington, D.C.?
No, el camino que usted quiere está a la derecha. No, the road you want is to the right.
¿A la izquierda? To the left?
No, vaya a la derecha y entonces a la izquierda. No, go to the right and then to the left.
Vaya a la derecha allí. Go to the right there.
Y entonces vaya a la izquierda en la Avenida Lincoln. And then go the left on Lincoln Avenue.
Vaya a la derecha allí en la Calle Primera y entonces vaya a la izquierda en la Avenida Lincoln. Go to the right there on First Street and then go to the left on Lincoln Avenue.
Vaya a la izquierda y entonces todo derecho. Go to the left and then straight ahead.

End of speaking/listening lesson. Continue with the reading for Lesson 32.

Reading for Lesson 32

Read the following sentences and phrases with your student, emphasizing the "th" sound in "birthday" and "withdraw". Remember, Spanish speakers tend to make this a "t" sound. When you are done, have the student read all the sentences and phrases out loud by herself. Correct any pronounciation you need to.

Reading Practice

What's wrong? (¿Qué le pasa?) You look upset (Se ve molesto).
I need to buy something for my uncle and the stores are closed.
Why do you need to buy something for your uncle?
It's his *birthday (cumpleaños)* tomorrow.
Oh really? I didn't know that.
Yes, well I want to buy him a birthday *present (regalo).*
Well Super Mart is open 24 hours. You can buy him something there.
Oh, that's right. I forgot about that.
You can find something good there. And it's not too expensive there.
Well I don't want to buy my uncle anything too cheap.
Right.
I think I'll go to the bank and *withdraw (sacar de la cuenta)* eighty dollars.
Eighty dollars? That is a lot of money for a birthday present.
Well I need the money for a book I want at the bookstore.
How much does the book cost?
About fifteen dollars. It's about how to speak English better.
How about if I go with you? I can help you *choose (escoger)* the present.
Would you like to have something to eat after?
Yes, there is a great pizza *place (lugar, sitio)* next to the bookstore.
Okay, we'll have some pizza after you buy your uncle's present and your book.

LEVEL 1: LESSON 33

Teaching Tip: This lesson can be titled the "th" pronounciation lesson because of the plethora of words containing th. Let the student know that you are going to stress correct pronunciation of this consonant blend. He will be introduced to the word "together" as well as continuing to practice the use of words like "think", "anything" and "either". Make sure he doesn't say pronounce these words like "togeder", "anyting" or "eider".

Say, "Siga derecho" in English. Go straight ahead.

Siga derecho por tres semáforos. Continue straight ahead for three traffic lights.

Siga derecho por dos semáforos. Continue straight ahead for two traffic lights.

Ask me in English if the department stores are open now. Are the department stores open now?

Repeat, "Are the department stores open now? Are the department stores open now?

No. Es tarde. Creo que las tiendas departamentales están cerradas". No. It's late. I think the department stores are closed.

No es tarde. It's not late.

Son las once. Sí es tarde. It's eleven o'clock. It is late.

Yo no creo. I don't think so.

¿De dónde es usted? Where are you from?

Soy de Nueva York. I'm from New York.

Con razón. No wonder.

Usted cree que no es tarde. You think it isn't late.

Con razón usted cree que no es tarde. No wonder you think it isn't late.

"Nunca" se dice "never" en inglés. Repita, "never". Never.

Repeat, "In New York it is never late". In New York it is never late.

En Nueva York nunca es tarde. In New York it is never late.

Nunca es tarde allí. It's never late there.

Tiene razón. You're right.

Nunca es tarde en Nueva York. It's never late in New York.

Nunca es tarde allí. It's never late there.
Pero es tarde aquí. But it's late here.
Y creo que las tiendas están cerradas. And I think the stores are closed.
Las tiendas aquí están cerradas. The stores here are closed.
Perdón, señorita. Excuse me, miss.
¿Es este el camino a Los Ángeles? Is this the road to Los Angeles?
El camino que usted quiere está todo derecho, al lado de la tienda de libros. The road you want is straight ahead, next to the book store.
¿Al lado de la tienda de libros? Next to the book store?
Sí, no puede perderlo. Yes, you can't miss it.
Siga derecho, y entonces a la izquierda. Continue straight ahead, then to the left.
How does one say "millas" in English? Miles.
Now ask "¿Cuántas millas?" How many miles?
¿Cuál es el camino a Los Ángeles? Which is the road to Los Angeles?
¿Es este el camino a Los Ángeles? Is this the road to Los Angeles?
¿Qué tan lejos está Los Ángeles? How far is Los Angeles?
Tell me that you need some gas. I need some gas.
"Por aquí" quiere decir "Around here". Repita, "Around here". Around here.
¿Cuánto cuesta por aquí? How much is it around here?
Un dólar por galón. One dollar per gallon.
"¿Es una broma?" se dice "Is this a joke?" en inglés. Repita "Is this a joke? Is this a joke?
¿Un dólar por galón? ¿Es un broma? One dollar per gallon? Is this a joke?
No es broma. It's no joke.
¿Cuánto cuesta? How much is it?
Un dólar por galón. One dollar per gallon.
Pero en Nueva York. But in New York.
La gasolina es más cara. Gas is more expensive.
Pero en Nueva York la gasolina es más cara. But in New York gas is more expensive.
Cuesta dos dólares por galón. It costs two dollars per gallon.
¿Dos dólares por galón? Two dollars per gallon?
Eso es nada. That's nothing.
En California cuesta cinco dólares por galón. In California it costs five dollars per gallon.
¿Cinco dólares por galón? ¡Qué ridículo! Five dollars per gallon? How ridiculous!
Eso todavía es nada. That's still nothing.
¿Eso todavía es nada? That's still nothing?

Sí. En Miami son seis dólares por galón. Yes. In Miami it's six dollars per gallon.
¿Cuánto por tres galones? How much for three gallons?
tres dólares. Three dollars.
¿tres dólares? ¿Es una broma? Three dollars? Is this a joke?
No es broma. Son tres dólares. It's not a joke. It's three dollars.
Tell me that tomorrow you're going to buy yourself a bicycle. Tomorrow I'm going to buy myself a bicycle.
Yo también. Me too.
Hoy voy a comprarme una bicicleta. Today I'm going to buy myself a bicycle.
Yo puedo. I can.
¿Puedo? Can I?
¿Puedo comprar algo? Can I buy something?
¿Puedo comprar algo en Nueva York? Can I buy something in New York?
No, no puede. No, you can't.
¿Por qué no? Why not?
Porque. Because.
Porque usted necesita el dinero. Because you need the money.
Para esta noche. For tonight.
Porque usted necesita el dinero para esta noche. Because you need the money for tonight.
Porque yo necesito. Because I need.
Necesito ochenta dólares. I need eighty dollars.
¿Usted necesita ochenta dólares? ¿Por qué? You need eighty dollars? Why?
Necesito comprar algo para mi tío. I need to buy something for my uncle.
Y las tiendas están cerradas. And the stores are closed.
Para decir en inglés, "Lo que necesito hacer" se dice "What I need to do". Repita "What I need to do". What I need to do.
¿Cómo se dice en inglés, "Lo que necesito hacer"? What I need to do.
Lo que necesito hacer es. What I need to do is.
Lo que necesito hacer es comprar. What I need to do is buy.
How does one say in English, "Lo que necesito hacer es comprarme una bicicleta"? What I need to do is buy myself a bicycle.
Necesito comprarme una bicicleta. I need to buy myself a bicycle.
¿Qué necesita? What do you need?
Yo necesito una bicicleta. I need a bicycle.
¿Qué necesita comprar? What do you need to buy?
Necesito comprarme una bicicleta. I need to buy myself a bicycle.

Hola, ¿cómo está? Hi, how are you?
Bien, gracias, ¿y usted? Fine thanks, and you?
En inglés, "Diga" se dice "Tell me". Repita, "Tell me". Tell me.
Ask in English, "Diga, ¿Cuándo va a Washington?" Tell me, when are you going to Washington?
Voy mañana por la noche. I'm going tomorrow night.
Do you remember how to say "Buenos días" in English? Good morning.
¿Cómo está? How are you?
Estoy bien. I'm fine.
¿Y usted? And you?
¿Cómo le va? How's it going?
Todo bien, gracias. It's going well, thanks.
Ask me in English if the stores are open. Are the stores open?
Now, in English tell me that they are closed. They're closed.
¿Por qué? Why?
Porque es tarde. Because it's late.
No es tarde. It's not late.
Say that it's eleven thirty. It's eleven thirty.
Sí es tarde. It is late.
Yo no creo. I don't think so.
Usted no cree. ¿De dónde es usted? You don't think so. Where are you from?
Soy de Miami. I'm from Miami.
Con razón usted no cree que es tarde. No wonder you don't think it's late.
Nunca es tarde en Miami. It's never late in Miami.
¿Va a trabajar? Are you going to work?
No creo. I don't think so.
Usted cree. You think.
Usted cree que no. You don't think so.
Yo no creo. I don't think so.
Yo voy a Nueva York. I'm going to New York.
Tal vez. Maybe.
Voy a Boston. I'm going to Boston.
Yo creo que voy a Boston. I think I'm going to Boston.
¿Qué va hacer allí? What are you going to do there?
Voy a ver algunos amigos. I'm going to see some friends.
Unos amigos. A few friends.
Tell me that you have a few friends there. I have a few friends there.

Now tell me that you are going to see your friends. I'm going to see my friends.
Y voy a trabajar. And I'm going to work.
How does one say "Tal vez o Puede ser" in English? Maybe.
Ochenta. Eighty.
Ochenta y cinco. Eighty five.
Noventa. Ninety.
Noventa y cinco. Ninety five.
Noventa y dos. Ninety two.
Noventa y nueve. Ninety nine.
Ochenta y nueve. Eighty nine.
¿Cuánto le debo? How much do I owe you?
Noventa dólares. Ninety dollars.
Aquí están cien dólares. Here are one hundred dollars.
¿Cuántos? How many?
Cien. One hundred.
Cien dólares. One hundred dollars.
Ciento cincuenta dólares. One hundred fifty dollars.
Ciento ochenta. One hundred eighty.
Ciento noventa. One hundred ninety.
Es demasiado. It's too much.
Ciento setenta. One hundred seventy.
Ciento sesenta y cinco. One hundred sixty five.
Ciento cuarenta y siete. One hundred forty seven.
¿Cuánto le debo? How much do I owe you?
Usted no me debe nada. You don't owe me anything.
Cien dólares. One hundred dollars.
Noventa dólares. Ninety dollars.
Tell me that I don't owe you anything. You don't owe me anything.
¿Por qué no? Why not?
¿Por qué? Why?
Porque. Because.
Porque su esposo. Because your husband.
Porque su esposo va a pagar más tarde. Because your husband is going to pay later.
¿Él va a pagar más tarde? He's going to pay later?
Say in English, "Sí, él va a pagar más tarde". Yes, he's going to pay later.
To say "Así que" you say "So then". Repeat, "So then". So then.
Así que usted no me debe nada. So then you don't owe me anything.

¿Qué quiere? What do you want?
Yo no quiero nada. I don't want anything.
Yo no tengo nada. I don't have anything.
¿Qué tiene usted? What do you have?
No tengo nada. I don't have anything.
Y no quiero nada. And I don't want anything.
Quiero cien dólares. I want one hundred dollars.
"Quiero irme" en inglés se dice "I want to leave". Repita, "I want to leave". I want to leave.
Tell me in English that you want to leave. I want to leave.
Ask in English, "Usted quiere irse?" You want to leave? (or) Do you want to leave?)
Sí, quiere irme. Yes, I want to leave.
Quiero irme ahora. I want to leave now.
¿Tan pronto? So soon?
Sí. Quiero irme. I want to leave.
How does one say "No quiero irme"? I don't want to leave.
No quiero. I don't want to.
Say that you're going to leave tomorrow. I'm going to leave tomorrow.
Nos vamos a ir. We're going to leave.
Nos vamos a ir mañana. We're going to leave tomorrow.
"Juntos" en inglés se dice "Together". Repita, "Together". Together.
Say "Nos vamos a ir juntos" in English. We're going to leave together.
Vamos juntos a Boston. We're going to Boston together.
Mi esposa y yo. My wife and I.
Vamos a Boston. Are going to Boston.
Juntos. Together.
Mi esposa quiere ver a unos amigos. My wife wants to see a few friends.
Y yo voy a trabajar. And I'm going to work.
Quiero irme con ustedes. I want to leave with you.
Pero no puedo. But I can't.
¿Por qué no? Why not?
Porque no tengo dinero. Because I don't have any money.
No tengo nada. I don't have anything.
Tengo mucho dinero. I have a lot of money.
Tengo noventa dólares. I have ninety dollars.
O cien dólares. Or one hundred dollars.
Usted puede irse con nosotros. You can leave with us.

Mañana. Tomorrow.

Vamos a Boston. We're going to Boston.

Juntos. Together.

Luego vamos a Washington, D. C. Then we're going to Washington, D. C.

Puede ser. Maybe.

Nos gustaría ver a nuestra amiga Mary. We'd like to see our friend Mary.

Ella vive en Washington, D.C. She lives in Washington, D. C.

Y ella trabaja allí. And she works there.

Ella no tiene coche. She doesn't have a car.

Ella no tiene uno. She doesn't have one.

Ella no tiene coche. She doesn't have a car.

Tell me in English that she doesn't need a car. She doesn't need a car.

Say "Ella necesita" in English. She needs.

Ella no necesita. She doesn't need.

Ella no tiene un coche. She doesn't have a car.

Now say in English, "Ella no necesita un coche porque usa bicicleta todo el tiempo". She doesn't need a car because she uses a bicycle all the time.

¿Ella usa una bicicleta? She uses a bicycle?

Sí, todo el tiempo. Yes, all the time.

Ask in English, "¿Tiene suficiente dinero?" Do you have enough money?

Answer in English, "Sí, creo que sí". Yes, I think so.

No necesitamos nada. We don't need anything.

No necesitamos nada y nuestro amigo no necesita nada. We don't need anything and our friend doesn't need anything.

La palabra "tampoco" se dice "either". Repita, "either". Either.

Él no necesita nada tampoco. He doesn't need anything either.

Nuestro amigo no necesita nada. Our friend doesn't need anything.

Nos vamos a ir. We're going to leave.

Mañana por la noche. Tomorrow night.

Pero nos gustaría ver Washington, D.C. But we'd like to see Washington, D.C.

Y a nuestra amiga Sofia. And our friend Sofia.

Nos gustaría ver Washington, D. C. y a nuestra amiga Sofia. We would like to see Washington, D. C. and our friend Sofia.

¿Están abiertas las tiendas departamentales ahora? Are the department stores open now?

No necesitamos nada. We don't need anything.

No necesitamos nada tampoco. We don't need anything either.

Pero queremos comprar algo. But we want to buy something.
Para nuestra amiga Mary. For our friend Mary.
Es demasiado tarde. It's too late.
Las tiendas departamentales están cerradas ahora. The department stores are closed now.
Están abiertas mañana. They're open tomorrow.
Nos vamos a ir mañana. We're going to leave tomorrow.
Do you remember how to say "Juntos" in English? Together.
Tell me that Boston is expensive. Boston is expensive.
Pero Washington, D.C. es más caro. But Washington D.C. is more expensive.
Tiene razón. Pero Washington es más caro. You're right. But Washington is more expensive.

End of speaking/listening lesson. Continue with the reading for Lesson 33.

Reading for Lesson 33

Please read the following sentences and phrases out loud with your student. Afterwards, have your student read them to you out loud.

Reading Practice

I need to buy myself a smaller car. I am spending too much money on gas.
Do you still drive that big Suburban?
Yes. I'm going to Boston this *weekend (fin de semana)* and I'm going to New York in two *weeks (semanas)*.
Are you going to drive *both times (ambas veces)*?
Yes, unfortunately. So I am going to spend at least five hundred dollars on gas!
You're kidding! (¡No me digas! o ¡Estás bromeando!)
No, I'm not. When *I drove (manejé)* to Los Angeles last summer, I spent a *thousand (mil)* dollars.
That's *crazy (loco)*. You're right then. You do need a smaller car.
I do, but the only bad thing is that the Suburban has a lot of *space (espacio)*. It has seven *seats (asientos)*, so I can take my wife, kids and parents with me on trips. It also has an enormous *trunk (cajuela)*.
That's true. You can't take all those people and *things (cosas)* with a smaller car.
Right.
So when are you going to Boston?
Tomorrow night after work. I'm going to visit my brother Ray and my uncle Tony. They live in Boston.
I'm going to visit my brother in Washington D.C. in July.
Which brother, your brother Sammy?
Yes, he's the one who doesn't drive.
I know. He's the one who *always goes on his bicycle (siempre va en su bicicleta)* everywhere. How is he?
He's fine. He just bought a new house. It is probably because of all the money he *saves (se ahorra)* from *using (usar)* his bicycle.
He *seems like a smart man (parece como un hombre listo)*.
He is.

LEVEL 1: LESSON 34

Teaching Tip: Many Spanish speakers will say, "What means this word?" instead of "What does this word mean?" In this lesson we will be using the word "means" and "mean" in regards to asking about what a word means. Please watch out for the student possibly adding an "s" when he shouldn't. Make sure he also asks "What does this word mean?" with the word "mean" in the right place. Correct him immediately in all these things so they don't become a habit.

Para decir "Vamos a aprender" en inglés, se dice "We are going to learn". Repita, "We are going to learn". We are going to learn.

¿Cómo se dice "Vamos a aprender" en inglés? We are going to learn.

Repita "We are". We are.

We are going. We are going.

We are going to learn. We are going to learn.

¿Cómo se dice "aprender" en inglés? To learn.

Repeat in English, "To learn". To learn.

Vamos a aprender. We are going to learn.

The word "some" means "algunas" en inglés. Diga "some". Some.

How does one say in English, "Vamos a aprender algunas". We are going to learn some.

Para decir "palabras nuevas", diga "new words". Diga, "new words". New words.

Tell me that we are going to learn some new words. We are going to learn some new words.

How does one say, "Algunas palabras nuevas" in English? Some new words.

"Expresiones" se dice "Expressions". Repita, "Expressions". Expressions.

Algunas palabras y expresiones nuevas. Some new words and expressions

Vamos a aprender algunas palabras y expresiones nuevas. We're going to learn some new words and exressions.

Algunas palabras y expresiones nuevas. Some new words and expressions

282

Vamos a aprender algunas palabras y expresiones nuevas. We're going to learn some new words and exressions.
Say "Hola" in English. Hello.
Now say hi. Hi.
Muchas gracias. Thanks a lot.
Usando la palabra "Hi", diga, "Hola, ¿cómo te va?" Hi, how's it going?
Bien, ¿y contigo? Fine, and with you?
Hola, ¿cómo te va? Es bueno verte. Hi, how's it going? It's good to see you.
Es bueno verte otra vez. It's good to see you again.
Es bueno verte también. It's good to see you too.
Muchas gracias. Thanks a lot.
Para preguntar a alguien, "¿Qué te pasa?" en inglés, se puede decir, "What's wrong?" Repeat, "What's wrong?" What's wrong?
Yo no sé. I don't know.
Repeat after me, "Maybe you work too much". Maybe you work too much.
Ask me what's wrong. What's wrong?
Puede ser que trabajas demasiado. Maybe you work too much.
Say that it's good to see me again. It's good to see you again.
How does one ask in English, "¿Qué te pasa? What's wrong?
Now say in English, "Vamos juntos". We're going together.
Vamos a Washington, D.C. We're going to Washington D.C.
"Nos vamos a ir" en inglés se dice "We're going to leave". Repita, "We're going to leave". We're going to leave.
Nos vamos a ir juntos. We're going to leave together.
Nos vamos a ir mañana. We're going to leave tomorrow.
Puede ser. Maybe.
Ask me how much money I have. How much money do you have?
The word "cien" means "one hundred". Repeat, "One hundred". One hundred.
Tell me that you have one hundred dollars. I have one hundred dollars.
Tengo cien dólares. I have one hundred dollars.
How does one say "cien" in English? One hundred.
Now tell me that you don't have anything. I don't have anything.
No tengo nada conmigo. I don't have anything on me.
Por favor deme noventa dólares. Please give me ninety dollars.
No quiero. I don't want to.
¿Por qué no? Why not?
Answer, "Because I need them." Because I need them.

Porque los necesito. Because I need them.
Quiero irme. I want to leave.
¿A dónde quiere ir? Where do you want to go?
Voy a Boston. I'm going to Boston.
Con mis amigos. With my friends.
Creo que no. I don't think so.
Puede ser. Maybe.
Creo que voy a Boston. I think I'm going to Boston.
¿Usted cree? You think?
¿No está segura? You're not sure?
Answer in English, "No, no estoy segura". No, I'm not sure.
Tell me in English that you want to see Boston. I want to see Boston.
Luego voy a trabajar. Then I'm going to work.
Puede ser. Maybe.
Creo que no. I don't think so.
Mi esposa quiere comprar algo. My wife wants to buy something.
Pero ella no tiene dólares. But she doesn't have any dollars.
Do you remember how to say "qué triste" in English? How sad.
No tiene dólares consigo. She doesn't have any dollars on her.
Ella no necesita nada. She doesn't need anything.
No necesitamos nada. We don't need anything.
Pero le gustaría comprar algo. But she'd like to buy something.
Para nuestros niños. For our children.
Yo no tengo dinero conmigo. I don't have any money on me.
Por favor deme noventa y cinco dólares. Please give me ninety five dollars.
Por favor deme noventa dólares. Please give me ninety dollars.
No quiero. I don't want to.
¿Por qué no? Why not?
Answer, "Because I need them." Because I need them.
Porque los necesito. Because I need them.
Yo no tengo dinero conmigo. I don't have any money on me.
Yo no tengo dinero conmigo tampoco. I don't have any money on me either.
Aquí están cien dólares. Here's one hundred dollars.
Usted puede irse ahora. You can leave now.
Para preguntar en inglés "¿Qué quiere decir eso?" diga, "What does that mean?" What does that mean?
Ask in English, "¿Qué quiere decir eso?" What does that mean?

¿Qué? What?
Para decir "la palabra" diga, "the word". Repita, "The word". The word.
La palabra "shoot". The word "shoot".
¿Qué quiere decir eso? What does that mean?
Say that it's an English word. It's an English word.
Diga en inglés, "Es una palabra en inglés". It's an English word.
¿Qué quiere decir eso? What does that mean?
Es una palabra en inglés. It's an English word.
Es una expresión en inglés. It's an English expression.
¿Es una palabra en inglés? Is it an English word?
Sí, creo que sí Yes, I think so.
Quiere decir 'caramba'. It means "caramba".
Creo que es una palabra en inglés. I think it's an English word.
Ask in English, "¿Qué quiere decir? What does it mean?
Now ask in English, "¿Son ustedes norteamericanos? Are you American?
Answer in English, "Sí, somos norteamericanos". Yes, we're American.
Somos. We are.
Somos Notreamericanos. We're American.
Tenemos un coche norteamericano. We have an American car.
Tenemos un coche norteamericano, un Chevy. We have an American car, a Chevy.
Do you remember how to say "Palabra" in English? Word.
Now say "La palabra". The word.
¿La palabra "shoot", qué quiere decir? The word, "shoot, what does it mean?
¿Qué quiere decir eso? What does that mean?
Es una expresión. It's an expression.
Quiere decir "caramba". It means "caramba".
¿De verdad? Really?
Sí, de verdad. Yes, really.
"Estamos aquí" en inglés se dice "We're here". Repita, "We're here". We're here.
Para decir "días", diga, "days". Repita, "days". Days.
Unos días. A few days.
Estamos aquí por unos días. We're here for a few days.
Yo estoy aquí por unos días. I'm here for a few days.
¿Cuántos días? How many days?
Por tres o cuatro días. For three or four days.
Estamos aquí por tres o cuatro días. We're here for three or four days.
¿Cuánto tiempo? How much time?

Por unos días. For a few days.

¿Cuánto tiempo? How long?

¿Qué quiere decir eso? What does that mean?

¿Qué quiere decir la palabra "stay"? What does the word "stay" mean?

Quiere decir "quedarse". It means "quedarse".

Oh, ahora entiendo. Oh, now I understand.

¿Cuánto tiempo van a quedarse? How long are you going to stay?

Por unos días. For a few days.

Vamos a quedarnos. We're going to stay.

Por unos días. For a few days.

Vamos a quedarnos por unos días. We're going to stay for a few days.

Porque no tenemos mucho tiempo. Because we don't have a lot of time.

Ask in English, "¿Qué quiere decir la palabra 'stay'?" What does the word "stay" mean?

Quiere decir "quedarse". It means "quedarse".

No tenemos mucho tiempo. We don't have much time.

No tenemos mucho tiempo hoy. We don't have much time today.

Entonces vamos a Boston. Then we're going to Boston.

Nos vamos a ir mañana. We're going to leave tomorrow.

Juntos. Together.

Nuestro amigo vive en Boston. Our friend lives in Boston.

Él trabaja allí también. He works there too.

Él necesita ochocientos dólares. He needs eight hundred dollars.

¿Ocho cientos? ¿Por qué? Eight hundred? Why?

Él no tiene coche. He doesn't have a car.

Él no necesita un coche. He doesn't need a car.

Pero él quiere comprar uno. But he wants to buy one.

Él quiere comprar un coche. He wants to buy a car.

Él quiere comprar un coche norteamericano. He wants to buy an American car.

Say in English, "No necesitamos nada". We don't need anything.

Now say in English, "Pero nos gustaría ver a nuestro amigo." But we'd like to see our friend.

Nos gustaría quedarnos en Boston. We'd like to stay in Boston.

Por tres días. For three days.

¿Cuánto tiempo? How long?

¿Cuánto tiempo va a quedarse? How long are you going to stay?

¿Cuánto tiempo va a quedarse en Boston? How long are you going to stay in Boston?

Nos gustaría quedarnos tres días. We'd like to stay three days.
No tenemos mucho tiempo. We don't have much time.
No podemos quedarnos. We can't stay.
No podemos quedarnos por cinco días. We can't stay for five days.
Disculpe. La palabra "shoot". ¿Qué quere decir? Excuse me. The word "shoot". What does it mean?
Quiere decir "caramba". It means "caramba".
Gracias. Thanks.
¿Qué? What?
La palabra "shoot". ¿Qué quiere decir? The word "shoot". What does it mean?
No sé que quiere decir eso. I don't know what that means.
Quiere decir "caramba". It means "caramba".
Nos gustaría quedarnos. We'd like to stay.
Nos gustaría quedarnos en los Estados Unidos. We'd like to stay in the United States.
Pero no tenemos mucho tiempo. But we don't have much time.
Mi esposa quiere irse. My wife wants to leave.
Ella quiere ver a nuestros niños. She wants to see our children.
Pero estamos aquí juntos. But we're here together.
La palabra "shoot". ¿Qué quiere decir? The word "shoot". What does it mean?
¿Qué quiere decir? What does it mean?
Quiere decir "caramba". It means "caramba".
Eso es lo que. That's what.
Eso es lo que quiere decir. That's what it means.
Eso es lo que "shoot" quiere decir. That's what "shoot" means.
¿En serio? Are you serious?
Sí, en serio. Yes, I'm serious.
Eso es lo que "shoot" quiere decir. That's what "shoot" means.
¿En serio? Are you serious?
Sí, en serio. Yes, I'm serious.

End of speaking/listening lesson. Continue with the reading for Lesson 34.

Reading for Lesson 34

The student should be able to read this and understand the conversation. If there is anything he doesn´t understand, encourage him to ask you to clear up anything he doesn´t understand.

Reading Practice

So *how do you and your family like Houston? (¿qué tal les gusta a usted y a su familia Houston?)*

We like it here very much but *it's a little too hot (es un poco demasiado caloroso)*.

That's Houston. It is *often (frecuentemente)* hot here.

I know. Well, we are going to stay another week before we go back home.

Only another week?

We'd like to stay *more time (más tiempo),* but my wife wants to go back. She *misses (extraña)* the children.

How many children do you have?

We have two sons and two daughters. The daughters are already grown up.

So the sons live with you still?

Yes. They are still young. One is twelve and the other is fourteen. They didn´t come with us this time because they *play football (juegan fútbol)* and they didn´t want to *miss (faltar)* any *games (juegos)*. They are staying with my brother. So we will probably go back next week. My wife misses the boys.

Return back (Regresar) to California?

Yes. The *weather (clima)* is nicer there, but everything is much more expensive.

I know.

Oh, do you know what the word "shoot" means?

Yeah, it means "caramba". People say it when something bad happens. It's just an expression.

That's what I thought it meant.

Yeah. *I use it all the time (Lo uso todo el tiempo)*. I said "shoot" yesterday after my son asked me for eight hundred dollars.

Eight hundred dollars? What does your son want eight hundred dollars for?

He wants to buy a new car.

He doesn't need a new car. He has that *beautiful (bonito)* Chevy Camaro.

Yeah, but he wants to buy a *truck (camioneta)*. He says he needs it for work.

LEVEL 1: LESSON 35

Teaching tip: Watch for the student's pronounciation of the word "August". Spanish speakers tend to pronounce the "a" and the "u" so it has two vowel sounds. Make sure the student pronounces is like a short "o" vowel which makes only one vowel sound. If your student has made it this far in the program, congratulate him and encourage him to continue in his English studies. He has already learned a lot and is showing an ability and focus to learn more and more!

How would you say, "Hola Nancy, ¿Cómo estás?" Hi Nancy, how are you?
"Not bad" quiere decir "no mal" o "nada mal" en inglés. Ahora diga "no mal" en inglés. Not bad.
Ask in English, "¿Cómo le va?" How's it going?
Nada mal. Not bad.
¿Qué quiere decir eso? What does that mean?
¿Qué? What?
La palabra "bad". The word "bad".
Eso quiere decir, "mal." That means "mal".
Nada mal. Not bad.
Oh, ahora entiendo. Oh, I understand now.
Pero yo no entiendo. But I don't understand.
Todavía no entiendo. I still don't understand.
Say in English, "Lo siento. Todavía no entiendo". I'm sorry. I still don't understand.
No entiendo. I don't understand.
How do you say, "Nada mal" en inglés? Not bad.
Estamos aquí. We're here.
Por unos días. For a few days.
Say in English, "Estamos aquí por unos días". We're here for a few days.
Ask how long. How long?

Now ask in English, "¿Cuánto tiempo se van a quedar". How long are you going to stay?
Nos vamos a quedar. We're going to stay.
Nos vamos a quedar por unos días. We're going to stay for a few days.
Entonces. Then.
Vamos a Boston. We're going to Boston.
Vamos a Boston para el festival. We're going to Boston for the festival.
¿Cuál festival? Which festival?
"El festival del tomate" en inglés se dice "The tomato festival". Repita, "The tomato festival". The tomato festival.
¿Cuándo es? When is it?
En inglés, "Agosto" se dice "August". Repita, "August". August.
Vamos a Boston para el festival. We're going to Boston for the festival.
¿Cuál festival? Which festival?
El festival del tomate. The tomato festival.
¿Cuándo es? When is it?
En Agosto. In August.
El mes de Agosto. The month of August.
¿El festival del tomate? Yo pensé que. The tomato festival? I thought that.
Yo pensé que el festival del tomate era en Julio. I thought the tomato festival was in July.
No, es este mes. No, it's this month.
Say again in English, "Yo pensé que el festival del tomate era en Julio". I thought the tomato festival was in July.
Yo pensé que era en Julio. I thought it was in July.
No, es este mes. No, it's this month.
No, es en Julio. No, it's in July.
¿En Julio o en Agosto? In July or in August?
Es este mes. It's this month.
El festival del tomate es en Julio. The tomato festival is in August.
Es este mes. It's this month.
Es en Julio. It's in July.
Say in English, "El festival del tomate es en Julio, no en Agosto". The tomato festival is in July, not in August.
¿No en Agosto? Not in August?
No, no en Agosto. No, not in August.
No en Agosto. En Julio. Not in August. In July.

Vamos a Boston para el festival del tomate. We're going to Boston for the tomato festival.
Juntos. Together.
No tenemos mucho tiempo. We don't have much time.
Tengo doscientos dólares. I have two hundred dollars.
Tell me in English that you have two hundred dollars for the festival. I have two hundred dollars for the festival.
Pero no necesito nada. But I don't need anything.
Mi esposo no necesita nada tampoco. My husband doesn't need anything either.
Y no tenemos mucho tiempo. And we don't have much time.
Vamos a quedarnos. We're going to stay.
Por unos días. For a few days.
Vamos a quedarnos por unos días. We're going to stay for a few days.
"Weeks", qué quiere decir esa palabra? "Weeks", what does that word mean?
¿Cuál palabra? Which word?
La palabra "weeks". The word weeks.
Quiere decir "semanas." It means "semanas".
¿Qué quiere decir? What does it mean?
Quiere decir "semanas". It means "weeks".
Quiere decir "semanas" en inglés. It means "weeks" in English.
Say "Unas semanas" in English. A few weeks.
Now say, "Una semana". One week.
¿Cuánto tiempo? How long?
Por una semana. For one week.
Vamos a quedarnos. We're going to stay.
Por una semana. For one week.
Juntos. Together.
Y entonces. And then.
Nos vamos a ir. We're going to leave.
¿Cuánto tiempo hace que ustedes están aquí? How long have you been here?
Unas semanas. A few weeks.
Ask me how long have I been here. How long have you been here?
Tell me you have been here for a few weeks. I have been here for a few weeks.
¿Cuánto tiempo hace que usted está aquí? How long have you been here?
He estado aquí. I have been here.
He estado aquí por unas semanas. I have been here for a few weeks.

Use the contraction "I've" to say in English, "He estado aquí por unas semanas". I've been here for a few weeks.
Say again, "He estado aquí por unas semanas". I've been here for a few weeks.
¿Cuánto tiempo ha estado en Boston? How long have you been in Boston?
La palabra "Ayer" se dice "Yesterday" en inglés. Repita, "Yesterday". Yesterday.
Para decir "Desde ayer" diga "Since yesterday". Since yesterday.
"Desde" quiere decir "Since" en inglés. Repita, "Since". Since.
How does one say "Desde ayer" in English? Since yesterday.
Hemos estado aquí desde ayer. We've been here since yesterday.
¿Desde cuándo? Since when?
Desde ayer. Since yesterday.
¿Qué compró ayer? What did you buy yesterday?
The word "nothing" means "nada" in English. Repeat, "Nothing". Nothing.
Ask me again, "¿Qué compró ayer?" What did you buy yesterday?
Nada. Nothing.
¿Nada? ¿Por qué no? Nothing? Why not?
"Compré" en inglés se dice "I bought". Repita, "I bought". I bought.
Compré algo. I bought something.
¿Qué compró? What did you buy?
Yo compré algo. I bought something.
Tell me that you bought something for your son. I bought something for my son.
Ahora repita "bought". Bought.
Compré algo para usted. I bought something for you.
¿Qué compró ayer? What did you buy yesterday?
¿Qué hizo ayer? What did you do yesterday?
Compré algo. I bought something.
¿Qué compró usted? What did you buy?
Algo para beber. Something to drink.
Compré algo para beber. I bought something to drink.
Compré algo de vino. I bought some wine.
"Newspaper" means "periódico" en inglés. Repeat, "Newspaper". Newspaper.
Tell me in English how to say "periódico". Newspaper.
Say in English, "Yo compré algo de vino y un periódico". I bought some wine and a newspaper.
¿Qué quiere decir eso? What does that mean?
¿Qué quiere decir "newspaper?" What does "newspaper" mean?

Say in English, "Newspaper means 'periódico' in English." "Newspaper" means "periódico" in English.
In English, tell me that you bought a newspaper. I bought a newspaper.
¿Un periódico norteamericano? An American newspaper?
Sí. Yes.
Y yo compré algo para beber. And I bought something to drink.
¿Cuánto tiempo ha estado aquí? How long have you been here?
Desde ayer. Since yesterday.
Estoy aquí desde ayer. I've been here since yesterday.
¿Qué hizo usted ayer? What did you do yesterday?
Compré algo de vino. I bought some wine.
Algo de vino caro. Some expensive wine.
Y un periódico norteamericano. And an American newspaper.
Eso no está mal. That's not bad.
Eso no está mal por el día. That's not bad for the day.
Mi esposo no tiene vino. My husband doesn't have any wine.
Tell me that you bought some wine. I bought some wine.
Para mi esposo. For my husband.
Say in English, "El periódico es para mí". The newspaper is for me.
Y el vino es para él. And the wine is for him.
Para él. For him.
El vino es para él. The wine is for him.
Para él. For him.
El vino es para él. The wine is for him.
Tell me in English that you bought some coffee too. I bought some coffee too.
El café es para mi amiga Mary. The coffee is for my friend Mary.
El café es para ella. The coffee is for her.
Para ella. For her.
Es para ella. It's for her.
El café es para ella. The coffee is for her.
Es para ella. It's for her.
Say in English, "El vino es para él. El café es para ella". The wine is for him. The coffee is for her.
Ask me in English if I like wine. Do you like wine?
Say "Me gusta" in English. I like.
Me gusta el vino. I like wine.
Sí, me gusta el vino. Yes, I like wine.

Me gusta. I like.

Me gustaría. I'd like.

Me gusta el vino, pero solo con la comida. I like wine, but only with food.

¿Le gusta el vino? Do you like wine?

Sí, pero solo con la comida. Yes, but only with food.

Me gusta el vino. I like wine.

Me gustaría algo de vino. I'd like some wine.

Ask me if I would like some wine. Would you like some wine?

No, gracias. No, thanks.

Tell me that you don't want anything. I don't want anything.

Pero a mi esposo le gustaría una cerveza. But my husband would like a beer.

Aquí está una cerveza. Here's a beer.

Es para él. It's for him.

Es para ella. It's for her.

Es para usted. It's for you.

End of speaking/listening lesson. Continue with the reading for Lesson 35.

Reading for Lesson 35

Have the student read the following out loud, using question or exclamation intonation as appropriate.

Reading Practice

Hi Nancy. How are you *these days (estos días)*?

Not bad. And you? *How have you been (¿Cómo has estado?)*?

Good. My family and I are getting ready to go to the Tomato Festival in San Francisco tomorrow.

The Tomato Festival?

Yes.

In San Francisco?

That's right.

I didn't know San Francisco had a Tomato Festival. *I didn't even know (Yo ni supe)* they had tomatoes there.

Well they do. It's great! Last year I bought some *tomato wine (vino de tomate)* and - .

Tomato wine? *You have got to be kidding (¡Tienes que estar bromeando!)*

No, I'm not. *It's actually (de hecho es)* very good. It is real wine with grapes and tomatoes.

Okay, that's enough. You don't have to tell me any more.

But it's really good. If you want, I can buy you a bottle.

No, it's all right. Maybe you can invite me to your place for a glass afterwards.

I'd be delighted (estaría encantada). Tomato wine is delicious. And it's only two hundred dollars a bottle *(la botella)* and -.

Two hundred dollars a bottle? That's crazy! How can you pay so much for something so ridiculous? *It's robbery (¡Es robo!)*

It's not robbery. *It's the art of wine at its best (Es el arte del vino en su mejor forma).*

Or at its worst (O en su peor forma). How can you spend so much money *for a bottle of anything (¿por una botella de cualquier cosa?)*?

You have to try (Tienes que probar) the wine *to know the answer (para saber la repuesta)* to that.

I'd rather not (Prefiero no).

Are you sure?

Yes, I'm sure. If you want to buy me anything, *buy me a tee shirt instead of the tomato wine. (cómprame una camiseta en vez del vino de tomate.)*

Okay. *I'll get you (te conseguiré)* a tomato wine tee shirt.

LEVEL 1: LESSON 36

Teaching tip: Remember, make sure the student pronounces the "y" correctly in saying "New York". Watch for his pronounciation being somewhere between a "y" and "j" sound.

Say in English, "Diga, Rosa. ¿Cuánto tiempo va a quedarse en Nueva York?" Tell me, Rosa, How long are you going to stay in New York?
¿Le gusta Nueva York? Do you like New York?
"Palabra" se dice "Word" en inglés. Repita, "Word". Word.
Now say in English, "La palabra". The word.
How do you say "Esa palabra"? That word.
¿Esa palabra? Es una palabra en inglés. That word? It's an English word.
¿Qué quiere decir esa palabra? What does that word mean?
¿Cómo se dice? How do you say?
Esa palabra. That word.
¿Cómo se dice esa palabra? How do you say that word?
¿En inglés? In English?
¿Cómo se dice esa palabra en inglés? How do you say that word in English?
Tell me that it's an English word. It's an English Word.
Now ask me what it means. What does it mean?
No tengo ninguna idea. I have no idea.
Nosotros somos Peruanos. We're Peruvian.
Estamos aquí desde hace unas semanas. We've been here for a few weeks.
¿Cuánto tiempo? How long?
¿Cuánto tiempo han estado aquí? How long have you been here?
Por unas semanas. For a few weeks.
Say in English, "Hemos estado aquí por unas semanas". We've been here for a few weeks.
Estamos aquí desde ayer. We've been here since yesterday.

Desde ayer. Since yesterday.
Vamos a quedarnos. We're going to stay.
Por unos días. For a few days.
¿Por cuántos días? For how many days?
Por unos días. For a few days.
Vamos a quedarnos por unos días. We're going to stay for a few days.
No tenemos mucho tiempo. We don't have much time.
Me gustan los Estados Unidos. I like the United States.
Ask me if I like New York. Do you like New York?
Say that yes, you like New York. Yes, I like New York.
Now say, "Me gusta mucho Nueva York" in English. I like New York very much.
Ustedes van a quedarse. You're going to stay.
¿Cuánto tiempo? How long?
¿Cuántos días? How many days?
Por una semana. For one week.
Por unas semanas. For a few weeks.
Eso no está mal. That's not bad.
Estamos aquí desde ayer. We've been here since yesterday.
Ask me what I did yesterday. What did you do yesterday?
Para preguntar "¿Cómpro usted algo?" en inglés se dice como "¿Compró usted cualquier cosa?" Se dice "Did you buy anything?" Repita, "Did you buy anything?" Did you buy anything?
Ask again in English, "¿Compró usted algo?" Did you buy anything?
¿Qué compró usted? What did you buy?
¿Compró usted un periódico norteamericano? Did you buy an American newspaper?
How doe one say "Yo compré" in English? I bought.
Muchas cosas. A lot of things.
Yo compré muchas cosas. I bought a lot of things.
Ask me if I bought anything. Did you buy anything?
Sí. Compré muchas cosas. Yes, I bought a lot of things.
¿Cómo qué? Like what?
Compré un periódico Americano para mi esposo. I bought an American newspaper for my husband.
¿Para quién? For who?
Para mi esposo. For my husband.
Compré un periódico para él. I bought a newspaper for him.
Y compré. And I bought.

Algo para beber. Something to drink.
Usted compró un periódico y algo para beber. You bought a newspaper and something to drink.
¿Qué? What?
Algo de vino. Some wine.
Eso no es mucho. That's not much.
Sí, lo es. Yes it is.
Usted compró un periódico y algo de vino. You bought a newspaper and some wine.
No es mucho. That's not much.
Sí, lo es. Yes, it is.
¿Sí es? ¿Por qué? It is? Why?
Porque compré cuarenta botellas de vino. Because I bought forty bottles of wine.
Entonces para usted. Then, for you.
Algo de vino. Some wine.
Algo de vino quiere decir. Some wine means.
Algo de vino quiere decir cuarenta botellas. Some wine means forty bottles.
Para usted algo de vino quiere decir cuarenta botellas de vino. For you, some wine means forty bottles.
Eso es mucho, entonces. That's a lot, then.
Sí, lo es. Yes, it is.
¿Y usted? And you?
¿Qué hizo usted ayer? What did you do yesterday?
¿Compró usted algo? Did you buy anything?
Ask me if I bought a lot of things. Did you buy a lot of things?
¿Compró usted algo para su esposa? Did you buy anything for your wife?
¿Compró usted algo de vino para ella? Did you buy some wine for her?
Conteste que no, brevemente. No, I didn't.
No necesito nada. I don't need anything.
Pero tal vez ella necesita algo. But maybe she needs something.
Yo no voy a comprar. I'm not going to buy.
No voy a comprar nada. I'm not going to buy anything.
Tell me you don't want to buy anything. I don't want to buy anything.
No vamos a comprar nada. We're not going to buy anything.
No queremos comprar nada. We don't want to buy anything.
¿Y ustedes? And you?
¿Compraron ustedes algo? Did you buy anything?
Compramos muchas cosas. We bought a lot of things.

¿Cómo qué? Like what?
Compramos vino, cerveza y algunos libros. We bought wine, beer and some books.
Estamos aquí desde ayer. We've been here since yesterday.
Hemos estado aquí por dos días. We've been here for two days.
Y compramos muchas cosas. And we bought a lot of things.
¿Compraron ustedes algo de vino? Did you buy any wine?
Sí, pero no cuarenta botellas. Yes, but not forty bottles.
¿Compraron ustedes algo de vino ayer? Did you buy any wine yesterday?
Sí, pero no cuarenta botellas. Yes, but not forty bottles.
Sí, pero no cuarenta botellas como usted. Yes, but not forty bottles like you.
"Como usted hizo" se dice "like you did" en inglés. Repita, "Like you did." Like you did.
Say in English, "Compramos algo de vino ayer." We bought some wine yesterday.
Pero no cuarenta botellas como usted hizo. Yes, but not forty bottles like you did.
¿Compraron ustedes algo de vino ayer? Did you buy any wine yesterday?
Si, pero no cuarenta botellas como usted hizo. Yes, but not forty bottles like you did.
Compramos muchas cosas. We bought a lot of things.
¿Cuándo? When?
Ayer. Yesterday.
No está mal. Not bad.
"Ustedes llegaron" se dice "You arrived" en inglés. Repita, "You arrived". You arrived.
How do you say, "Ustedes llegaron" in English? You arrived.
¿Llegaron ustedes? Did you arrive?
¿Cuándo llegaron ustedes? When did you arrive?
Llegamos ayer. We arrived yesterday.
Llegamos ayer a las tres. We arrived yesterday at three o'clock.
Llegamos ayer a las tres de la tarde. We arrived yesterday at three o'clock in the afternoon.
Llegamos ayer a las dos de la tarde. We arrived yesterday at two o'clock in the afternoon.
Say again in English, "Llegamos ayer." We arrived yesterday.
Ayer por la mañana. Yesterday morning.
Llegamos ayer por la mañana. We arrived yesterday morning.
Buenos días. Good morning.
Ustedes llegaron. You arrived.
¿Cuándo llegaron ustedes? When did you arrive?

¿Cuándo llegaron ustedes a Nueva York? When did you arrive in New York?
A Nueva York. In New York.
Llegamos ayer. We arrived yesterday.
Llegamos ayer por la mañana. We arrived yesterday morning.
Yo llegué. I arrived.
Llegué a Nueva York. I arrived in New York.
Con mi familia. With my family.
Con mis tres hijos. With my three children.
Con mis dos niños. With my two boys.
Mi niña pequeña. My little girl.
Y mi esposo. And my husband.
Llegamos juntos. We arrived together.
Ask in English, "¿A qué hora? At what time?
Llegamos a las ocho. We arrived at eight o'clock.
Yo llegué ayer por la mañana. I arrived yesterday morning.
Yo llegué a las nueve. I arrived at nine o'clock.
¿Y usted? ¿Cuándo llegó a Nueva York? And you? When did you arrive in New York?
Ayer por la mañana. Yesterday morning.
A las ocho. At eight o'clock.
¿Y cuando llegaron en los Estados Unidos? And when did you arrive in the United States?
Llegamos ayer. We arrived yesterday.
Vamos a quedarnos. We're going to stay.
Por una semana. For one week.
Y luego vamos a irnos. And then we're going to leave.
Mañana. Tomorrow.
Nos vamos a ir mañana por la mañana. We're going to leave tomorrow morning.
Ask me if I like New Yrok. Do you like New York?
Conteste que sí brevemente. Yes, I do.
A mi me gusta Nueva York. I like New York.
Pero no tenemos mucho tiempo. But we don't have much time.
Y vamos a irnos. And we're going to leave.
Mañana por la mañana. Tomorrow morning.
Ask me if I bought anything. Did you buy anything?
Say in English that you bought a lot of things. I bought a lot of things.
Ask in English, "¿Qué compró usted?" What did you buy?

Un periódico norteamericano. An American newspaper.

Para mi esposo. For my husband.

Compré un periódico para él. I bought a newspaper for him.

Y compré algo. And I bought something.

Para mi amiga. For my friend.

Nos vamos a ir mañana por la mañana. We're going to leave tomorrow morning.

Tell me that you'll see me tonight. I'll see you tonight.

¿Quiere cenar con nostros esta noche? Do you want to have dinner with us tonight?

Conteste que sí, brevemente. Yes, I do.

Estaría encantado se dice, "I'd be delighted". Repita, "I'd be delighted". I'd be delighted.

Te veré esta noche. I'll see you tonight.

Pregunte en inglés si quiero cenar con ustedes esta noche. Do you want to have dinner with us tonight?

Say in English that you'd be delighted. I'd be delighted.

Te veré esta noche, entonces. I'll see you tonight, then.

De acuerdo. Okay.

End of speaking/listening lesson. Continue with the reading for Lesson 36.

Reading for Lesson 36

Have the student read the following sentences and phrases to you out loud. Teaching tip: Use the student's pronounciation of the name "Martha" as an opportunity for him to practice his "th". At this point he should be minimizing pronouncing "th" as a hard "t".

Reading Practice

Hello Mary. It's Martha.

Hi Martha. How are you?

Not bad. I can't complain.

You can't complain? *That's good to know (Es bueno saberlo). It never does any good to complain (Nunca hace bien quejarse).*

You're right. I have a cousin who complains all the time.

So do I (También yo).

Yeah, well my cousin is *always sick (siempre enfermo).* It's probably because he complains all the time.

You're probably right.

So how is your family?

They're well, thanks. My daughter Sofia *will be eight years old tomorrow (va a cumplir ocho años mañana).*

It's her birthday tomorrow? That's great! So *how are you going to celebrate (cómo vas a celebrar)?*

We are taking her to the zoo (La vamos a llevar al zoológico) with some of her friends. The zoo here is very nice.

Yes, we know. Anyway, we are having a dinner at our house afterwards. Would you like to come?

Absolutely. At what time?

How about five thirty?

Great. That will give me enough time *to run a few errands (hacer unos mandados).* I need to do some shopping near Park Avenue and North Fifty Third Street.

How are your husband and son?

Well Rocky is already grown up and going to San Jose State University. *He is studying to be a dentist (Está estudiando para ser dentista).*

Good for him. I'm sure *he'll do well (él lo hará bien).*

Tell your husband that he's invited to dinner with us too.

I will. See you tomorrow at five thirty.

I'll see you then. *Take care (Cuídate).*

LEVEL 1: LESSON 37 (LESSONS 33 – 36 REVIEW)

Teaching tip: Note: As in the previous review lessons, this lesson is quite long as well. It is broken up into sections again so you can take one section per day or more, depending on the mastery of the student. up in the sections as seen in this lesson. In this way, this long lesson is completed over a period of 4 – 5 days. With each section completed, the student can review a Reading Practice from the past that was more challenging for the student. When you get to the final section, do the Reading Practice that comes at the end.

Section One

¿Cómo se dice en inglés, "Lo que necesito hacer"? What I need to do.
Diga en inglés, "Lo que necesito hacer es comprar". What I need to do is buy.
Tell me in English, "Lo que necesito hacer es comprarme una bicicleta". What I need to do is buy myself a bicycle.
Necesito comprarme una bicicleta. I need to buy myself a bicycle.
Ask me what I need. What do you need?
Tell me that you need a bicycle. I need a bicycle.
¿Qué necesita comprar? What do you need to buy?
Necesito comprarme una bicicleta. I need to buy myself a bicycle.
Do you remember how to say in English, "Hola, ¿cómo está?" Hi, how are you?
Bien, gracias, ¿y usted? Fine thanks, and you?
Dígame, cuando va a Washington? Tell me, when are you going to Washington?
Voy mañana por la noche. I'm going tomorrow night.
Say "Buenos días" in English. Good morning.
In English, ask me how I am. How are you?
Answer in English, "Estoy bien. ¿Y usted?" I'm fine. And you?
¿Cómo le va? How's it going?
Todo bien, gracias. It's going well, thanks.
Ask me if the stores are open. Are the stores open?
Están cerradas. They're closed.

¿Por qué? Why?
Porque es tarde. Because it's late.
No es tarde. It's not late.
Son las once y media. It's eleven thirty.
Sí es tarde. It is late.
Yo no creo. I don't think so.
Ask me where I'm from. Where are you from?
Tell me that you're from Miami. I'm from Miami.
Con razón usted no cree que es tarde. No wonder you don't think it's late.
Nunca es tarde en Miami. It's never late in Miami.
Ask me if I'm going to work. Are you going to work?
No creo. I don't think so.
Usted cree. You think.
Usted cree que no. You don't think so.
Yo no creo. I don't think so.
Yo voy a Nueva York. I'm going to New York.
Puede ser. Maybe.
Voy a Houston. I'm going to Houston.
Yo creo que voy a Houston. I think I'm going to Houston.
Ask me what I'm going to do there. What are you going to do there?
Voy a ver algunos amigos. I'm going to see some friends.
Unos amigos. A few friends.
Tengo unos amigos allí. I have a few friends there.
Tell me you're going to see your friends. I'm going to see my friends.
Y voy a trabajar. And I'm going to work.
Puede ser. Maybe.
Say "Ochenta" in English. Eighty.
Now say "Ochenta y cinco" in English. Eighty five.
Noventa. Ninety.
Noventa y cinco. Ninety five.
Noventa y dos. Ninety two.
Noventa y nueve. Ninety nine.
Ochenta y nueve. Eighty nine.
Ask me how much do I owe you. How much do I owe you?
Noventa dólares. Ninety dollars.
Aquí están cien dólares. Here are one hundred dollars.
¿Cuántos? How many?

Cien. One hundred.
Ciento cincuenta dólares. One hundred fifty dollars.
Ciento ochenta. One hundred eighty.
Ciento noventa. One hundred ninety.
Es demasiado. It's too much.
Ciento setenta. One hundred seventy.
Ciento sesenta y cinco. One hundred sixty five.
Ciento cuarenta y siete. One hundred forty seven.
Ask me in English how much you owe me. How much do I owe you?
Usted no me debe nada. You don't owe me anything.
Cien dólares. One hundred dollars.
Tell me that I don't owe you anything. You don't owe me anything.
¿Por qué no? Why not?
¿Por qué? Why?
Porque. Because.
Porque usted no me debe nada. Because you don't owe me anything.
Porque su esposo. Because your husband.
Porque su esposo va a pagar más tarde. Because your husband is going to pay later.
¿Él va a pagar más tarde? He's going to pay later?
Sí, él va a pagar más tarde. Yes, he's going to pay later.
Así que usted no me debe nada. So then you don't owe me anything.
¿Qué quiere? What do you want?
Yo no quiero nada. I don't want anything.
Yo no tengo nada. I don't have anything.
¿Qué tiene usted? What do you have?
No tengo nada. I don't have anything.
Y no quiero nada. And I don't want anything.
Quiero cien dólares. I want one hundred dollars.
Ask me if I want to leave. You want to leave?
Sí, quiero irme. Yes, I want to leave.
Tell me in English that you want to leave now. I want to leave now.
How does one say "¿Tan pronto?" in English? So soon?
Sí. Quiero irme. I want to leave.
No quiero irme. I don't want to leave.
Say that you don't want to. I don't want to.
Tell me that you're going to leave tomorrow. I'm going to leave tomorrow.
Nos vamos a ir. We're going to leave.

Nos vamos a ir mañana. We're going to leave tomorrow.
Nos vamos a ir juntos. We're going to leave together.
Vamos juntos a Houston. We're going to Houston together.
Mi esposa y yo vamos a Houston. My wife and I are going to Houston.
Juntos. Together.
Mi esposa quiere ver a unos amigos. My wife wants to see a few friends.
Y yo voy a trabajar. And I'm going to work.
Say that you want to leave with me. I want to leave with you.
Pero no puedo. But I can't.
¿Por qué? Why?
Porque no tengo dinero. Because I don't have any money.
No tengo nada. I don't have anything.
Say, "Tengo mucho dinero" in English. I have a lot of money.
Now say, "Tengo noventa dólares". I have ninety dollars.
O cien dólares. Or one hundred dollars.
Usted puede irse con nosotros. You can leave with us.
Mañana. Tomorrow.
Vamos a Boston. We're going to Houston.
Juntos. Together.
Luego vamos a Washington, D. C. Then we're going to Washington, D. C.
Do you remember how to say "Puede ser" in English? Maybe.
Nos gustaría ver a nuestra amiga Mary. We'd like to see our friend Mary.
Ella vive en Washington, D. C. She lives in Washington, D. C.
Y ella trabaja allí. And she works there.
Ella no tiene coche. She doesn't have a car.
Ella no tiene uno. She doesn't have one.
Tell me that she doesn't need a car. She doesn't need a car.
Ella necesita. She needs.
Ella no necesita. She doesn't need.
Ella no necesita un coche. She doesn't need a car.
Ella no necesita un coche porque usa una bicicleta todo el tiempo. She doesn't need a car because she uses a bicycle all the time.
¿Ella usa una bicicleta? She uses a bicycle?
Sí, todo el tiempo. Yes, all the time.
Ask me in English if I have enough money. Do you have enough money?
Answer in English, "Sí, creo que sí". Yes, I think so.
No necesitamos nada. We don't need anything.

No necesitamos nada y nuestro amigo no necesita nada. We don't need anything and our friend doesn't need anything.
Él no necesita nada tampoco. He doesn't need anything either.
Nuestro amigo no necesita nada. Our friend doesn't need anything.
Nos vamos a ir. We're going to leave.
Mañana por la noche. Tomorrow night.
Pero nos gustaría ver Washington, D. C. But we'd like to see Washington, D. C.
Y a nuestra amiga. And our friend.
Ask if the department stores are open now. Are the department stores open now?
¿Por qué? No necesitamos nada. Why? We don't need anything.
Pero queremos comprar algo. But we want to buy something.
Para nuestra amiga Mary. For our friend Mary.
Es demasiado tarde. It's too late.
Tell me that the department stores are closed now. The department stores are closed now.
Estan abiertas mañana. They're open tomorrow.
Nos vamos a ir mañana. We're going to leave tomorrow.
Juntos. Together.
Houston es caro. Houston is expensive.
Pero Washington, D. C. es más caro. But Washington, D. C. is more expensive.
Tiene razón. Washington, D. C. es más caro. You're right. Washington, D. C. is more expensive.
¿Cómo se dice "Vamos a aprender" en inglés? We are going to learn.
Repita "We are". We are.
Say, "We are going". We are going.
Now say, "We are going to learn". We are going to learn.
¿Cómo se dice "aprender" en inglés? To learn.
Vamos a aprender. We are going to learn.
Vamos a aprender algunas. We are going to learn some.
Vamos a aprender algunas palabras nuevas. We are going to learn some new words.
Remember that "expresiones" is "expressions" in English. Repeat, "expressions". Expressions.
Algunas palabras y expresiones nuevas. Some new words and expressions
Vamos a aprender algunas palabras y expresiones nuevas. We're going to learn some new words and exressions.
Muchas gracias. Thanks a lot.
De nada. You're welcome.

Hola, ¿cómo te va? Hi, how's it going?
Bien, ¿y contigo? Fine, and with you?
Hola, ¿cómo te va? Es bueno verte. Hi, how's it going? It's good to see you.
Es bueno verte otra vez. It's good to see you again.
Es bueno verte también. It's good to see you too.
Muchas gracias. Thanks a lot.
¿Qué te pasa? What's wrong?
Yo no sé. I don't know.
Puede ser que trabajas demasiado. Maybe you work too much.
Tal vez. Maybe.
Vamos a Washington, D.C. We're going to Washington, D.C.
Nos vamos a ir juntos. We're going to leave together.
Nos vamos a ir mañana. We're going to leave tomorrow.
Ask me how much money I have. How much money do you have?
Tengo cien dólares. I have one hundred dollars.
No tengo nada. I don't have anything.
No tengo nada conmigo. I don't have anything on me.
Por favor deme noventa dólares. Please give me ninety dollars.
Say that you don't want to. I don't want to.
¿Por qué no? Why not?
Porque necesito el dinero. Because I need the money.
Y quiero irme. And I want to leave.
Ask me where I want to go. Where do you want to go?
Tell me that you're going to Houston. I'm going to Houston.
Con mis amigos. With my friends.
Creo que no. I don't think so.
Puede ser. Maybe.
Now say that you think you're going to Boston. I think I'm going to Boston.
¿Usted cree? You think?
¿No está seguro? You're not sure?
No, no estoy seguro. No, I'm not sure.
Quiero ver a Boston. I want to see Boston.
Luego voy a trabajar. Then I'm going to work.
Puede ser. Maybe.
Say that you don't think so. I don't think so.
Mi esposa quiere comprar algo. My wife wants to buy something.
Pero ella no tiene dólares. But she doesn't have any dollars.

No tiene dólares consigo. She doesn't have any dollars on her.
Ella no necesita nada. She doesn't need anything.
No necesitamos nada. We don't need anything.
Pero le gustaría comprar algo. But she'd like to buy something.
Para nuestros niños. For our children.
Say that you don't have any money on you. I don't have any money on me.
Por favor deme noventa y cinco dólares. Please give me ninety five dollars.
Yo no tengo dinero conmigo. I don't have any money on me.
Yo no tengo dinero conmigo tampoco. I don't have any money on me either
Aquí están cien dólares. Here's one hundred dollars.
Usted puede irse ahora. You can leave now.
¿Qué quiere decir eso? What does that mean?
¿Qué? What?
La palabra "shoot". The word "shoot".
Say that it's an English word. It's an English word.
Ask in English, "¿Qué quiere decir eso? What does that mean?
Tell me in English, "Es una expresión en inglés." It's an English expression.
No es una expresión. Es una palabra. It's not an expression. It's a word.
¿Es una palabra en inglés? Is it an English word?
Sí, creo que sí. Yes, I think so.
Quiere decir 'caramba'. It means "caramba".
Creo que es una palabra en inglés. I think it's an English word.
¿Qué quiere decir? What does it mean?
¿Son ustedes norteamericanos? Are you American?
¿Sí, somos norteamericanos. Yes, we're American.
Somos. We are.
Somos Notreamericanos. We're American.
Tenemos un coche norteamericano. We have an American car.
Tenemos un coche norteamericano, un Chevy. We have an American car, a Chevy.
Say "Palabra" in English. Word.
How does one say, "La palabra"? The word.
Ask in English, "La palabra 'shoot', qué quiere decir?" The word, "shoot", what does it mean?

Section Two
¿Qué quiere decir eso? What does that mean?
Es una expresión. It's an expression.

Say that it's a word, not an expression. It's a word, not an expression.
Quiere decir "caramba". It means "caramba".
Estamos aqúi por unos días. We're here for a few days.
¿Cuántos días? How many days?
Por tres o cuatro días. For three or four days.
Estamos aquí por tres o cuatro días. We're here for three or four days.
¿Cuánto tiempo? How long?
Por unos días. For a few days.
How does one ask, "¿Qué quiere decir eso?" in English? What does that mean?
¿Qué quiere decir la palabra "stay"? What does the word "stay" mean?
Quiere decir "quedarse". It means "quedarse".
Oh, ahora entiendo. Oh, now I understand.
¿Cuánto tiempo? How long?
Ask how long we are going to stay. How long are you going to stay?
Por unos días. For a few days.
Vamos a quedarnos por unos días. We're going to stay for a few days.
Porque no tenemos mucho tiempo. Because we don't have a lot of time.
No tenemos mucho tiempo. We don't have much time.
No tenemos mucho tiempo hoy. We don't have much time today.
Entonces vamos a Houston. Then we're going to Houston.
Nos vamos a ir mañana. We're going to leave tomorrow.
Juntos. Together.
Nuestro amigo vive en Houston. Our friend lives in Houston.
Él trabaja allí también. He works there too.
Él necesita ochocientos dollares. He needs eight hundred dollars.
¿Ochocientos? ¿Por qué? Eight hundred? Why?
Él no tiene coche. He doesn't have a car.
Tell me that he doesn't need a car. He doesn't need a car.
Pero él quiere comprar uno. But he wants to buy one.
Él quiere comprar un coche. He wants to buy a car.
Say in English, "Él quiere comprar un coche norteamericano". He wants to buy an American car.
Now say in English, "No necesitamos nada". We don't need anything.
Pero nos gustaría ver a nuestro amigo. But we'd like to see our friend.
Nos gustaría quedarnos en Houston. We'd like to stay in Houston.
Por tres días. For three days.
¿Cuánto tiempo? How long?

Ask how long we are going to stay in Boston. How long are you going to stay?
¿Cuánto tiempo va a quedarse en Boston? How long are you going to stay in Boston?
Nos gustaría quedarnos por tres días. We'd like to stay three days.
No tenemos mucho tiempo. We don't have much time.
No podemos quedarnos. We can't stay.
No podemos quedarnos por cinco días. We can't stay for five days.
¿Qué quere decir eso? What does that mean?
¿Qué? What?
La palabra "shoot". The word "shoot".
Say that you don't know what that means. I don't know what that means.
Nos gustaría quedarnos. We'd like to stay.
Nos gustaría quedarnos en los Estados Unidos. We'd like to stay in the United States.
Pero no tenemos mucho tiempo. But we don't have much time.
Mi esposa quiere irse. My wife wants to leave.
Say that she wants to see our children. She wants to see our children.
Pero estamos aquí juntos. But we're here together.
Ask in English, "¿Qué quiere decir esta palabra?" What does this word mean?
¿Disculpe? Excuse me?
"Shoot". ¿Qué quiere decir eso? Shoot. What does that mean?
La palabra "shoot", qué quiere decir? The word "shoot", what does it mean?
¿Qué quiere decir? What does it mean?
Quiere decir. It means.
Quiere decir "caramba". It means "caramba".
Eso es lo que. That's what.
Eso es lo que quiere decir. That's what it means.
Eso es lo que "shoot" quiere decir. That's what "shoot" means.
Para preguntar "¿En serio?" se dice en inglés, "Are you serious?" Diga, "Are you serious?" Are you serious?
Sí, en serio. Yes, I'm serious.
Eso es lo que "shoot" quiere decir. That's what "shoot" means.
La palabra "shoot" quiere decir, "caramba". The word "shoot" means "caramba".
¿En serio? Are you serious?
Sí, en serio. Yes, I'm serious?
Hola Nancy, ¿Cómo estás? Hi Nancy, how are you?
How would she say "nada mal" in English? Not bad.
Ask in English, "¿Cómo le va?" How's it going?
Nada mal. Not bad.

¿Qué quiere decir eso? What does that mean?
¿Qué? What?
La palabra "bad". The word "bad".
Eso quiere decir, "mal." That means "mal".
Nada mal. Not bad.
O, ahora entiendo. Oh, I understand now.
Now say that you don't understand. I don't understand.
Todavía no entiendo. I still don't understand.
Lo siento. Todavía no entiendo. I'm sorry. I still don't understand.
No entiendo. I don't understand.
No mal. Not bad.
Estamos aquí. We're here.
Por unos días. For a few days.
Diga en inglés, "Estamos aquí por unos días". We're here for a few days.
Ask how long. How long?
Ask in English, "¿Cuánto tiempo se van a quedarse?" How long are you going to stay?
Nos vamos a quedar. We're going to stay.
Nos vamos a quedar por unos días. We're going to stay for a few days.
Entonces. Then.
Nos vamos a ir. We're going to leave.
Vamos a Sacramento. We're going to Sacramento.
Vamos a Sacramento para el festival. We're going to Sacramento for the festival.
¿Cuál festival? Which festival?
"El festival del tomate" en inglés se dice "The tomato festival". Repita, "The tomato festival". The tomato festival.
¿Cuándo es? When is it?
"Agosto" se dice "August" en inglés. Repita,"August". August.
Vamos a Boston para el festival. We're going to Sacramento for the festival.
¿Cuál festival? Which festival?
El festival del tomate. The tomato festival.
¿Cuándo es? When is it?
En Agosto. In August.
El mes de Agosto. The month of August.
¿El festival del tomate? Yo pensé que. The tomato festival? I thought that.
Yo pensé que el festival del tomate era en Agosto. I thought the tomato festival was in August.

No, es este mes. No, it's this month.
Yo pensé que el festival del tomate era en Agosto. I thought the tomato festival was in August.
Yo pensé que era en Agosto. I thought it was in August.
No, es este mes. No, it's this month.
"Julio" en inglés se dice "July". Repita,"July". July.
No, es en Julio. No, it's in July.
¿En Julio o en Agosto? In July or in August?
Es este mes. It's this month.
El festival del tomate es en Julio. The tomato festival is in July.
Es este mes. It's this month.
Es en Julio. It's in July.
Tell me that the tomato festival is in July, not in August. The tomato festival is in July, not in August.
¿No en Agosto? Not in August?
No, no en Agosto. No, not in August.
No en Agosto. En Julio. Not in August. In July.
Say in English, "Vamos a Sacramento para el festival del tomate". We're going to Sacramento for the tomato festival.
How does one say "Juntos" in English? Together.
No tenemos mucho tiempo. We don't have much time.
Tengo dos cientos dólares. I have two hundred dollars.
Tell me you have two hundred dollars for the festival. I have two hundred dollars for the festival.
Pero no necesito nada. But I don't need anything.
Mi esposo no necesita nada. My husband doesn't need anything.
Y no tenemos mucho tiempo. And we don't have much time.
Vamos a quedarnos. We're going to stay.
Por unos días. For a few days.
Vamos a quedarnos por unos días. We're going to stay for a few days.
"Weeks", ¿qué quiere decir esa palabra? "Weeks", what does that word mean?
¿Cuál palabra? Which word?
La palabra "weeks". The word "weeks".
Quiere decir "semanas." It means "semanas".
¿Qué quiere decir eso? What does that mean?
Quiere decir "semanas". It means "weeks".
Say "Unas semanas" in English. A few weeks.

Una semana. One week.

¿Cuánto tiempo? How long?

Por una semana. For one week.

Vamos a quedarnos. We're going to stay.

Por una semana. For one week.

Juntos. Together.

Y entonces. And then.

Nos vamos a ir. We're going to leave.

Ask how long we have been here. How long have you been here?

Answer in English, "Por unas semanas". For a few weeks.

Now ask how long I have been here. How long have you been here?

He estado aquí. I have been here.

He estado aquí por unas semanas. I have been here for a few weeks.

Usando la contracción "I've", otra vez diga "He estado aquí por unas semanas". I've been here for a few weeks.

Una vez más, diga, "He estado aquí por unas semanas". I've been here for a few weeks.

Ask me how long I have been in Houston. How long have you been in Houston?

Say, "Ayer" in English. Yesterday.

"Desde" se dice "Since" en inglés. Repita,"Since". Since.

Desde ayer. Since yesterday.

Hemos estado aquí desde ayer. We've been here since yesterday.

Ask me what I bought yesterday. What did you buy yesterday?

Say, "Nada" in English. Nothing.

¿Nada? ¿Por qué no? Nothing? Why not?

¿Qué compró ayer? What did you buy yesterday?

"Compré" en inglés se dice "I bought". Repita,"I bought". I bought.

Compré algo. I bought something.

¿Qué compró? What did you buy?

Yo compré algo. I bought something.

Say in English, "Yo compré algo para mi hijo". I bought something for my son.

Tell me in English that you bought something for me. I bought something for you.

In English, ask me what I bought yesterday. What did you buy yesterday?

Now ask me what I did yesterday. What did you do yesterday?

Compré algo. I bought something.

¿Qué compró usted? What did you buy?

Algo para beber. Something to drink.

Compré algo para beber. I bought something to drink.
Compré algo de vino. I bought some wine.
Y un periódico. And a newspaper.
¿Qué quiere decir eso? What does that mean?
¿Qué? What?
¿Qué quiere decir "periódico". What does "periódico" mean?
Quiere decir "newspaper". It means "newspaper".
Compré un periódico. I bought a newspaper.
¿Un periódico norteamericano? An American newspaper?
Y yo compré algo para beber. And I bought something to drink.
¿Cuánto tiempo hace que usted está aquí? How long have you been here?
Desde ayer. Since yesterday.
Tell me that you've been here since yesterday. I've been here since yesterday.
¿Qué hizo usted ayer? What did you do yesterday?
Compré algo de vino. I bought some wine.
Algo de vino caro. Some expensive wine.
Y un periódico norteamericano. And an American newspaper.
Eso no está mal para un día. That's not bad for one day.
Eso no está mal. That's not bad.
Mi esposo no tiene vino. My husband doesn't have any wine.
Compré algo de vino. I bought some wine.
Para mi esposo. For my husband.
El periódico es para mí. The newspaper is for me.
Y el vino es para él. And the wine is for him.
Para él. For him.
El vino es para él. The wine is for him.
Compré también algo de café. I bought some coffee too.
Say that the coffee is for your friend Mary. The coffee is for my friend Mary.
El café es para ella. The coffee is for her.
Es para ella. It's for her.
Say in English, "El vino es para él. El café es para ella". The wine is for him. The coffee is for her.
Ask me if I like wine. Do you like wine?
Me gusta. I like.
Me gusta el vino. I like wine.
Sí, me gusta el vino. Yes, I like wine.
Me gusta el vino, pero solo con la comida. I like wine, but only with food.

¿Le gusta el vino? Do you like wine?
Sí, pero solo con la comida. Yes, but only with food.
Me gustaría algo de vino. I'd like some wine.
Ask me if I would like some wine. Would you like some wine?
No, gracias. No, thanks.
No quiero nada. I don't want anything.
Pero a mi esposo le gustaría una cerveza. But my husband would like a beer.
Aquí está una cerveza. Here's a beer.
Es para él. It's for him.
Es para ella. It's for her.
Diga, Rosa, ¿cuánto tiempo va a quedarse en Nueva York? Tell me, Rosa, How long are you going to stay in New York?
Ask me if I like New York. Do you like New York?
How do you say "Esa palabra"? That word.
¿Esa palabra? Es una palabra en inglés. That word? It's an English word.
¿Qué quiere decir esa palabra? What does that word mean?
¿Cómo se dice? How do you say?
Esa palabra. That word.
¿Cómo se dice esa palabra? How do you say that word?
¿En inglés? In English?
¿Cómo se dice esa palabra en inglés? How do you say that word in English?
Es una palabra en inglés. It's an English Word.
¿Qué quiere decir? What does it mean?
No tengo ningún idea. I have no idea.
Nosotros somos mexicanos. We're Mexican.
Hemos estado aquí por unas semanas. We've been here for a few weeks.

Section Three

¿Cuánto tiempo? How long?
¿Cuánto tiempo han estado aquí? How long have you been here?
Por unas semanas. For a few weeks.
Hemos estado aquí por unas semanas. We've been here for a few weeks.
Estamos aquí desde ayer. We've been here since yesterday.
Desde ayer. Since yesterday.
Vamos a quedarnos. We're going to stay.
Por unos días. For a few days.
¿Por cuántos días? For how many days?

Por unos días. For a few days.
Vamos a quedarnos por unos días. We're going to stay for a few days.
Say in English, "No tenemos mucho tiempo". We don't have much time.
Tell me you like the United States. I like the United States.
Ask me if I like New York. Do you like New York?
Answer in English, "Sí, me gusta Nueva York". Yes, I like New York.
Me gusta mucho Nueva York. I like New York very much.
Hemos estado aquí desde ayer. We've been here since yesterday.
Ask me what I did yesterday. What did you do yesterday?
Ask me if I bought something. Did you buy anything?
Sí. Unas cosas. Yes. A few things.
¿Qué compró usted? What did you buy?
Ask me if I bought an American newspaper. Did you buy an American newspaper?
Tell me you bought a lot of things. I bought a lot of things.
Ask me if I bought anything. Did you buy anything?
Sí. Compré muchas cosas. Yes, I bought a lot of things.
Compré un periódico Americano para mi esposo. I bought an American newspaper for my husband.
¿Para quién? For who?
Para mi esposo. For my husband.
Compré un periódico para él. I bought a newspaper for him.
Y compré. And I bought.
Algo para beber. Something to drink.
Say in English, "Usted compró un periódico y algo para beber". You bought a newspaper and something to drink.
¿Qué? What?
Algo de vino. Some wine.
Eso no es mucho. That's not much.
Sí, lo es. Yes it is.
Usted compró un periódico y algo de vino. You bought a newspaper and some wine.
¿Es? ¿Por qué? It is? Why?
Porque compré cuarenta botellas de vino. Because I bought forty bottles of wine.
Entonces para usted. Then, for you.
Algo de vino. Some wine.
Algo de vino quiere decir. Some wine means.
Algo de vino quiere decir cuarenta botellas. Some wine means forty bottles.

Para usted algo de vino quiere decir cuarenta botellas de vino. For you, some wine means forty bottles.

Eso es mucho, entonces. That's a lot, then.

Sí, lo es. Yes, it is.

Eso es mucho, entonces. That's a lot, then.

Sí, lo es. Yes, it is.

¿Y usted? And you?

¿Qué hizo usted ayer? What did you do yesterday?

In English, ask me if I bought anything. Did you buy anything?

Ask me if I bought a lot of things. Did you buy a lot of things?

¿Compró usted algo para su esposa? Did you buy anything for your wife?

¿Compró usted algo de vino para ella? Did you buy some wine for her?

En inglés, conteste que no, brevemente. No, I didn't.

No necesito nada. I don't need anything.

Yo no voy a comprar. I'm not going to buy.

No voy a comprar nada. I'm not going to buy anything.

No quiero comprar nada. I don't want to buy anything.

No vamos a comprar nada. We're not going to buy anything.

No queremos comprar nada. We don't want to buy anything.

¿Y ustedes? And you?

¿Compraron ustedes algo? Did you buy anything?

Compramos muchas cosas. We bought a lot of things.

Hemos estado aquí desde ayer. We've been here since yesterday.

Hemos estado aquí por dos días. We've been here for two days.

Y compramos muchas cosas. And we bought a lot of things.

¿Compraron ustedes algo de vino? Did you buy any wine?

Sí, pero no cuarenta botellas. Yes, but not forty bottles.

Ask me if we bought any wine yesterday. Did you buy any wine yesterday?

Sí, pero no cuarenta botellas. Yes, but not forty bottles.

Sí, pero no cuarenta botellas como usted. Yes, but not forty bottles like you.

Sí, pero no cuarenta botellas como usted lo hizo. Yes, but not forty bottles like you did.

¿Compraron ustedes algo de vino ayer? Did you buy any wine yesterday?

Sí, pero no cuarenta botellas como usted lo hizo. Yes, but not forty bottles like you did.

Compramos muchas cosas. We bought a lot of things.

¿Cuándo? When?

Ayer. Yesterday.
Nada mal. Not bad.
How do you say, "ustedes llegaron"? You arrived.
¿Llegaron ustedes? Did you arrive?
In English, ask me when we arrived. When did you arrive?
How does one say in English, "Llegamos ayer". We arrived yesterday.
Now say in English, "Llegamos ayer a las tres". We arrived yesterday at three o'clock.
Llegamos ayer a las tres de la tarde. We arrived yesterday at three o'clock in the afternoon.
Llegamos ayer a las dos de la tarde. We arrived yesterday at two o'clock in the afternoon.
Llegamos ayer por la mañana. We arrived yesterday morning.
Buenos días. Good morning.
Ustedes llegaron. You arrived.
¿Cuándo llegaron ustedes? When did you arrive?
In English, ask me when we arrived in New York. When did you arrive in New York?
Llegamos ayer. We arrived yesterday.
Llegamos ayer por la mañana. We arrived yesterday morning.
Yo llegué. I arrived.
Llegué a Nueva York. I arrived in New York.
Con mi familia. With my family.
Con mis tres hijos. With my three children.
Con mis dos niños. With my two boys.
Mi niña pequeña. My little girl.
Y mi esposo. And my husband.
Llegamos juntos. We arrived together.
Ask in English, "¿A qué hora?" At what time?
Answer in English, "Llegamos a las ocho". We arrived at eight o'clock.
Tell me you arrived yesterday morning. I arrived yesterday morning.
Yo llegué a las nueve. I arrived at nine o'clock.
¿Y usted? ¿Cuándo llegó a Nueva York? And you? When did you arrive in New York?
Ayer por la mañana. Yesterday morning.
A las ocho. At eight o'clock.
¿Y cuando llegaron a los Estados Unidos? And when did you arrive in the United States?

Llegamos ayer. We arrived yesterday.
Vamos a quedarnos. We're going to stay.
Por una semana. For one week.
Y luego vamos a irnos. And then we're going to leave.
Mañana. Tomorrow.
Nos vamos a ir mañana por la mañana. We're going to leave tomorrow morning.
Ask me if I like New York. Do you like New York?
Answer briefly that yes, you do. Yes, I do.
Tell me that you like New York. I like New York.
Pero no tenemos mucho tiempo. But we don't have much time.
Y vamos a irnos. And we're going to leave.
Mañana por la mañana. Tomorrow morning.
In English, ask me if I bought anything. Did you buy anything?
Tell me that you bought a lot of things. I bought a lot of things.
Now ask me what I bought. What did you buy?
Un periódico norteamericano. An American newspaper.
Para mi esposo. For my husband.
Compré un periódico para él. I bought a newspaper for him.
Y compré algo. And I bought something.
Para mi amiga. For my friend.
Nos vamos a ir mañana por la mañana. We're going to leave tomorrow morning.
Te veré esta noche. I'll see you tonight.
¿Quiere cenar con nostros esta noche? Do you want to have dinner with us tonight?
Conteste que sí, brevemente. Yes, I do.
Estaría encantado. I'd be delighted.
Te veré esta noche, entonces. I'll see you tonight, then.
De acuerdo. Okay.

End of speaking/listening lesson. Continue with the reading for Lesson 37.

Reading for Lesson 37

There are a lot of questions in this reading. Make sure the student uses correct intonation in each of them.

Reading Practice
Hello Ralph. How are you doing?
I'm fine, Andy. And you?
I'm doing well, thanks. Do you know what time it is?
It's nine fifteen. *Are you in a hurry (Vas de prisa)?*
Maybe. Do you know if the stores open?
They're all closed. *All of them except for the 24 hour ones (Todos ellas menos las de 24 horas).*
Why?
What do you mean (Que quieres decir), "why"? Because it's late.
It's not late.
It's nine fifteen. *That's late for most stores (Eso es tarde para la mayoría de las tiendas).*
I don't think so.
You don't think so? Where are you from?
I'm from Miami.
No wonder you don't think it's late. It's never late in Miami.
That's true (Eso es verdad).
I'm going to Houston tomorrow to visit a friend.
Really? Houston is nice at this time of year *(Houston es agradable en esta época del año).*
I know. *It's too hot to go in the summer (Hace demasiado calor para ir en el verano).*
How long are you staying there?
I'm staying a week.
Well I hope you have fun.
Thanks.
It was good seeing you.
Take care.
Goodbye now.

LEVEL 1: LESSON 38 (BONUS LESSON)

This is a low key, "Relax and put your feet up, compadre," lesson. After those boot camp review lessons, this will be refreshing! It's a nice calm way to finish up Level 1. Teaching tip: Often times Spanish speakers say "childrens" instead of "children". If this happens, stop the student and have her resay the word. Pressing the tip of the tongue against the back of the teeth helps emphasize the final "n" sound.

Say hello to me and ask me how I am. Hi, how are you?
Answer for me in English, "Estoy bien, gracias. ¿Y usted? ¿Cómo ha estado?" I'm fine, thanks. And you? How have you been?
How does one say, "Muy bien" in English? Very well.
Ask me where I'm from. Where are you from?
Yo soy de Brazil. ¿Y usted? I'm from Brazil. And you?
Soy norteamericano. I'm American.
Tell me you're from Los Angeles. I'm from Los Angeles.
Usted habla inglés muy bien. You speak English very well.
Mi esposo es de Los Ángeles también. My husband is from Los Angeles too.
¿Dónde está? Where is he?
Está por aquí en un lugar. He's around here somewhere.
¿Habla español su esposo? Does your husband speak Spanish?
Solo un poco. Only a little.
¿Y usted? ¿Habla español? And you? Do you speak Spanish?
Say that you speak Spanish very well. I speak Spanish very well
Ask me where I'm from. Where are you from?
Mis padres son de Costa Rica pero yo soy de aquí. My parents are from Costa Rica but I'm from here.
Tell me that you're not from here. I'm not from here.
Yo no soy mexicano. I'm not Mexican.
No soy mexicano tampoco. I'm not Mexican either.

Ask me if I'm hungry. Are you hungry?
En inglés si uno tiene mucha hambre, dice "I'm starving." Es como decir, "Estoy hambriento". Repita, "I'm starving". I'm starving.
¿Tiene hambre? Are you hungry?
Estoy hambriento. I'm starving.
Entonces, ¿le gustaría comer algo? Then, would you like to have something to eat?
Sí, por favor. Yes, please.
¿Qué quiere comer? What do you want to eat?
Me gustaría almorzar en un restaurante chino. I'd like to have lunch at a Chinese Restaurant.
Y me gustaría beber algo en el hotel después. And I'd like to have something to drink at the hotel afterwards.
De acuerdo. Okay.
Me gustaría desayunar en el hotel. I would like to have breakfast at the hotel.
Me gustaría cenar en un restaurante italiano. I'd like to have dinner at an Italian restaurant.
¿Cuál restaurante italiano? Which Italian restaurant?
El restaurante italiano en la Calle Primera. The Italian restaurant on First Street.
A mí me gustaría cenar en el restaurante italiano en la Calle Cincuenta y tres Norte. I'd like to have dinner at the Italian restaurant on North Fifty Third Street.
Perdón, ¿qué hora es? Excuse me, what time is it?
Son las cinco. It's five o'clock.
¿Sabe usted qué hora es? Do you know what time it is?
Son las siete. It's seven o'clock.
¿Por qué pregunta? Why do you ask?
En inglés, "Es que" se dice, "It's that". Repita, "It's that". It's that.
Es que tengo que ir a trabajar a las ocho. It's that I have to go to work at eight o'clock.
¿Qué quiere hacer más tarde? What do you want to do later?
Quiero ir al cine y al parque en la calle Cincuenta y tres Norte. I want to go to the movies and to the park on North Fifty Third Street.
¿Y usted? ¿Qué le gustaría hacer esta tarde? And you? What would you like to do this afternoon?
I want to go to the movies too, but I can't. Quiero ir al cine también pero no puedo.
¿Por qué no? Why not?
Es que tengo que comprar un regalo. It's that I have to buy a present.

Say in English "Me gustaría comprar un regalo para mi hijo". I would like to buy a present for my son.

¿Cuál hijo? ¿Marcos o Ruben? Which son? Marcos or Ruben?

Ruben. Es su cumpleaños. Ruben. It's his birthday.

Puede ir a la tienda en la Calle Tercera. You can go to the store on Third Street.

Puede comprar muchas cosas buenas allí. You can buy many good things there.

Ask in English "¿Cuántos hijos tiene usted?" How many children do you have?

Answer in English, "Tengo tres hijos. Dos niñas y un niño". I have three children. Two girls and one boy.

¿Y usted? ¿Tiene hijos usted? And you? Do you have any children?

Tengo solo un hijo. Pero ya ha crecido. I have only one son. But he's already grown up.

¿Ya ha crecido? He's already grown up?

Sí, ya ha crecido. Tiene veinte años. Yes, he's already grown up. He's twenty years old.

Say in English "Mi niña tiene ocho años." My daughter is eight years old.

Mi hijo es pequeño. Solo tiene seis años. My son is small. He only is six years old.

¿Cuánto dinero le debo? How much money do I owe you?

Usted me debe cinco dólares. You owe me five dollars.

¿Cinco dólares? ¿Es todo? ¿Está seguro? Five dollars? That's all? Are you sure?

Sí, estoy seguro. Yes, I'm sure.

Buenas tardes, Señor Martinez. ¿Cómo está hoy? Good afternoon, Mr. Martinez. How are you today?

Muy bien, gracias. ¿Y usted? ¿Cómo ha estado? Very well, thanks. And you? How have you been?

Pase, por favor. Pase. Come in, please. Come in.

Tome un asiento. Take a seat.

Es bueno verlo. It's good to see you.

Es bueno verla también. It's good to see you too.

¿Cómo está su familia? How is your family?

Bien, gracias. Fine, thanks.

"¿Tiene sed?" se dice "Are you thirsty?" Pregunte, "Are you thirsty?" Are you thirsty?

¿Tiene sed? ¿Le gustaría beber algo? Are you thirsty? Would you like to have something to drink?

"Tengo sed" se dice "I'm thirsty". Repita, "I'm thirsty". I'm thirsty.

Pregunte "¿Tiene sed?" Are you thirsty?

Un poco. A little.

¿Tiene sed? Are you thirsty?

Sí, tengo sed. Yes, I'm thirsty.

"Tengo mucha sed" se dice "I'm very thirsty". Repita, "I'm very thirsty." I'm very thirsty.

How do you say "Tengo mucha sed" in English? I'm very thirsty.

Ask me if I'm thirsty. Are you thirsty?

Try to say, "Un poco" in English. A little.

Ask me what I have. What do you have?

"Jugo de naranja" se dice "Orange juice". Repita, "Orange juice". Orange juice.

Tengo agua, jugo de naranja, té helado y café. I have water, orange juice, iced tea and coffee.

¿Qué le gustaría? What would you like?

Me gustaría un vaso de agua, por favor. Pero sin hielo. I'd like a glass of water, please. But without ice.

Me gustaría un vaso de jugo de naranja, por favor. I'd like a glass of orange juice, please.

¿Con hielo? With ice?

Sí, por favor. Yes, please.

¿Y usted? And you?

Tengo agua, jugo de naranja, té helado y café. I have water, orange juice, iced tea and coffee.

No, gracias. No tengo sed. No, thank you. I'm not thirsty.

¿Le gustaría beber algo? Would you like to drink something?

No, gracias. No tengo sed. No, thank you. I'm not thirsty.

Tell me that you would like to have breakfast at the hotel this morning. I would like to have breakfast at the hotel this morning.

¿Y usted? ¿Dónde le gustaría desayunar? And you? Where would you like to have breakfast?

"No importa" en inglés se dice "It doesn't matter". Repita, "It doesn't matter". It doesn't matter.

Ask in English, "¿Dónde le gustaría desayunar? Where would you like to have breakfast?

No importa. It doesn't matter.

Ask me if I'm sure. Are you sure?

Sí, estoy seguro. Yes, I'm sure.

Repeat after me, "We can have breakfast at the hotel today, and tomorrow at the Indian restaurant. We can have breakfast at the hotel today, and tomorrow at the Indian restaurant.

Diga en inglés, "Podemos desayunar en el hotel hoy, y mañana en el restaurante Indio". We can have breakfast at the hotel today, and tomorrow at the Indian restaurant.

¿Cuál restaurante Indio? El que está en la Calle Primera o el que está en la Avenida Hamilton? Which Indian restaurant? The one that's on First Street or the one that's on Hamilton Avenue?

Answer in English, "El de la Calle Primera". The one on First Street.

Quiero almorzar con mi hijo hoy. I want to have lunch with my son today.

¿Quiere venir con nosotros? Do you want to come with us?

Conteste que sí, brevemente. Yes, I do.

Mañana voy a cenar con mis padres. Tomorrow I'm going to have dinner with my parents.

¿Dónde? Where?

En el restaurante italiano en la Avenida Parque. At the Italian restaurant on Park Avenue.

¿Qué hora es? What time is it?

Son las dos. It's two o'clock.

¿Sabe usted qué hora es? Do you know what time it is?

Sí, son las tres. Yes, it's three o'clock.

Me gustaría comprar algo para mi esposo más tarde. I would like to buy something for my husband later.

¿A qué hora? At what time?

A las cuatro. At four o'clock.

Ask in English, "¿Sabe usted dónde está la Calle Cincuenta y tres Norte?" Do you know where North Fifty Third Street is?

Answer in English, "No está aquí. Está por allá". It's not here. It's over there.

¿Está seguro? Are you sure?

"No se preocupe" se dice "Don't worry" en inglés. Repita, "Don't worry". Don't worry.

Ask me if I'm sure. Are you sure?

Sí. No se preocupe. Está por allá. Yes. Don't worry. It's over there.

Muchas gracias. Thank you very much.

De nada. You're welcome.

¿Cuánto le debo? How much do I owe you?

¿Cuánto le debo por el vino? How much do I owe you for the wine?

Diez dólares y cincuenta centavos. Ten dollars and fifty cents.
¿Diez dólares y cincuenta centavos? ¿Es todo? Ten dollars and fifty cents? That's all?
Sí. Es todo. Yes. That's all.
Say "Eso es barato" in English. That's cheap.
Say in English, "Yo sé. El vino no es caro aquí". I know. The wine isn't expensive here.
¿Por qué no? Why not?
No sé por qué es tan barato. I don't know why it's so cheap.
Bueno. No importa. All right. It doesn't matter.
¿Cuánto cuesta eso? How much does that cost?
Es uno veinte y cinco. It's one twenty five.
¿Y esto? And this?
Cuesta seis dólares. It costs six dollars.
Eso es demasiado. That's too much.
Tell me you don't have enough money. I don't have enough money.
Tengo todo mi dinero en el hotel. I have all my money at the hotel.
¿Cuánto dinero tiene? How much money do you have?
No mucho. Not much.
Solo veinte dólares y once pesos. Only twenty dollars and eleven pesos.
No es mucho. It's not much.
Tengo más dinero en el cajón. I have more money in the drawer.
¿Tenemos suficiente para un taxi? Do we have enough for a taxi?
Sí, tenemos suficiente para un taxi. Yes, we have enough for a taxi.
Soy el Señor Rafael Mendoza. I'm Mr. Rafael Mendoza.
Mucho gusto conocerlo, Sr. Mendoza. Pleased to meet you, Mr. Mendoza.
¿Cómo está su familia? How is your family?
Muy bien, gracias. ¿Y usted? ¿Cómo ha estado? Very well, thanks. And you? How have you been?
Usted me debe trece dólares, por favor. You owe me thirteen dollars, please.
Tenga. Here.
Muchas gracias. Thank you very much.
De nada. You're welcome.
Es bueno verlo otra vez. It's good to see you again.
Gracias. Es bueno verlo también. Thanks. It's good to see you too.
¿Cómo está su esposa? How is your wife?
Muy bien. Very well.
¿Y sus hijos? And your children?

Muy bien también, gracias. Ya han crecido. Very well too, thanks. They're already grown up.

End of speaking/listening lesson. Continue with the reading for Lesson 38.

Reading for Lesson 38

Read the following sentences and phrases with your student. Please make sure that proper intonation is used for all questions.

Reading Practice

Are you from a big family (Eres de una familia grande), Mark? How many brothers and sisters do you have?

My family isn't very big. I only have two brothers. One lives here and the other is in Sacramento.

I only have one sister. But she's only twelve, so she still lives at home in Oregon.

Do you ever visit her (La visitas)?

Yes, *during the summer (durante el verano)*. Oregon is nice then. *It is pretty cold the rest of the year (Es algo frío el resto del año).*

How about you? Do you ever visit Sacramento?

Yes. I go about three or four times a year.

How long does it take to get there from here?

It takes about two hours.

That's not too bad.

Yeah. At least gas costs a little less then before.

Yes. It's about a dollar fifty per gallon where I live.

How are your mother and father?

My parents are fine. They work a little. *My mother works fifteen hours a week at a store (Mi mamá trabaja quince horas a la semana en una tienda).* My father works sixteen hours a week at a restaurant on First Street.

Hey, would you like to have something to drink?

Where, at the hotel?

Yeah.

That sounds good. But I don't have much money on me, only ten or eleven dollars.

That's enough. You can buy five beers with that.

I can?

Yes, but *on second thought (pensándolo otra vez),* maybe ten or eleven dollars isn't enough.

It is enough because I don't want too much beer. Two or three beers is enough for me.

Relax. I was just joking.

I know.

Congratulations!
You have completed Level 1
Thank You!

Look for "How to Teach English to a Spanish Speaker Level 2
On Amazon now!

ALSO BY THE AUTHOR:

AVAILABLE ON AMAZON!

ABOUT THE AUTHOR

Ephrain Tristan Ortiz is a graduate of UC Davis (Bachelor of Arts), National University (CA State Teaching Credential) and Andersonville Theological Seminary (Master/Doctorate in Christian Education). He worked as an elementary school teacher for 9 years and as an ESL teacher for adults 2 years through his local county of education office, and another 4 years through his private company, the De la Vega Language Institute. He has also taught Biblical Hebrew to local church leaders and theologians for 4 years. Dr. Ortiz has published over 20 books, one of which is the Amazon best seller "Extraordinary Intelligence: How to Increase your Brain Power and Bless a Life," and several of which are English language instructional books. His publications are centered around making life easier, safer, successful and more enjoyable for his readers. You can connect with Dr. Ortiz via LinkedIn.com.

Made in the USA
Middletown, DE
21 April 2024